KU-649-937

endorsed for
BTEC

REVISE BTEC NATIONAL
Health and Social Care

REVISION GUIDE

Series Consultant: Harry Smith

Authors: Brenda Baker, James O'Leary, Marie Whitehouse
and Georgina Shaw

For the full range of Pearson revision titles across KS2, KS3, GCSE, Functional Skills, AS/A Level and BTEC visit:
www.pearsonschools.co.uk/revise

Pearson

Introduction

Which units should you revise?

This Revision Guide has been designed to support you in preparing for the externally assessed units of your course. Remember that you won't necessarily be studying all the units included here – it will depend on the qualification you are taking.

BTEC National Qualification	Externally assessed units
Certificate	1 Human Lifespan Development
For both: Extended Certificate Foundation Diploma	1 Human Lifespan Development 2 Working in Health and Social Care
Diploma	1 Human Lifespan Development 2 Working in Health and Social Care 4 Enquiries into Current Research in Health and Social Care
For both: Extended Diploma Extended Diploma (HS)	1 Human Lifespan Development 2 Working in Health and Social Care 3 Anatomy and Physiology for Health and Social Care 4 Enquiries into Current Research in Health and Social Care

Your Revision Guide

Each unit in this Revision Guide contains two types of pages, shown below.

Content **pages** help you revise the essential content you need to know for each unit.

Skills **pages** help you prepare for your exam or assessed task. Skills pages have a coloured edge and are shaded in the table of contents.

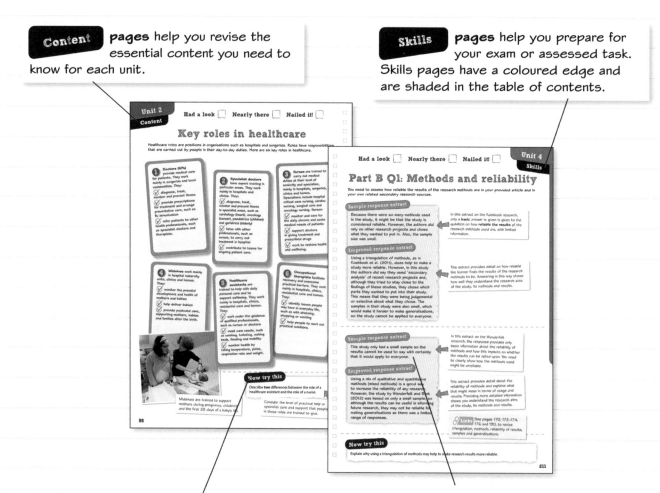

Use the **Now try this** activities on every page to help you test your knowledge and practise the relevant skills.

Look out for the **sample response extracts** to exam questions or set tasks on the skills pages. Post-its will explain their strengths and weaknesses.

Contents

Unit 1: Human Lifespan Development

1 Principles of growth
2 Principles of development
3 Gross motor skills, 0-8 years
4 Fine motor skills, 0-8 years
5 Physical development in adolescence
6 Physical development in early adulthood
7 Physical development in middle adulthood
8 Physical development in later adulthood
9 Intellectual development
10 Stages of cognitive development – Piaget
11 Piaget – how children think
12 Language development
13 Theories of attachment
14 Emotional development – self-concept
15 Stages of play
16 Friendships and relationships
17 Social development and independence
18 Maturation theory
19 Social learning theory
20 Nature versus nurture
21 Genetic factors
22 Biological factors
23 Environmental factors
24 Health and social care services
25 Social factors – family dysfunction
26 Social factors – bullying
27 The influence of culture and religion
28 Economic factors
29 Life events
30 The effects of life events
31 Cardiovascular disease and ageing
32 Degeneration of the nervous tissue
33 Degeneration of the sense organs
34 Osteoarthritis and nutrition
35 Dementia
36 Effects of illness common in ageing
37 Psychological effects of ageing
38 Theories of ageing
39 Provision for the aged
40 Ageing and economic effects
41 Your Unit 1 exam
42 Using case studies
43 Short-answer questions
44 'Which' and 'Identify' questions
45 'Explain' questions
46 'Outline' questions
47 'Describe' questions
48 Extended case study
49 Long-answer questions
50 Applying theories
51 'Discuss' questions
52 'Evaluate' questions
53 'Justify' questions
54 'To what extent' questions
55 Concise answers

Unit 2: Working in Health and Social Care

56 Key roles in healthcare
57 Healthcare settings
58 Key roles in social care
59 Social care settings
60 Responsibilities in healthcare
61 Responsibilities in social care
62 Supporting routines
63 Anti-discriminatory practice
64 Adapting provision of services
65 Empowering individuals
66 Empowerment in practice
67 Ensuring safety in care
68 Reports and complaints procedures
69 The Data Protection Act 1998
70 Ensuring confidentiality
71 Accountability to professional bodies
72 Safeguarding regulations
73 Working in partnerships
74 Holistic approaches
75 Monitoring care internally
76 Monitoring care externally
77 Public sector services
78 Private and voluntary services
79 Hospitals and daycare units
80 Hospice care
81 Residential care
82 Domiciliary and workplace care
83 Access to services
84 Barriers to services
85 Representing service-user interests
86 Advocacy
87 Regulation and inspection process
88 Regulation and inspection in England
89 Regulation and inspection in Wales
90 Regulation and inspection in Northern Ireland
91 Regulation of professions
92 Meeting standards
93 Training for health and social care workers
94 Safeguarding employees
95 Ill health and specific needs
96 Caring for people with mental ill health
97 Caring for people with a learning disability
98 Caring for people with physical and sensory disability
99 Early years care
100 Later adulthood care
101 Policies, procedures and regulations
102 Working practices in healthcare
103 Working practices in social care
104 Your Unit 2 exam
105 Responding to scenarios
106 'Identify' and 'Outline' questions
107 'Describe' questions
108 'Explain' questions
109 'Discuss' questions
110 Long-answer questions
111 Concise answers

Unit 3: Anatomy and Physiology for Health and Social Care

112 Cell structure and function
113 Tissue types: connective tissue
114 Tissue types: epithelial tissue
115 Tissue types: muscle and nervous tissue
116 Major body organs
117 Energy metabolism
118 Inheritance and genetic variation
119 Mendelian principles
120 Genetic and chromosome disorders, and testing
121 Homeostasis: temperature and blood pressure
122 Homeostasis: glucose and fluids
123 The heart structure and function
124 The cardiovascular system
125 Blood structure and function
126 Cardiovascular disorders
127 Respiratory system structure
128 Respiratory system function
129 Respiratory disorders
130 The skeletal system
131 Joints and movements
132 Skeletal disorders
133 The muscular system and disorders
134 Major muscles
135 The digestive system
136 Enzymes and products of digestion
137 Absorption of digestive products
138 Digestive disorders
139 The nervous system
140 Disorders of the nervous system
141 The endocrine system

142 Endocrine disorders
143 Lymphatic and immune systems
144 Lymphatic organs and disorders
145 The renal system and disorders
146 The female reproductive system
147 The male reproductive system
148 Reproductive system disorders
149 Gametes, fertilisation, conception and growth
150 Foetal growth through the trimesters
151 Prenatal development and teratogens
152 Congenital disorders
153 Clinical trials
154 Epidemiological studies and data analysis
155 Data analysis skills: statistics, bar charts and histograms
156 Data analysis skills: graphs and tables
157 Data analysis skills: pictorial presentation
158 Your Unit 3 exam
159 'State' and 'Which' questions
160 'Identify' and 'Complete' questions
161 'Outline' and 'In which'/'To which' questions
162 'Describe' questions
163 'Explain' questions
164 'Compare and contrast' questions
165 'Provide a key' and 'What' questions
166 'Deduce' questions
167 'By how many' and 'To what extent' questions

Unit 4: Enquiries into Current Research in Health and Social Care

168 Purpose of research
169 Issues in health and social care
170 Planning research
171 Rationale for research
172 Quantitative methods
173 Qualitative methods
174 Advantages and disadvantages
175 Research questions
176 Target groups and samples
177 Ethical principles
178 Safeguarding ethics
179 Confidentiality
180 Informed consent
181 Legislation
182 Non-judgemental practice
183 Primary and secondary research
184 Literature review
185 Notes and records of sources
186 Reading techniques
187 Academic reading and analysis
188 Referencing conventions
189 Referencing techniques
190 Selecting reliable sources
191 Electronic searches
192 Connecting sources
193 Suitability of sources
194 Interpreting quantitative data
195 Interpreting graphs and tables
196 Bias in quantitative data
197 Interpreting qualitative data
198 Interpreting words
199 Bias in qualitative data
200 Recommendations for practice
201 Recommendations for provision
202 Identifying future research
203 Reflecting on research
204 Your Unit 4 set task
205 Part A: Planning research
206 Part A: Assessing sources
207 Part A: Making notes
208 Part B: Listing sources
209 Part B Q1: Research methods
210 Part B Q1: Suitability of methods
211 Part B Q1: Methods and reliability
212 Part B Q2: Research issues and significance
213 Part B Q2: Research conclusions
214 Part B Q3: Further research and methods
215 Part B Q3: Further research and ethics
216 Part B Q3: Further research and planning
217 Part B Q4: Implications for practice and provision
218 Part B Q4: Recommendations for practice and provision

219 Answers

A small bit of small print
Pearson publishes Sample Assessment Material and the Specification on its website. This is the official content and this book should be used in conjunction with it. The questions in *Now try this* have been written to help you test your knowledge and skills. Remember: the real assessment may not look like this.

Principles of growth

Growth is sometimes referred to as physiological change. It describes an increase in length or height, weight and dimensions.

Measuring height

1 **Infants** grow rapidly and will reach roughly half their adult height by the age of two.

2 **Adolescents** (9 to 18 years) experience growth spurts (when height increases rapidly over a short period) during puberty.

3 Full height is reached by the start of early **adulthood** (19 to 45 years).

The four principles of growth

1 Growth rates are not constant.

2 Different parts of the body grow at different rates.

3 Growth rates vary between children.

4 The growth rate of boys is usually faster on average than that of girls, as men tend to be taller than women.

Head dimensions

Head circumference is measured at birth and at 6–8 weeks to identify any abnormality in brain or skull growth. Skull growth is faster in the first two years of life but continues into early adulthood.

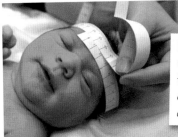

Head circumference is measured across the forehead, just above the ears and at the midpoint of the back of the head.

Length or height?

- In the first two years, an infant's **length** is measured when lying down.
- From 2 years old their **height** is measured when standing.

Recording growth

Growth is an indicator of children's health and wellbeing.

Measurements are plotted on a growth chart. Centile lines represent the values of measurement from a large number of children to show 'norms' of growth in each age group.

- Growth charts give the length or height, weight and head dimensions expected at a particular age.
- Comparing children's growth against norms is important to identify signs of ill-health and development problems.
- Growth charts are different for boys and girls as their expected rate of growth varies.

Now try this

Baby Brad is 8 weeks old. He has been taken to the clinic to check that he is growing at the expected rate. A nurse checks his weight and will plot it on a chart. She is aware that infants triple their weight in their first year.

Identify **two** other measurements that the nurse will take.

Principles of development

Development describes the acquisition of skills and abilities through the life stages.

Areas of development

Physical development – growth and other physical changes that happen to our body throughout life.

Intellectual/cognitive development – the development of language, memory and thinking skills.

Emotional development – the ability to cope with feelings about ourselves and towards others.

Social development – the ability to form friendships and relationships, and to learn to be independent.

Development milestones

The rate of development may vary between individuals but it follows the same sequence, with each stage called a milestone (developmental norm). The diagram shows language milestones up to 8 years.

Development is **observed** and cannot be measured in the same way as growth.

Links Look at page 3 to revise the sequence of physical development in infants.

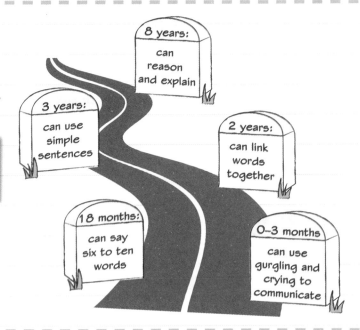

8 years: can reason and explain

3 years: can use simple sentences

2 years: can link words together

18 months: can say six to ten words

0–3 months can use gurgling and crying to communicate

Now try this

Henry is 4 years old and attends nursery. His key person is worried that his development is not progressing as well as expected for his age.

Outline the role of observation in understanding Henry's development.

Observation involves an assessment of children's abilities, learning and behaviour to ensure that children are making expected progress against milestones.

Gross motor skills, 0–8 years

Gross motor skills allow children to control the large muscles in their torso, arms, legs, hands and feet.

Infancy, 0–2 years

1 Infants develop their gross motor skills from the head down.

2 Around six months, infants gradually control muscles in their neck and back so they can roll, sit and crawl.

3 At around 11–13 months, the muscles in their legs develop so that they can stand, cruise and walk.

4 At 2 years, infants can climb onto low furniture and propel a sit-on toy, and at 2½ years they can kick a ball.

Using gross motor skills

Crawling
Walking
Running
Balancing
Skipping
Gross motor activity
Coordinating
Jumping
Bending
Scooting
Kicking
Pushing
Pulling
Climbing

Early childhood, 3–8 years

From about 3–4 years old they can balance and walk along a line. At about 5–8 years old they can balance on a low beam.

From about 3–4 years old they can run forwards and backwards. At about 5–8 years old they can skip with a rope.

Children continue to develop gross motor skills

From about 3 years old they can pedal and control a tricycle. By about 6 years old they can ride a bicycle.

From about 3–4 years old they can hop on one foot. At about 5–8 years old they can hop, skip and jump with confidence.

From about 3 years old they can throw a ball and by about 4 years old they can aim it. At about 5–8 years old they can accurately throw and catch a ball.

Now try this

Bobby is 5 months old. He has just started to roll over to his front from his back.

Identify **two** gross motor skills that Bobby is likely to acquire in the next three months.

Fine motor skills, 0–8 years

Fine motor skills are important for controlling and coordinating the movement of the small muscles in the fingers and hands.

How fine motor skills develop

18 months

This 18-month-old can build with small blocks, use a spoon and make marks with crayons using a **palmar grasp**. At 2 years old she will pull on her shoes and control her crayon to draw circles and dots.

Newborn

This newborn is able to grasp an adult's finger. By 3 months he will hold a rattle for a short time and at 6 months he will grasp a toy and pass it to his other hand. At 12 months he will pick up small objects using a **pincer grasp**.

The development of the small muscles in the fingers and hands

This 5-year-old can control the muscles in her fingers to manipulate the construction block and use hand–eye coordination to fit the piece into the correct place. She writes her own name forming letters correctly and by the time she is 8 she will use joined-up writing.

3 years

This 3-year-old is developing a **tripod grasp**. He can use a fork and spoon, turn the pages of a book, and button and unbutton clothing. At 4 years old he will be able to thread small beads and colour in pictures.

5 years

Activities that support fine motor skills

Skill	Description	Activity
Gripping	Having the strength in fingers and hands to hold an object firmly.	Holding a rattle, tricycle handle or spoon.
Manipulation	Skilful movement of objects using fingers and hands, such as turning, twisting and passing objects from one hand to another.	Building with blocks, playing a musical instrument, playing with and placing farm animals or cars.
Hand–eye coordination	Control of eye movement at the same time as finger and hand movement.	Writing, sewing or completing jigsaw puzzles.

Now try this

Connor is 18 months old. His sister Amy is 3 years old. They are both meeting the expected milestones for their age.

Outline the differences in their fine motor skills.

Ensure that you make links between the children described in the case study and the developmental milestones expected at their age.

Physical development in adolescence

Adolescence is the life stage between 9 and 18 years old.

Puberty

During adolescence, young people experience a physical change called puberty. This takes place in girls around 11–13 years and in boys around 13–15 years.

Puberty starts when a hormone in the brain sends a signal to the pituitary gland, which releases hormones that stimulate the ovaries in girls and the testes in boys to produce sex hormones.

During this life stage a young person's height can increase rapidly over a short time – this is known as a growth spurt. In girls this happens around 11–13 years and in boys around 13–15 years.

The role of hormones in sexual development

In boys

The hormone **testosterone** is produced by the testes. It stimulates growth of the penis and testes, pubic hair growth, the development of muscle and lowering of the voice.

In girls

The hormones oestrogen and progesterone are produced by the ovaries. They stimulate growth of the breasts and reproductive system and helps to regulate the menstrual cycle.

Primary sexual characteristics

These are the processes that are related to the sex organs that are present at birth and mature when sex hormones are released.

Secondary sexual characteristics

These are not necessary for reproduction. They develop when sex hormones are released.

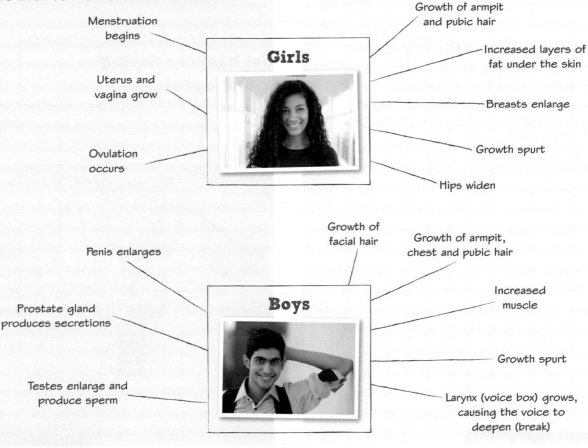

Girls
- Menstruation begins
- Uterus and vagina grow
- Ovulation occurs
- Growth of armpit and pubic hair
- Increased layers of fat under the skin
- Breasts enlarge
- Growth spurt
- Hips widen

Boys
- Penis enlarges
- Prostate gland produces secretions
- Testes enlarge and produce sperm
- Growth of facial hair
- Growth of armpit, chest and pubic hair
- Increased muscle
- Growth spurt
- Larynx (voice box) grows, causing the voice to deepen (break)

Now try this

Explain the difference between primary and secondary sexual characteristics.

Physical development in early adulthood

Early adulthood describes the life stage between 19 and 45 years of age.

Maturation

Individuals reach physical maturity (**maturation**) in early adulthood.

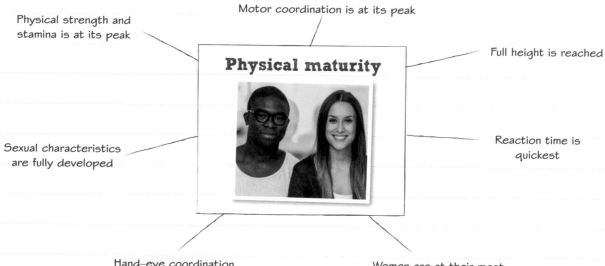

Physical strength and stamina is at its peak

Motor coordination is at its peak

Full height is reached

Physical maturity

Sexual characteristics are fully developed

Reaction time is quickest

Hand–eye coordination is at its peak

Women are at their most fertile and can become pregnant and lactate

Fertility and perimenopause

At the beginning of this life stage, women are at their most fertile. Around 40–45 years old they reach the end of their reproductive years. This period is called **perimenopause**.

During menopause, the reduction in oestrogen causes physical and emotional symptoms that include:

- hot flushes
- night sweats
- mood swings
- loss of libido
- vaginal dryness.

What happens during perimenopause?

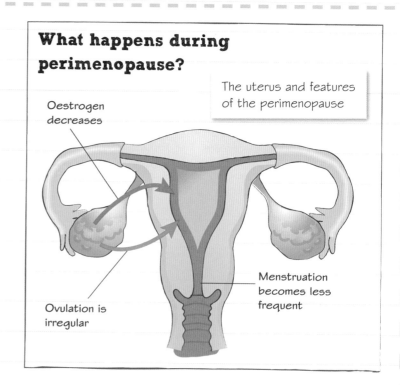

The uterus and features of the perimenopause

Oestrogen decreases

Menstruation becomes less frequent

Ovulation is irregular

Now try this

Most professional athletes will reach a career peak during the first part of early adulthood.

Explain why their success happens at this time, with reference to their physical stage of development.

Physical development in middle adulthood

Middle adulthood describes the life stage between 46 and 65 years of age.

Ageing

The ageing process mainly begins in middle adulthood

Signs of ageing include:
- greying hair
- loss of muscle tone, strength and stamina
- body shape may change with an increase in or loss of weight
- men begin to lose hair
- women are no longer fertile as menstruation ends
- loss of height.

Menopause

Menopause is a natural physiological change experienced by women during the middle adult life stage. It happens over several years with the gradual ending of menstruation.

The role of sex hormones in females

✓ **Oestrogen** plays the most important role in female sexuality and regulates ovulation.

✓ **Progesterone** is necessary for the implantation of fertilised eggs in the uterus, the maintenance of pregnancy and sexual heath.

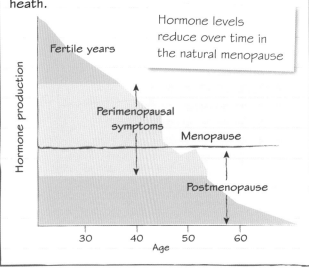

Hormone levels reduce over time in the natural menopause

The symptoms of menopause are the result of hormonal changes

A reduction in oestrogen causes:
- the ovaries to stop producing eggs
- thinning and shrinkage of the vagina.

A reduction in oestrogen and progesterone:
- gradually stops menstruation
- impacts libido.

A reduction in oestrogen:
- affects the hypothalamus in the brain, which regulates temperature, causing hot flushes and night sweats
- affects the health of hair, skin and nails
- may cause mood swings, as oestrogen regulates neurotransmitters that affect mood.

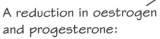

Now try this

Outline the role of oestrogen in menopause.

Physical development in later adulthood

Later adulthood describes the life stage from 65 years old onwards.

The effects of ageing

The ageing process is the natural deterioration of the body.

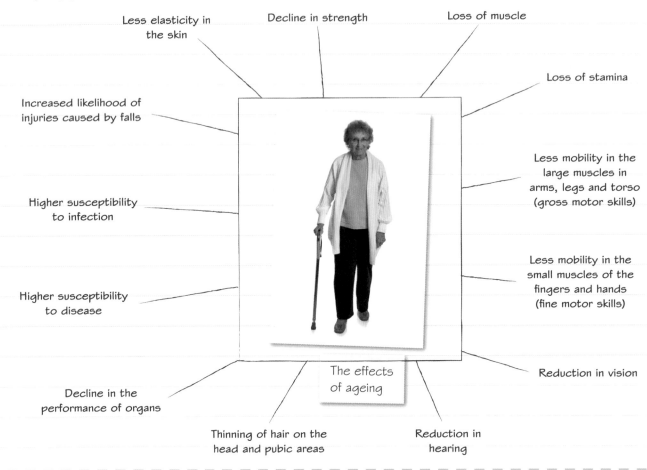

Less elasticity in the skin

Decline in strength

Loss of muscle

Loss of stamina

Increased likelihood of injuries caused by falls

Less mobility in the large muscles in arms, legs and torso (gross motor skills)

Higher susceptibility to infection

Less mobility in the small muscles of the fingers and hands (fine motor skills)

Higher susceptibility to disease

The effects of ageing

Reduction in vision

Decline in the performance of organs

Thinning of hair on the head and pubic areas

Reduction in hearing

Height loss

It is usual to start to lose height in middle adulthood, which continues into later life. By the age of 80 individuals may have lost as much as 5cm. This is caused by changes in posture and compression of the spinal discs and joints.

Intellectual ability

Ageing does not always impact on cognitive ability, but it can negatively affect how individuals process information, for example:

- memory
- recall
- speed of thinking.

Now try this

Peter is 69 years old. He is retired. He used to play football for a local team but now has to watch rather than taking part.

Identify **two** possible effects of Peter's life stage on his physical development.

 Make sure you relate your answer to the facts given about Peter so that you identify the physical changes that prevent Peter from taking part in sport.

Intellectual development

Intellectual development is about how individuals organise ideas and make sense of the world around them.

Problem solving – needed to work things out and make predictions about what might happen

Moral development – needed for reasoning and making choices about how to act towards self and others

Types of intellectual development

Language development – essential to organise and express thoughts

Memory – essential for storing and recalling information

Abstract thought and creative thinking – essential for thinking and discussing things that can't be observed

Stages of life

Intellectual skills develop differently at different stages of life.

Intellectual development continues in early adulthood. By early adulthood individuals have gained knowledge, skills and experience. They use past experiences to make judgements. Thinking is logical and realistic. Individuals are able to think through problems and make decisions.

| Infancy and early childhood | → | Early adulthood | → | Later adulthood |

Neurones may also be known as neurons.

This is a time of rapid intellectual development. 90% of neurone (brain cell) connections are in place by the time children are 5 years old.

Individuals continue to learn new skills and knowledge into later adulthood. Intelligence does not change but short-term memory and thinking speed may decline.

Worked example

Alyssa is 26 years old. She has been a website designer for five years and is good at her job. She has just got a promotion and is managing a new team.

Outline features of Alyssa's intellectual development in relation to her ability to carry out her new job.

Sample response extract

Alyssa will have gained a great deal of knowledge about the job as she has been doing it for five years. She will also have gained skills and knowledge that she can apply to the new job. She will be able to think rationally about any problems using past experiences to help her make decisions and find solutions.

Intellectual milestones 0–8 years

☑ From birth – can use all their senses to help understand the world around them.

☑ At 3 years – can ask questions, count, recognise colours and sort objects.

☑ At 5 years – starting to read and write and draw in detail, can talk about the past and future.

☑ At 8 years – can think more deeply, reason, talk about abstract ideas and plan.

Now try this

Sami is 3 years old and has just started nursery. Sami is meeting the expected milestones in intellectual development. Sami loves to paint, play with sand and build towers with wooden blocks.

Make sure you choose intellectual skills relevant to the context of Sami's play activities.

Identify **three** features of Sami's intellectual development in relation to the play activities at nursery.

Stages of cognitive development – Piaget

Piaget believed that children pass through distinct developmental stages in sequence. He thought that children should be allowed to discover things for themselves through spontaneous play.

Criticisms of Piaget's stages

Some critics believe that Piaget underestimated children's development and that with support they can move more quickly to the next stage of development.

4. Formal operations: from 11 up to 18 years. Young people have the capacity for abstract thought, rational thought and problem solving.

3. Concrete operations: from 7 to 11 years. Children use practical resources to help them to understand the world, such as counters for mathematics. They classify, categorise and use logic to understand things they see.

2. Pre-operational: from 2 to 7 years. Children begin to control their environment by using symbolic behaviour, including representational words and drawings and pretend play, but are not yet able to think logically.

1. Sensorimotor: from birth to 2 years. Infants learn about their environment and develop early schemas (concepts) by using all their senses to physically explore the world.

Piaget's development stages

Piaget's schematic development theory

This theory explains how children use their experiences to **construct** their understanding of the world around them.

Assimilation: the child constructs an understanding or concept (schema).	The child has developed a schema about sand.
▼	
Equilibrium: the child's experience fits with their schema.	The child's experience in the nursery sandpit fits with their schema.
▼	
Disequilibrium: a new experience disturbs the child's schema.	Water is added to the sandpit. The sand behaves differently, which upsets the child's schema.
▼	
Accommodation: the child's understanding (schema) changes to take account of the new experience.	The child changes their schema to accommodate their new experience of sand. They develop a new schema.

Now try this

Explain, giving an example, what Piaget means by 'schema'.

Piaget – how children think

Piaget believed that children think differently from adults.

Conservation

Piaget carried out tests to show the stage when children begin to reason and think logically.

1 This child is 4. He is shown two identical glasses with the same amount of water in each.

2 The water from one glass is poured into a tall, narrow beaker.

3 The child believes that the tall, narrow beaker contains more water.

Piaget's test shows that:

- Children under 7 years old cannot conserve because they cannot think about more than one aspect of a situation at one time.
- By the operational stage at 7 years old, children can think logically so understand that the quantity of water stays the same when poured into a differently shaped container.

Conservation

Conservation refers to children's understanding that the amount remains the same even when the container's shape has changed. Piaget also used tests using solids, weight and number.

Egocentrism

Piaget believed that, until children are 7 years old, they only see things from their own perspective (point of view). He used his Swiss mountain test to prove his theory of **egocentrism**.

This child is under 7. The test showed that children of this age cannot describe the mountain from the doll's perspective.

Criticisms of Piaget

- Piaget sometimes underestimated children's rate of development.
- With support, children can develop more advanced concepts.
- Children can be given experiences that help them to move through the stages at a faster rate.
- Some children can see things from the perspective of others before the age of 7.

Now try this

Nathan, aged 3 years, enjoys playing outdoors on the wheeled toys but gets frustrated when he has to wait his turn for a tricycle.

With reference to Piaget's theory:

1 explain why Nathan might find it difficult to wait for his turn
2 describe when he will start to see things from other children's perspectives.

11

Language development

Language development involves communication through articulation (speech) and receptive speech (understanding).

Stages of language development

Infancy	0–3 months	✓ Makes mouth movements in response to parent. ✓ Cries to ask for food or comfort.
	6–12 months	✓ Understands some words, such as 'byebye'. ✓ Makes sounds such as 'gaga'.
	18 months	✓ Can say between six and ten words. ✓ Can follow simple instructions.
Early childhood	2–3 years	✓ Links words together, for example 'me car'. ✓ Vocabulary increasing to approximately 200 words at 2½ years.
	3–5 years	✓ Uses simple sentences. ✓ Asks questions. ✓ May use incorrect forms of words, for example 'I good'.
	8 years	✓ Speaks in complex sentences. ✓ Can reason and explain.
Adolescence	9–19 years	✓ Developing vocabulary. ✓ Uses language to explore abstract ideas.

Language Acquisition Device (LAD)

Noam Chomsky proposed the LAD as the hypothetical part of the human mind that allows infants to acquire and produce language. He suggested that humans:

- are born with a structure in their brain that enables them to acquire language
- have a critical period for first language development in the first years of life
- all follow the same pattern of language development
- have an innate understanding of the structure of language (called **universal grammar**) that is the basis for all languages (subject, verb, object).

Chomsky's LAD theory helps to explain how children develop language skills. It is based on **nativist theory**, which suggests that individuals are pre-programmed to develop in a certain way.

Criticisms of Chomsky

1 Lack of scientific evidence of innate understanding of structure of language.

2 The rate of language development is affected by the degree of interactions with others.

3 Does not take into account that a language acquisition support system is required.

4 Chomsky put emphasis on grammar in sentence development rather than meanings.

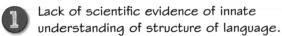

Now try this

Saira is 3 years old. Explain two possible features of language development that help to explain how Saira has instinctively acquired language at her life stage, according to Chomsky.

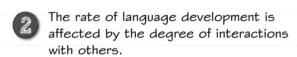

Link the identified skills to how Saira might use them.

Theories of attachment

Attachment is the emotional bond that is formed between infants and young children and their main caregiver.

Bowlby's theory of attachment

In their early months, infants form one primary attachment.

Attachment to the primary caregiver is essential.

A disruption to attachment has a negative impact on development.

Infants are biologically pre-programmed to form attachments

Infancy is a critical period for developing attachments.

Attachment to the primary caregiver is a model for future attachments.

Schaffer and Emerson's stages of attachment

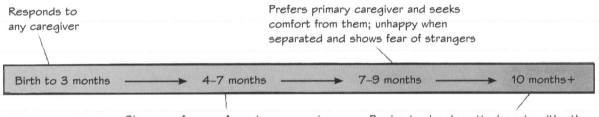

Responds to any caregiver

Prefers primary caregiver and seeks comfort from them; unhappy when separated and shows fear of strangers

Birth to 3 months → 4–7 months → 7–9 months → 10 months+

Shows preference for primary caregiver but accepts care from others

Begins to develop attachments with others who respond to them. By 18 months most infants have formed multiple attachments.

Ainsworth's Strange Situation Classification (SSC)

Mary Ainsworth classified attachments into three main types, based on a study of children's reactions when parted from a parent.

Types of attachment	Secure	Insecure / avoidant	Insecure / resistant
Parenting style	In tune with the child and their emotions	Unavailable to child / rejects them	Inconsistent in meeting the child's needs
Infants' behaviour	Will show distress when primary caregiver leaves, and greets them when they return; seeks comfort from caregiver when upset; happy with strangers when caregiver is present	Does not show distress when primary caregiver leaves; continues to explore the environment; may go to a stranger for comfort	Shows distress when primary caregiver leaves but resists contact on their return; shows anxiety and insecurity

Disrupted attachment

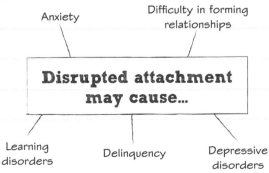

Anxiety

Difficulty in forming relationships

Disrupted attachment may cause...

Learning disorders

Delinquency

Depressive disorders

Now try this

Ruby is 1 month old. She lives with her mother but is sometimes looked after by her grandmother. Ruby's mum intends to return to work in a few months, so Ruby will go to a nursery.

Use Schaffer and Emerson's stages of attachment and Bowlby's theory to produce a flow chart to show how Ruby's attachment will develop during the infancy stage.

Emotional development – self-concept

Self-concept is an individual's evaluation of their own self-worth.

The difference between self-image, self-concept and self-esteem

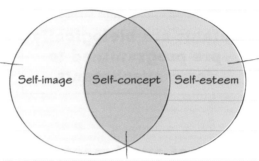

How individuals view themselves, influenced by how they are perceived by others. For example, a slim person might perceive themselves as overweight.

Self-image   Self-concept   Self-esteem

How individuals value and feel about the knowledge they have of themselves. One person might think, 'I can't do it, I'm not good enough, people don't like me'. Another person might think, 'I can, I'm special, I'm clever, friends like me.'

The combination of self-image and self-esteem

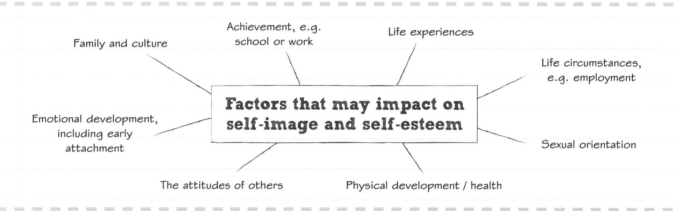

Family and culture

Achievement, e.g. school or work

Life experiences

Life circumstances, e.g. employment

Factors that may impact on self-image and self-esteem

Emotional development, including early attachment

The attitudes of others

Physical development / health

Sexual orientation

Self-image and self-esteem

	Positive self-image		Negative self-image
👍	Feels happy about personal appearance and abilities	👎	Feels unattractive or less intelligent than others
👍	Receives good feedback from others about appearance and abilities	👎	Receives negative comments from others about appearance or abilities
👍	Compares self favourably with others	👎	Compares self negatively against 'perfect' images in magazines/on TV

	High self-esteem		Low self-esteem
👍	Feels confident	👎	Feels worthless
👍	Willing to try new things	👎	Less likely to try new things
👍	Copes well under pressure	👎	Less likely to cope well in new or difficult situations

A person's self-esteem is not constant and may change from time to time depending on an individual's circumstances.

Now try this

Carly is 13 years old. She has not yet reached puberty, but her two best friends have. They are both much taller than her, have started to develop breasts and are menstruating. Carly is receiving comments about her lack of development on social media.

How might Carly's experience affect her self-image?

Think about how Carly might compare her appearance with her friends and how she may be affected by others' comments.

Stages of play

The stages of play are closely linked with stages of social development and language.

Play in infancy and early childhood

- All children play.
- Infants start to play when they are just a few months old.
- Play promotes physical, intellectual, emotional and social development.

Varying stages of play

The stages of play may vary between children. All children will pass through these stages. Stages are influenced by children's language and intellectual development. Initially children play alone, then alongside other children, and eventually share and co-operate during play.

Stages of play in infancy and early childhood

2–3 years, **parallel play**: these children are playing next to each other but are involved in their own play.

Children are aware of other children. They may copy each other but they do not interact.

Stages of play

0–2 years, **solo play**: this infant is engrossed in his own play.

Children play alone with toys such as rattles, shakers and balls. They may be aware that other infants are present but do not attempt to play with them.

3 years and over, **co-operative play**: these children are sharing, talking and playing together.

Children share ideas and resources in the same activity. They interact and agree roles to develop their play towards a shared goal.

Language and play

Refer to the stages of language development and Chomsky's Language Acquisition Device (LAD) theory on page 12 to remind yourself that:

✓ play is important for children to develop their vocabulary

✓ children need language to be able to communicate and negotiate during co-operative play.

Symbols and play

Refer to Piaget's stages on page 10 to remind yourself of how children learn.

✓ Infants use all their senses to find out about the world around them (heuristic play).

✓ Children in the pre-operational stage (2 to 7) learn best through exploratory play. The provision of natural materials indoors and outdoors encourages curiosity and exploratory learning.

Now try this

Eli is 20 months old. Identify suitable toys and resources that could be provided to encourage parallel play alongside his brother Kian, aged 3 years.

Friendships and relationships

Friendships and relationships are essential for healthy human development.

Building friendships

Building friendships involves learning to value others and developing skills to interact with individuals and groups.

Close friendships	
	• From around 3 years old, children start to develop special friendships. • These make individuals feel secure and confident. • They also promote independence and self-esteem.
Friendships with a wider group of friends 	• As children widen their circle of friends, they become more confident and independent. • Adolescents are greatly influenced by the views of their friends, which may affect their self-image. • Wider friendships continue to be important in adulthood for positive emotional and social development.

Relationship breakdowns

A breakdown in relationships can have a negative impact on social and emotional development and health.

Developing relationships

Relationships involve developing skills to interact with others in different situations.

Formal relationships develop between non-related individuals such as colleagues or teacher and pupil. Positive formal relationships are important for good self-esteem and self-image.

Intimate relationships may begin in adolescence and continue, and new ones form throughout life. Close intimate relationships result in greater contentment, emotional security and positive self-image.

Relationships

Informal relationships are built between individuals and family or significant people. They start with attachments in infancy. Strong informal relationships promote contentment and the confidence to deal with life events. They help to build other informal, formal and intimate relationships throughout life.

Healthy relationships

Healthy relationships may result in:

👍 acceptance   👍 respect
👍 trust   👍 responsibility
👍 compromise   👍 honesty.

Unhealthy relationships

Unhealthy relationships may result in:

👎 stress   👎 blame
👎 isolation   👎 low self-esteem
👎 distrust   👎 insecurity.

Now try this

Saeed is 4 years old and has just started school. He has a best friend called Nathan.

Explain the possible effects of building friendships on Saeed's social and emotional development.

Information on page 15 will help you with this answer.

Social development and independence

Independence involves doing things for oneself and making decisions without relying on others. It is closely linked to social and emotional development.

The development of independence through the life stages

Infancy
- Depends on others for care.
- Will play alone but likes a familiar adult close by.

Early childhood
- Develops the necessary skills to become more independent in personal care.
- Develops likes and dislikes and can make limited decisions.

Adolescence
- Enjoys more freedom, can make independent decisions (e.g. about lifestyle and education), but emotions may affect this ability.
- Takes responsibility for own actions but influenced by others.

Early adulthood
- May live with parents but is independent.
- Makes own decisions about personal life and career.
- Often a time for relationships, marriage and starting a family.

Middle adulthood
- Becomes increasingly independent.
- Increased freedom with life changes, e.g. dependent children leave home; retirement.

Later adulthood
- Continues to make own decisions.
- May have financial constraints if relying on state pension.
- Changes in mental and physical capacity may gradually reduce ability to make own decisions and care for self.

Independence (y-axis) — *Life stage* (x-axis)

Levels of independence follow a pattern but vary between individuals

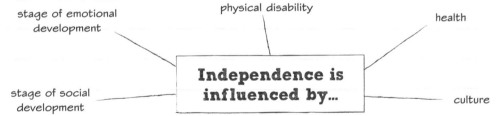

stage of emotional development — physical disability — health — **Independence is influenced by…** — stage of social development — culture

Peer pressure

Peer pressure describes a person or group influencing an individual to change their behaviour, values or beliefs so they conform to, and become socially accepted by, a peer group. Adolescents may pressurise others to follow their lead on school rules, home rules and lifestyle.

Negative and positive behaviours

Possible negative behaviours due to peer pressure:
- smoking, using alcohol and drugs
- truancy
- bullying
- vandalising
- stealing
- disrespect

Possible positive behaviours due to peer pressure:
- taking part in sport
- studying
- befriending
- respecting others
- learning a new skill
- eating healthy foods
- keeping safe if taking part in sex

Now try this

Identify **three** features of social development in adolescence.

 Use the information on this page and page 16 to help you.

Maturation theory

Gesell's theory helps to explain how biological maturation (the process of maturing) is related to overall development.

Gesell's maturation theory

Gesell based his theory on his belief that:
- development is genetically determined from birth – a biological process
- children follow the same orderly sequence in their development
- the pace of development may vary depending on physical and intellectual development.

'The child's personality is a product of slow gradual growth. His nervous system matures by stages and natural sequences.'

Gessell observed the behaviours of many children, from which he determined averages or 'norms' which he called milestones of development. His milestones describe children's physical, social and emotional development.

Gesell (1880–1961)

Gesell was a psychologist and paediatrician. He was a pioneer in child development and remains influential in our understanding of child development.

Gesell was the first person to use observation of children to understand their development.

Positive and negative views of Gesell's theory

👍 He determined typical norms of development that are still used today.

👍 He used advanced methodology in observations of behaviour of large numbers of children.

👎 He did not consider the influence of individual or cultural differences in children.

👎 He believed that the 'norms' of development he described were desirable.

Now try this

Outline how Gesell's milestones can help early years practitioners support and promote children's development.

Social learning theory

Social learning theory suggests that the way children behave is an interaction between personal and environmental factors.

Bandura's theory

Social learning theory is based on a belief that learning happens through observing, imitating and modelling the behaviours of others.

1 Attention: learning takes place when a child focuses their attention on a person who 'models' the behaviour. Children are more likely to imitate the behaviour of someone they identify with or admire.

2 Retention: what the child has observed is retained in their memory to be used when an opportunity occurs.

3 Reproduction: what has been learned is reproduced or imitated. It may be rehearsed in the child's mind first and then imitated later when there is an opportunity.

4 Motivation: children feel motivated because they anticipate intrinsic or extrinsic rewards (vicarious reinforcement). Children will be motivated to repeat or stop the behaviour, depending on intrinsic or extrinsic reinforcement.

The four principles of social learning

Reinforcement

Behaviour may be repeated or resisted – this is reinforcement and may be positive or negative.

Positive reinforcement: the behaviour is repeated because of personal satisfaction (intrinsic reinforcement) or rewards (extrinsic reinforcement).

Negative reinforcement: the behaviour is not repeated to avoid an adverse experience such as lack of satisfaction or being told off.

Vicarious reinforcement:

- Children may be motivated because they see that the person or 'model' they observe is getting satisfaction or positive feedback.
- Children may resist imitating the action because the model receives negative feedback from their action.

Remember: negative reinforcement is not the same as punishment.

Bobo doll experiment

Children were shown adults being aggressive or non-aggressive towards the Bobo doll. The aggressive adults were either rewarded, reprimanded or had no consequence for their behaviour. The experiment was designed by Bandura to show that:

☑ children would copy the aggressive behaviour of another person

☑ the outcome for the adult impacted on the likelihood of children copying the behaviour.

The result

☑ Children learned aggressive behaviour through observation.

☑ Children were more likely to imitate an adult who was rewarded for aggressive behaviour than one who was reprimanded.

Now try this

Use an observation of your own to explain Bandura's principles of learning.

Observe a child watching and imitating an adult's actions, for example using a computer or a telephone, or digging in the garden.

Nature versus nurture

It is widely accepted that both nature and nurture play a role in human development.

Nature versus nurture debate

Nature (nativism):
the influence of innate/inherited features on development. Based on the assumption that children are genetically pre-programmed. They have inherited skills, abilities and behaviours from their parents.

Nature and nurture:
Piaget accepted that children develop in a predestined way (stages of cognitive development), but believed experiences help them to develop new concepts.

Nurture (empiricism or behaviourism):
the influence of the environment and nurturing. Based on the assumption that characteristics are acquired and can be shaped through experiences.

Nature   Nurture

Look again at nativist theories, such as Gesell's maturation theory on page 18, Bowlby's attachment theory on page 13 and Chomsky's theory of Language Acquisition Device (LAD) on page 12.

Look again at Piaget's theories on page 10.

Look again at behaviourist theories, such as Bandura's social learning theory on page 19.

Genetic predisposition

An individual's **genetic predisposition** (nature) can be triggered by their environment and life experiences (nurture).

Genetic inheritance — The individual — Environment/ lifestyle

Stress–diathesis model

This explains how both nature and nurture play a part in the development of psychological disorders.

Nature — **Diathesis:** a predisposition or vulnerability to mental disorders due to an abnormality of the brain or neurotransmitters (genetic / biological factors) →

Psychological disorders

Nurture — **Stresses:** traumatic events in a person's life, e.g. relationships, abuse, culture (environmental factors) →

Now try this

Outline **one** theory that is based on a nature (nativist) approach and **one** theory that is based on a nurture (behaviourist) approach.

Links Look at pages 12, 13, 18 and 19 to remind yourself of the theories.

Genetic factors

Genetic factors can affect physical growth, development, health and appearance.

Genetic predisposition to conditions

Genes are sets of instructions to the cells that determine growth and development. Individuals inherit 23 pairs (one from each parent) of chromosomes, which contain genes. Health conditions can arise from defective inherited genes.

Dominant genes

A **defective gene** can be passed on from **one parent or both**. The likelihood of developing a condition depends upon whether the defective gene is recessive or dominant. A **dominant gene** needs only to be passed on by one parent for the child to develop a condition, for example:

* **Brittle bone disease**: causes bones to break easily.
* **Huntington's disease**: causes involuntary movement, cognitive and psychiatric disorders.

Recessive genes

A **recessive gene** must be passed on from **both parents** for the child to develop the condition. For example:

* **Cystic fibrosis**: causes a build-up of thick, sticky mucous that can damage the lungs.
* **Phenylketonuria (PKU)**: causes intellectual disability and developmental delay.
* **Duchenne muscular dystrophy**: causes muscle weakness and wasting resulting in difficulty with motor skills and walking.

If the defective gene is passed from one parent only, the child becomes a **carrier**.

Conditions caused by an abnormality in an individual's chromosomes

* **Down's syndrome**: individuals have an extra copy of chromosome 21. This causes characteristic facial features, growth delay and intellectual disability.
* **Klinefelter syndrome**: boys have an extra X chromosome, causing problems during, or a delay in, puberty.
* **Colour blindness**: caused by mutations in the X chromosome, so is more common in males. It makes it difficult to distinguish colours.

Down's syndrome is caused by an extra chromosome.

Genetic susceptibility to disease

This means an increased likelihood of developing a disease because of an individual's genetic makeup. It can lead to diseases such as:

* cancer
* high blood cholesterol
* diabetes.

Other factors affecting disease

The likelihood of developing diseases can be increased or reduced by:

* ☑ environmental factors
* ☑ lifestyle
* ☑ life events
* ☑ availability of preventative treatment.

Now try this

Outline what is meant by:

1 genetic predisposition to conditions
2 susceptibility to disease.

Condition: an abnormal state of health that impacts on wellbeing.

Disease: a disorder of the function or structure of the body.

Biological factors

Biological factors are those that affect the development of a living organism.

Biological factors

The mother's **lifestyle** during pregnancy can affect the health and development of the unborn child. Poor lifestyle factors that may affect the unborn child include:

- poor diet
- drug use
- alcohol use
- smoking.

Effects on developing child

The effects of poor lifestyle choices in pregnancy include:

- low birth weight
- premature birth
- long-term health problems
- learning disabilities
- developmental delay
- congenital defects (defects in the developing foetus).

Maternal infections

Infections such as rubella or cytomegalovirus (CMV) can be passed to the baby in the womb and may cause:

- health problems
- congenital defects
- still birth
- miscarriage.

Foetal alcohol syndrome

This syndrome is caused by exposure to alcohol in the womb. Symptoms include:

- small head circumference
- neurological problems
- abnormal growth
- developmental delay
- facial abnormalities.

Congenital anomalies

These are defects or anomalies in the developing foetus, such as congenital heart disease or club foot. Anomalies may be detected before birth, during birth or in later life.

Genetic, such as Down's Syndrome

Nutritional, such as a deficiency in folate, which increases the risk of neural tube defect (spina bifida)

Factors contributing to congenital anomalies

Environmental, such as maternal exposure to pesticides, chemicals, radiation or alcohol or tobacco, causing abnormal growth

Infections, such as rubella, resulting in deafness and health problems

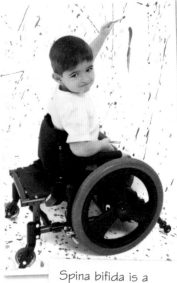

Spina bifida is a congenital anomaly.

Now try this

Identify **three** possible effects of foetal alcohol syndrome.

Environmental factors

Factors affecting human growth and development

Inherited · Environmental · Social · Economic · Biological · Life events

Pollution

Pollution happens when harmful substances contaminate the atmosphere. Pollutants are taken into the body via the nose and mouth or through the skin.

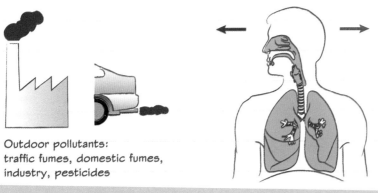

Outdoor pollutants:
traffic fumes, domestic fumes,
industry, pesticides

Indoor pollutants:
cleaning chemicals,
aerosols, cigarette
smoke, mould/bacteria

Conditions caused by pollutants:
- respiratory disorders: bronchitis, asthma, emphysema, lung cancer
- cardiovascular problems: artery blockage, heart attack
- allergies: wheezing, rashes, allergic rhinitis, anaphylactic shock.

Poor housing conditions

These can lead to short-term or longer-term health problems.

Poor ventilation / damp and
mould: respiratory disorders

Overcrowding:
anxiety / depression

**Possible effects of
housing conditions**

Inadequate heating:
hypothermia

Poor sanitation / vermin:
risk of infection

Lack of outdoor space:
cardiovascular problems

People at risk

Infants, people with existing respiratory disorders and the elderly are more at risk from pollution.

Now try this

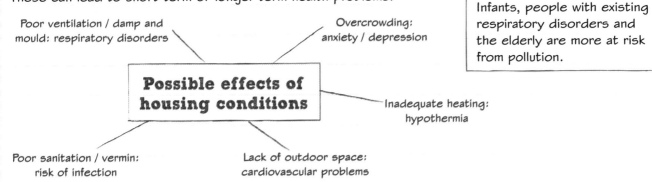

Will is 52 years old. He lives with his wife, son and grandson in a small flat in a busy part of London. Will's father died of a heart attack in his 40s. Will has now been diagnosed with heart disease. He has a healthy diet and has never smoked.

Using your knowledge of genetic and environmental factors, identify three reasons why Will may have developed heart disease.

Health and social care services

Health care services are available to support individuals with their health and social care needs. Access to services can be difficult as availability can vary between different geographical areas.

The relationship between health and social care services

Health services

Urgent /emergency care
Sexual health
Mental health
Pharmacy
Dental
Eye care
Walk-in centres (for minor illness and injury)
Home nursing
Chronic health care
Community health (for screening and preventative care)
Maternity services
Paediatric care

Advisory services
Advocacy
Discharge planning
Transport
Nursing home
End-of-life care
Safeguarding

Adult and children's social care

Day centres and luncheon clubs
Supported living
Residential care
Benefits: financial support
Home care
Housing
Children's services

Access to services can prove difficult for some people

1 Service availability

- Specialist services or drugs are not available in some geographical areas.
- There may be restrictions on delivery or service opening times.
- Pressures on services because of increased demand, e.g. winter flu, may limit availability.
- Waiting times are affected by lack of availability of specialists and hospital beds.
- Lack of public transport to take individuals to and from services.

2 Individual circumstances

- Mobility difficulties restrict physical access.
- Learning and/or communication difficulties can impact on a person's understanding of and contact with available services.
- Sensory difficulties impact on a person's ability to find out about and access services.
- Personal circumstances, such as caring for others or working long hours, can make attending services difficult.

Now try this

Rajif is 48 and has learning and communication difficulties. He smokes, which is starting to give him breathing difficulties.

Explain **two** reasons why Rajif may have difficulty in accessing services.

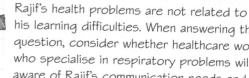

Rajif's health problems are not related to his learning difficulties. When answering this question, consider whether healthcare workers who specialise in respiratory problems will be aware of Rajif's communication needs and, if not, the possible effects.

Social factors – family dysfunction

The quality of family relationships has a long-term impact on development.

Dysfunctional families

Characteristics of a dysfunctional family include:

- members of the family do not carry out their responsibilities
- needs of family members are not met
- family members display negativity towards each other
- sibling rivalry and conflict
- abuse may happen
- use of coercion and blame.

Reasons

Reasons for family dysfunction include:

- parents perpetuate their own dysfunctional upbringing
- untreated mental illness in one or more family members
- alcohol or drug abuse by one or more members of the family.

Impact of dysfunction

Members of dysfunctional families have negative self-image and low self-esteem, and difficulty building friendships and relationships.

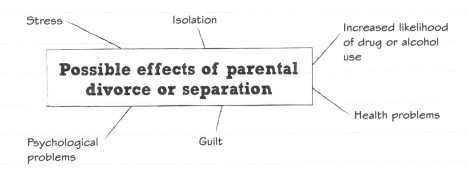

Stress

Isolation

Increased likelihood of drug or alcohol use

Possible effects of parental divorce or separation

Health problems

Psychological problems

Guilt

Parenting styles

Children are often self-controlled, confident and have high self-esteem.

Children may have poor social skills and low self-esteem.

	Supportive	Unsupportive
Demanding	**Authoritative** Children are accepted for who they are. There is mutual love and respect.	**Authoritarian** Parents assert their authority. Children are controlled.
Undemanding	**Permissive** Parents are indulgent. They do not attempt to control behaviour.	**Disengaged / uninvolved** Parents are neglectful and show a lack of interest. There is poor attachment.

Children may be self-confident, impulsive and have difficulty building friendships.

Children may have low confidence and self-esteem and hide their emotions.

Now try this

Consider the scenarios below:

1   Kieran is 14 years old. He enjoys being out with friends and is allowed to get home late. He is often rude to his parents, but they do not take action because they feel that it is his life stage and he will grow out of it.

2   Zofia is 11 years old. She is doing well at school. Her mum talks to her about her homework each evening and she is encouraged to finish it before she sees her friends.

Identify the parenting style used for each young person.

Social factors – bullying

Bullying can happen at any stage of life. It has a negative effect on everyone involved: the victim, the bully and any onlookers.

Bullying can take different forms

 Verbal: using words to hurt, including:
- name calling
- making racist, sexist or disablist comments / slurs
- making hurtful comments
- making threats
- ridiculing.

 Emotional: causing psychological hurt, including:
- spreading rumours
- excluding
- ignoring
- stalking.

3 Physical: using force, including:
- hitting
- pushing
- slapping
- kicking
- taking / hiding / damaging another's belongings.

4 Cyber bullying: using technology to hurt, including:
- sending hurtful messages via the internet
- sharing personal information without permission
- posting inappropriate photos
- hurtful / anonymous text messaging.

Short-term effects of bullying

Inability to cope with life events

Stress/anxiety

Poor self-image

Short-term effects of bullying

Withdrawal from school, work and activities

Low self-esteem

Eating disorders

Long-term effects of bullying

Bullying can have a significant psychological effect on development and wellbeing, including:
- difficulties in forming relationships
- poor academic achievement
- substance misuse
- self-harm
- increased risk of suicide.

Now try this

Zak has just started secondary school. He has started receiving hurtful text messages but does not know who they are from.

Explain **one** possible short-term effect and one possible long-term effect on Zak's **social** development, and one possible short-term effect and one possible long-term effect on his **emotional** development.

The influence of culture and religion

Development is influenced by an individual's culture, the community in which they live and their beliefs (religious or spiritual).

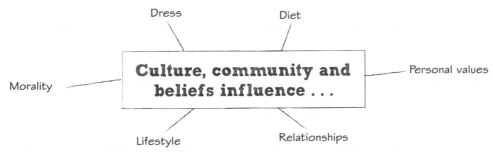

Dress   Diet

Morality

Culture, community and beliefs influence ...

Personal values

Lifestyle   Relationships

Lifestyle rules

Many religions and beliefs have lifestyle rules which followers abide by.

	Examples	Possible health benefits	Possible health risks
Dietary restrictions	Some religions forbid the consumption of certain foods, such as shellfish for Jews or pork for Muslims. Buddhists and many Hindus are vegetarian.	High fibre and/or low fat diets lower risk of high cholesterol, heart disease and high blood pressure. Reduced risk of cancers and heart disease if alcohol or stimulants are restricted.	Nutritional deficiencies, such as lack of calcium (bones and teeth), iron and vitamin B12 (for red blood cells), vitamin D (for healthy bone growth) and protein (for maintenance of muscles, organs, skin and bones).
Fasting	Several religions have periods of fasting, such as Muslims during Ramadan, Jews for several days in the year and Mormons on the first Sunday of each month.	Loss of weight, reduced cholesterol levels, detoxification.	Heartburn, constipation, malnourishment, dehydration, exacerbation of existing conditions such as diabetes and stress.
Medical interventions	For example, Christian scientists believe in healing through prayer and Jehovah's Witnesses do not receive blood transfusions.		Deterioration to health and possible death.

Possible social and emotional effects of culture and beliefs

Positive effects

👍 People share the same values, beliefs and religion.

👍 People feel accepted and are supported by others.

👍 People feel valued by others because of their values, beliefs and religion.

Negative effects

👎 People are discriminated against because of their values, beliefs or religion.

👎 People feel excluded because of their values, beliefs or religion.

👎 A person's culture is ignored or not understood.

Now try this

Many Hindus and Buddhists are vegetarian. Identify **two** health benefits and **two** possible health risks of vegetarianism.

Economic factors

Economic factors are all the aspects of life related to money, including educational achievement, our job, how we choose to live and the amount of money we make.

Income and expenditure: a person's level of income and personal wealth.

Education: the stage of education reached, educational opportunities and achievements.

Economic factors

Lifestyle and health: being able to afford a healthy diet or access to exercise, making choices about sexual practices, alcohol, smoking and drug use that affect personal finance and the ability to keep and sustain employment.

Employment status: whether a person is in work or not, the type of work (manual, non-manual, professional), whether it is full- or part-time, job security and future prospects.

Effects of economic factors

Factor	Positive effects	Negative effects
Physical	👍 Manual/active jobs improve muscle tone and stamina. 👍 Lifestyle: being able to afford a healthy diet and regular exercise to keep digestive systems, circulatory systems and joints healthy.	👎 Manual jobs may cause muscular and skeletal problems. 👎 Sedentary/desk-based jobs can cause back problems, repetitive strain injury, lack of fitness and increased risk of joint problems and heart disease.
Intellectual	👍 Being in work, education or training promotes creative thinking and problem-solving skills. 👍 Being able to afford a good diet and exercise can promote cognitive development.	👎 Being out of work, retired or in a non-demanding job may cause deterioration of memory and problem-solving skills. 👎 Low income and a low-quality lifestyle can lead to stress and loss of concentration.
Emotional	👍 Being in a high-status job and having a good income and education may lead to high self-image and positive self-esteem. 👍 Having an adequate income and job provides opportunities and independence.	👎 Being unemployed, having a low-status job and poor academic achievement can lead to poor lifestyle choices (e.g. drug use, unhealthy diet), negative self-image and low self-esteem. 👎 Low income and poor health due to lifestyle can lead to lack of choice and independence. 👎 Concerns about lack of work or finances can lead to stress.
Social	👍 Being at school, college, or in training or work provides opportunities to develop friendships. 👍 Being able to afford a healthy lifestyle can lead to friendships.	👎 Low income or unemployment offers fewer opportunities for building relationships. 👎 Poor lifestyle may lead to breakdown in relationships.

Now try this

Think of at least **four** more examples of effects that could be added to this table – two positive and two negative.

Life events

Everyone experiences major events during their life. These can be predictable or unpredictable, depending on the person's life course.

Examples of life events

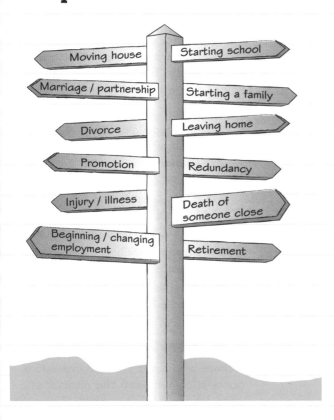

Moving house
Starting school
Marriage / partnership
Starting a family
Divorce
Leaving home
Promotion
Redundancy
Injury / illness
Death of someone close
Beginning / changing employment
Retirement

Types of transition

Life events are also known as transitions.

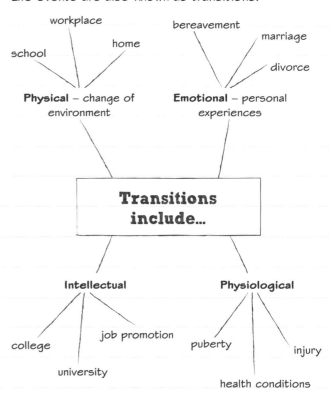

workplace
school
home
Physical – change of environment

bereavement
marriage
divorce
Emotional – personal experiences

Transitions include...

Intellectual
college
university
job promotion

Physiological
puberty
injury
health conditions

What are predictable life events?

These are life events that:
- are likely to happen to most people, such as starting school or work
- can be anticipated and prepared for.

Predictable events often have positive effects such as building self-esteem, developing confidence, providing security or furthering learning. However, the changes can still cause anxiety, which may affect health and wellbeing.

What are unpredictable life events?

These are life events that:
- are not expected, such as an accident or serious illness
- happen with little or no warning so cannot be prepared for.

Some life events will happen to many people but not everyone, for example marriage, having children, getting a promotion or serious illness.

Now try this

Anya is 29 years old. Draw a timeline for Anya from birth to her present age.

Identify the predictable life events that she is likely to have experienced in her life so far.

The effects of life events

Life events can cause stress that results in health problems. The level of stress depends on the event, the situation of the individual and their ability to cope with the demands of life.

Life events can impact on health and wellbeing

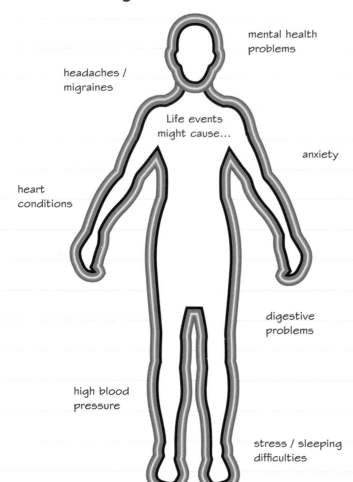

mental health problems

headaches / migraines

Life events might cause...

anxiety

heart conditions

digestive problems

high blood pressure

stress / sleeping difficulties

Holmes-Rahe social adjustment rating scale

Thomas Holmes and Richard Rahe believed there was a correlation (relationship) between psychological illness and stressful events.

The study

1. Holmes and Rahe listed 43 life events that individuals may experience.
2. They applied a score (unit) to each life event, depending on the level of stress it was likely to cause.
3. Patients were asked to indicate the life events they had experienced from the list.
4. Patients added up the scores from their life events.

The result of the study

Holmes and Rahe found there was a correlation between the number of units (the level and number of stressful events the individual experienced) and their illness.

Predictable and unpredictable

Predictable and unpredictable life events can cause stress at any life stage. Extreme stress from unpredictable life events can cause serious mental and physical problems.

Events listed by Holmes and Rahe

Holmes and Rahe listed both predictable and unpredictable events. The units allocated to each event varied depending on the event.

Here are some examples of life events and their associated units:

- ✓ death of a partner = 100 units
- ✓ marriage = 50 units
- ✓ retirement = 45 units
- ✓ change of school = 20 units

Now try this

Look at the life events in the diagram on page 29. List them in order of the likely level of stress you think they will cause, starting with the most stressful. Compare your list with the Holmes-Rahe list.

Cardiovascular disease and ageing

The risk of cardiovascular disease increases with age, but the likelihood may be increased or reduced by other factors.

Changes in the heart with ageing

1. The heart may increase in size, causing the heart wall to thicken, making it more difficult for the heart muscles to relax and fill with blood between beats.

2. Artery walls narrow due to clogging by fats called cholesterol, preventing blood from passing easily.

3. Pacemaker cells decrease, causing problems in the rhythm of the heart.

4. The valves inside the heart that control the flow of blood thicken and become stiffer.

These changes increase the likelihood of angina, hypertension (high blood pressure), heart murmurs, stroke, heart attack and heart failure.

Factors affecting cardiovascular health in older age

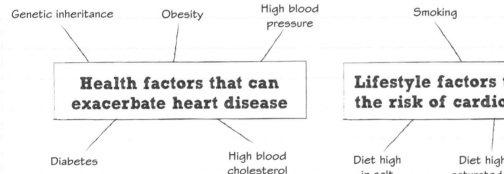

Genetic inheritance   Obesity   High blood pressure   Smoking   Alcohol

Health factors that can exacerbate heart disease

Lifestyle factors that can increase the risk of cardiovascular disease

Diabetes   High blood cholesterol   Diet high in salt   Diet high in saturated fats   Lack of exercise

The effects of cardiovascular disease in later life

Negative effects
- 👎 loss of independence
- 👎 anxiety about health
- 👎 depression
- 👎 anger
- 👎 frustration
- 👎 reduced mobility
- 👎 loss of opportunity to develop new friendships

Positive effects
- 👍 closer relationships with family members and friends
- 👍 choosing to improve lifestyle

Now try this

Janet will soon be 65. Her mother died from cardiovascular disease aged 67.

List examples of **five** things that Janet can do to reduce the likelihood of cardiovascular disease.

Degeneration of the nervous tissue

Nerves are pathways that carry messages along the spinal cord between the brain and the different parts of the body. The loss of neurones in the brain leads to a decrease in the capacity of the brain to send and receive nerve impulses.

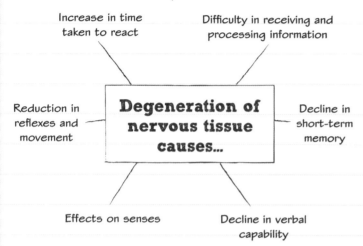

Increase in time taken to react

Difficulty in receiving and processing information

Reduction in reflexes and movement

Degeneration of nervous tissue causes...

Decline in short-term memory

Effects on senses

Decline in verbal capability

Facts about nervous tissue

- The pace of degeneration varies between older people.
- The same symptoms may be caused by illness such as Alzheimer's disease.
- The brain can produce new brain cells into older age (e.g. stroke patients learn to speak again).
- New connections between nerve cells can develop.
- Exercising, not smoking and cognitive activity can slow the degeneration of the nervous tissue in older people.

Loss of neurones and degenerative diseases

Loss of neurones from structures of the brain that control movement may cause degenerative diseases such as Parkinson's disease. The average age for the onset of Parkinson's is 60.

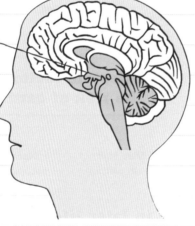

Substantia nigra: dopamine-producing cells

Parkinson's disease affects neurones in an area of the brain called the substantia nigra. As the neurones die, the production of a chemical called dopamine decreases. Dopamine sends messages to the part of the brain that controls movement and coordination.

Tremor: uncontrollable shaking, beginning in the hand and arm

Depression   Anxiety

Physical effects of Parkinson's disease

Cognitive effects of Parkinson's disease

Mobility: slowness of movement and muscle stiffness

Impairment in thinking and problem solving

Now try this

Identify the effects of degeneration of the nervous tissue. Suggest **three** ways that individuals can reduce the decline.

Degeneration of the sense organs

The senses help individuals to receive information from the environment. As we get older our senses become less sharp.

 Taste

With age:

- the number of taste buds decreases, reducing the enjoyment of food and perhaps resulting in poor diet
- production of saliva decreases, affecting the taste and enjoyment of food
- the ability to smell decreases, reducing the ability to detect dangerous odours such as fumes or foods that have gone off.

 Sight

With age:

- vision becomes less sharp
- cataracts may develop, causing cloudiness in vision
- the vitreous (gel-like substance) in the eye starts to shrink, causing floaters
- peripheral vision deteriorates
- eye muscles become weaker, reducing the field of vision
- pupils react more slowly in bright light or darkness
- there is an increased risk of age-related macular degeneration (AMD), which causes a gradual loss of sight.

Older people experience physiological change in sense organs.

 Touch

A decrease in the number of receptor cells in older age leads to:

- reduced sensitivity to temperature, which can lead to burns, frostbite or hypothermia
- reduced sensitivity to injury, which can lead to untreated pressure sores or ulcers
- increased sensitivity to touch, which can cause bruising
- skin becoming more sensitive to the sun, which can lead to sunburn or skin cancer.

 Hearing

With age:

- fluid-filled tubes in the inner ear, which help to maintain balance, become affected, which may cause dizziness and falls
- the ability to hear high-frequency sounds deteriorates
- distinguishing between sounds is more difficult
- tinnitus (persistent noise) is experienced because of a build-up of wax or damage to the ear.

Social and emotional effects of degeneration of sense organs

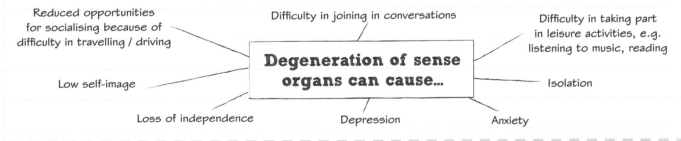

Reduced opportunities for socialising because of difficulty in travelling / driving

Difficulty in joining in conversations

Difficulty in taking part in leisure activities, e.g. listening to music, reading

Degeneration of sense organs can cause...

Low self-image

Isolation

Loss of independence   Depression   Anxiety

Now try this

Outline:

1 reasons why a person's diet can be negatively affected by a degeneration of the senses
2 the effects of a poor diet on other aspects of physical development.

Osteoarthritis and nutrition

Two common physical effects in older age are osteoarthritis and a reduction in the absorption of nutrients.

What is osteoarthritis?

The physical effects of osteoarthritis are:

- swelling and pain in joints
- damage to the soft tissue around joints
- difficulty in walking
- difficulty in climbing stairs.

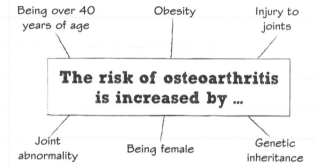

Being over 40 years of age   Obesity   Injury to joints

The risk of osteoarthritis is increased by ...

Joint abnormality   Being female   Genetic inheritance

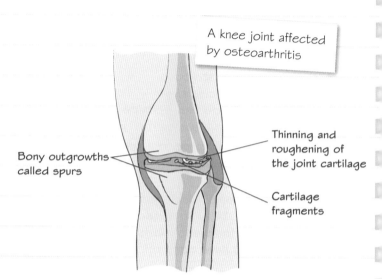

A knee joint affected by osteoarthritis

Bony outgrowths called spurs

Thinning and roughening of the joint cartilage

Cartilage fragments

Absorption of nutrients

With age, the body is less efficient at absorbing the nutrients it requires. This can result in malnutrition, even if the person's diet remains the same as when they were younger. The reduction of the absorption of nutrients is caused by:

- reduced production of gastric hydrochloric acid, which prevents the breakdown of proteins, fats and carbohydrates
- the deterioration of the function of the digestive organs and digestive lining.

The effects of deficiencies in essential nutrients

Essential nutrients	The effects of deficiency
Vitamin D	Increases risk of osteoporosis, cancer and diabetes, and reduces the body's ability to absorb calcium.
Calcium	Causes bone loss and increases the risk of osteoporosis and fractures.
Vitamin B12	Slows the creation of red blood cells and reduces nerve function.
Magnesium	Impacts on the immune system and function of the heart.
Omega-3	Increases the risk of rheumatoid arthritis and macular degeneration.
Potassium	Weakens bones and reduces cell function and kidney function.
Vitamin C	Slows healing and the development of healthy tissue.
Iron	Increases the risk of anaemia.

Older people have an increased risk of dehydration as their sensation of thirst decreases. Fluid intake is essential for healthy organs and digestive system.

Now try this

Give **three** reasons why an older person may have an increased risk of osteoarthritis.

Dementia

Dementia is a term that is used to describe symptoms associated with damage to the function of the brain, such as memory loss.

Facts about dementia

A stroke may cause dementia because when the brain's blood supply is restricted, brain cells begin to die.

Lifestyle factors such as smoking, an unhealthy diet and lack of exercise can increase the risk of dementia.

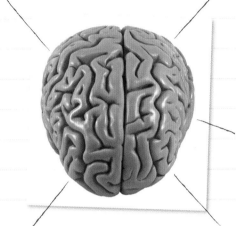

The risk of dementia increases with age.

Alzheimer's disease is the most common form of dementia.

Dementia is a progressive disease – more parts of the brain are damaged over time.

Alzheimer's disease

Alzheimer's disease is the most common cause of dementia. It mainly affects people over the age of 65. Proteins called plaques and tangles build up in the brain. This leads to a shortage of chemicals in the brain, which affects the transmission of signals.

Normal brain

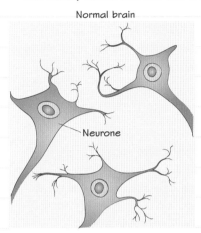

Neurone

Brain with Alzheimer's disease

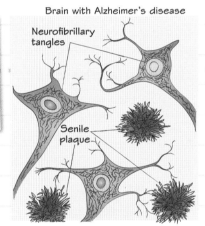

Neurofibrillary tangles

Senile plaque

Comparison of normal neurones and those of someone with Alzheimer's disease.

The effects of Alzheimer's disease

Early stage
- Decline in short-term memory
- Difficulty completing routine tasks
- Impairment in thinking / problem solving

Later stage
- Language impairment
- Lack of judgement
- Emotional outbursts
- Changes in behaviour
- Agitation

Final stage
- Unable to recognise family members
- Unable to feed or care for self
- Lack of control of bodily functions
- Almost total loss of memory
- Death

Support needs for Alzheimer's disease

Early stage
- Informal help with everyday tasks
- Medication
- Counselling
- Memory clinics

Later stage
- Community / specialist nurse visits
- Respite care
- Medication
- Support in the home with personal care

Final stage
- Residential/hospice care
- Personal/continence care
- End-of-life care

Now try this

Identify **two** services that could support an individual at each stage of Alzheimer's disease.

Effects of illness common in ageing

The physical effects of illness impact on all other areas of a person's development.

 Physical effects

Illness may:

- make the body less able to fight infection
- reduce stamina
- result in lost mobility
- cause pain and discomfort
- impact on the senses, making them less sharp
- affect vision and cause dizziness that could lead to falls.

2 Intellectual effects

Illness may:

- cause short-term memory loss
- affect decision-making skills
- slow the ability to respond and react to information
- cause difficulty in verbal communication.

3 Social effects

Illness may:

- reduce the opportunity and ability to socialise with friends
- impact on senses or neural capacity, making socialising difficult
- affect ability to communicate in groups.

4 Emotional effects

Illness may:

- cause emotional distress, e.g. incontinence, communication difficulties
- result in dependence on others for personal care
- cause feelings of lack of control
- bring families closer together
- result in low self-esteem.

Lifestyle choices

Provides the additional nutrients needed to reduce a decline in health.

Healthy diet

Maintains a healthy weight to reduce stress on the heart and other organs.

Keeps the joints mobile.

Lifestyle choices may improve or exacerbate the impact of ill health on older people.

Exercise

Maintains muscle and strength.

Keeps the heart healthy.

Medication that is prescribed correctly should control illness and not make it worse.

Taking recreational drugs can negatively affect intellectual development and mood.

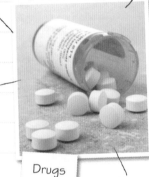

Drugs

Not smoking reduces the impact of age-related disease.

Now try this

Yohan is 62 years old. He recently had a heart attack and has just been discharged from hospital.

1 Identify **one** effect that Yohan's health may have on his social development and **one** effect on his emotional development.

2 Identify **two** ways that Yohan can reduce the risk of a decline to the health of his heart.

Psychological effects of ageing

Social change in older age can bring about a sense of loss, anxiety, reduced confidence and low self-esteem.

Social changes

Loss of job and status: retirement may reduce self-esteem because of a feeling of lack of purpose, but increases leisure time and opportunities to try new things such as travel, enjoy grandchildren and hobbies.

Reduced mobility/fitness: inability to move around and continue to carry out physical tasks can result in cognitive decline and reduce wellbeing.

Losing own home: affects contentment and security when forced to move, e.g. into smaller house, in with family or into residential care.

Social changes and their effects

Loss of independence: reliance on others increases a feeling of helplessness.

Death of partner/friends: grief can cause a loss of sense of safety and security, increased isolation and loss of intimacy.

Reduced access to social networks: difficulty in meeting and taking part in social activity can prevent development of the brain, cause or worsen depression and other mental conditions.

Financial concerns

Research by Age UK has shown that, in 2016, 29% of retired people did not have financial concerns and 26% said they were just getting by. This means that almost half of the older population do have financial concerns, with 14% living in poverty. This can result in:

- less opportunity to socialise
- less money to buy food
- less money to pay for adequate heating
- worry and stress.

Loneliness and dependence

36% of people over 65 years live alone. Taking advantage of free bus travel or continuing to drive can help older adults to feel part of the community, and reduce the feeling of loneliness and dependence.

No longer being able to travel adversely affects independence and self-esteem.

Self-esteem

Health, employment and financial security are essential for high self-esteem. If these things are lost, an individual can feel:

- that they are no longer useful
- that they are no longer independent and can't do things for themselves
- financially insecure and anxious about how they will pay for things.

All of these will reduce self-esteem.

Effects of culture religion and beliefs

Culture, religion and beliefs can have a positive impact on ageing because:

- individuals feel part of a group or community, so less isolated
- beliefs help people to make sense of their ageing and come to terms with mortality
- some cultures and religions place more value on older people.

Now try this

Neena's husband died recently. He was Neena's carer, so she is now moving from her home where she has lived for 40 years into residential care.

Explain **two** possible effects of these events on Neena's psychological health.

Theories of ageing

Ageing is a natural process that takes place over a long period of time. Theories help to explain what is happening during that process.

Activity theory

Individuals can achieve healthy ageing through continued social activity.

Social disengagement theory

A reduction in social contact is natural in older age.

Activity theory (Robert Havighurst, 1960s) is based on a belief that:

* the social and psychological needs of individuals remain the same
* people need activity and social interactions
* individuals adjust to their declining health and mobility and/or strength
* people continue to involve themselves in the community.

Social disengagement theory is based on a belief that:

* people naturally withdraw from social contact in older age
* society withdraws from older people
* people focus on their previous life and activities
* family expects less from older people
* older people become more dependent
* ageing can result in tranquillity and be a positive development.

Getting the most out of later life

Older people can be supported to continue to get satisfaction from life by encouraging:

👍 involvement in new activities, such as hobbies and volunteering

👍 the planning of new goals

👍 the development of new relationships

👍 decision making and choices about their own care.

Now try this

Clive is 72. He had a good job managing an IT department. He retired 4 years ago.

Use activity theory to outline ways that Clive can continue to enjoy life.

Provision for the aged

The number of older people has increased. They have specific health and social care needs and rely on a range of different services to meet their needs and help them to remain independent.

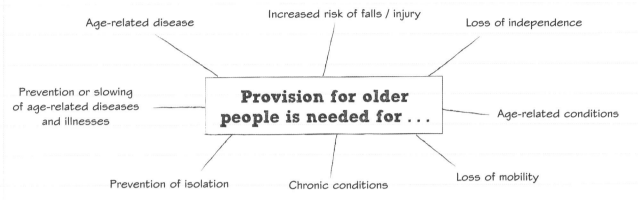

What type of provision is available?

1 **Acute care**: meeting immediate health needs, such as broken hips, heart attacks.
2 **Healthcare**: medication, support for long-term conditions, palliative care, continence care, specialist nursing / units.
3 **Social care**: own home, day care or residential, assessing needs, supporting independence, personal care, day-to-day care, respite care.
4 **Community equipment**: keeping people mobile and independent in their own home, e.g. mobility aids, aids for daily living.
5 **Psychological care**: counsellors, mental health nursing.
6 **Benefits and entitlements**: adaptions to home, transport to and from appointments, financial support.
7 **End-of-life care**: pain relief, psychological support.

Provisions to help maintain health

Integrated services

Older people may need different services to work together to assess and provide for their health and care needs.

Formal and informal services are integrated to provide a holistic care package:

- **Formal health care**: statutory, private, voluntary
- **Informal health care**: provided by family, community or religious groups.

Now try this

Add one more example to each of the seven types of provision listed above.

Ageing and economic effects

Life expectancy has increased each decade over the last 100 years and the birth rate has fallen. This means there are more older people, which increases pressure on the economics of the UK.

An ageing population in the UK

- Life expectancy is now 79.2 years for males and 83.3 years for females.
- There are as many people over 65 years old as under 16 years old.
- One in three babies born today will reach 100 years of age.
- The old age dependency ratio has risen.

Old age dependency ratio

This describes the ratio of people older than 65 (so assumed to be retired) to the number of people of working age, which is defined as between 15 and 64. An increase in the older population and longer life expectancy has resulted in fewer people of working age being available to support the needs of older people.

What the changes mean for the economy

 Health and welfare: older people already use more health and care services. A rise in numbers means a higher demand and increased costs.

 Pension costs: more people receive a state pension, leaving less money for economic investment.

> **Impacts of the percentage rise in older people on the economy**

 Employment: more retired people means a shortage of skilled workers. There are changes to working patterns as older people work part-time.

 Housing: more retirement homes and sheltered housing are required. People stay in their own homes longer so fewer larger homes are available for families.

Government responses

The government has responded to these changes by:

- raising the retirement age
- making it easier for older people to stay in work and/or work part-time
- encouraging people in work to take out private pensions
- increasing taxes to pay for state pensions and welfare.

Pressures on services

Additional pressure is put on services due to:

- advances in medicine that help people to live longer
- families being unable or less willing to care for older family members at home
- an increase in the numbers of older people with chronic conditions.

Now try this

Identify **three** possible effects on the economy of changes in the old age dependency ratio.

Your Unit 1 exam

You will have 1 hour and 30 minutes to complete your Unit 1 exam paper. You need to answer every question.

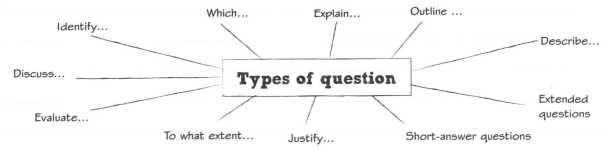

Identify...　Which...　Explain...　Outline ...

Discuss...

Describe...

Types of question

Evaluate...

Extended questions

To what extent...　Justify...　Short-answer questions

Number of marks

The paper is worth 90 marks in total. The marks are shown in brackets and will range from 1 to 12 marks per question.

The number of marks indicates the amount of time you should spend on each question.

Remember to take a **black** pen into your exam. It's a good idea to have a spare pen as well.

Spelling, punctuation and grammar

Make sure that your answers are clear and use accurate spelling, punctuation and grammar.

✓ **Spelling:** you should know how to spell key technical terms, such as 'cognitive development'.

✓ **Grammar:** for example, you can use paragraphs in longer answers to help structure your points.

✓ **Punctuation:** when writing in full sentences, use commas and full stops where needed to make your meaning clear.

Worked example

Carl and his friend Saeed are 12 years old. A year ago they were the same height and weight. Carl is now 5 centimetres taller than Saeed but is still the same weight as his friend.

Use the principles of growth to explain Carl's pattern of growth at his life stage.　`4 marks`

Sample response extract

Carl may have had a growth spurt because he is experiencing puberty. Different parts of his body will grow at different rates, so Carl's weight may be increasing more slowly than his height.

This question is worth 4 marks. You should aim to spend only 3 or 4 minutes reading about Carl and writing the answer.

This is an **explain** question. You need to show that you understand the topic and give reasons to support your opinion or argument. Make sure you give enough detail to justify your answer.

Links Look at pages 1 and 5 to revise the content covered in this question.

There is more about 'explain' questions on page 45.

Now try this

Identify **three** primary sexual characteristics that a boy will develop during puberty.

You need to briefly state two different examples.

Links Revise this topic on page 5.

Using case studies

All the questions in your exam will relate to members of **one family**. As you work through the exam you will gradually find out more about each person so that you can answer questions about their development. Information will include details such as **age, relationships, lifestyle choices**, their **environment** or their **life events**. In the second half of the exam paper you will be given an extended case study relating to one member of the family. There is more about this on page 48. You should always read case studies carefully.

Why case studies are important

Case studies are used so that you can apply your knowledge and understanding of the content of this unit to **realistic situations** and **contexts**. You will need to apply knowledge and understanding about:

- ✓ key features of development across the life stages
- ✓ factors that impact on human growth and development
- ✓ theories that help to explain human growth and development
- ✓ life events that can impact on human growth and development
- ✓ the effects of ageing for the individual and for society.

Worked example

Konrad is 49 years old. He has two children, Nina aged 12 and Micah, who is 3 years old. Micah has just started nursery. The nursery has an outdoor play area with a climbing frame, ride-on toys and a selection of bats, balls and hoops.

Describe Micah's gross motor skills in relation to how his ability to take part in outdoor play should develop.

6 marks

Sample response extract

Micah will have developed the large muscles in his arms and legs, which will help him to hold on to the climbing frame and push up with his legs to climb higher. He will be able to use the large muscles in his hands to hold a ball and use the muscles in his arms and legs to throw or kick it. Micah will be developing his leg strength, balance and coordination, so will be able to pedal and control ride-on toys.

In your exam paper you will be given information about family members in a case study to help you to answer the questions. You can underline key words to help you to answer the question.

This tells you that Konrad is in the middle adult life stage, Nina is in the adolescent life stage and Micah is in the early childhood life stage.

For this **describe** question, you need to show your knowledge of the **age/life stage** of the child and the types of **activities** he might be doing. Recall your knowledge of the physical skills a child has acquired at this age/stage and make links to how he uses them to take part in the activities.

Links Look at page 3 to revise the content covered in this question. There is more about 'describe' questions on page 47.

Now try this

Micah is meeting his expected milestones in social development.

Outline Micah's stage of play.

You already know Micah's age. The information in this question tells you more about Micah so that you can answer another question about his social development.

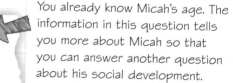

 Links Revise page 15 to answer this question.

Short-answer questions

Short-answer questions will test your knowledge and understanding of a topic. They are worth between 1 and 6 marks.

Typical short-answer question types

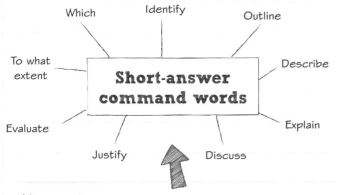

Which · Identify · Outline · To what extent · Describe · Short-answer command words · Evaluate · Explain · Justify · Discuss

You may also see some of these command words in questions worth 10–12 marks, where the information about the topics is more complex.

Answering the questions

- Questions where you need to use your **knowledge** range from 3–6 marks.
- Questions where you need to show your **understanding** of topics range from 1–6 marks.
- Spending too long answering questions that are worth 1 or 2 marks can mean that you run out of time for later questions that are worth 10–12 marks.

Worked example

Drew has just left university with a good degree. He has been offered a job at a local IT company.

Identify three possible reasons why Drew has a positive self-image. **3 marks**

This question asks you to **identify**, which means giving a brief relevant fact linking Drew's situation to the development of positive self-image.

You need to give realistic facts for Drew's situation.

Sample response extract

1. Drew has a sense of achievement.
2. Drew has improved status.
3. Drew will feel financially secure.

Links See pages 14 and 28 to revise the content in this question.

Worked example

Carla, aged 28, has just found out that she is pregnant. She is visiting the midwife to get advice.

Outline the importance of a healthy lifestyle during pregnancy for the developing baby. **6 marks**

This short-answer question is worth 6 marks.

You need to briefly outline the key points about the mother's healthy lifestyle and the impact on the baby. This answer mentions diet and smoking as two aspects of lifestyle. To answer the question fully, another aspect of lifestyle would be needed in the answer.

Sample response extract

A healthy diet is important, as nutritional deficiencies can impair brain development and cause abnormalities. Carla should avoid tobacco as nicotine and carbon monoxide will pass into her blood stream to the foetus, which can cause premature birth. Carla should not...

Now try this

Complete the answer about Carla's pregnancy by writing another sentence or two outlining the importance of not drinking alcohol during pregnancy.

Links See page 22 to revise the content covered in this question.

'Which' and 'Identify' questions

'Which' and 'identify' questions require you to quickly recall facts or main features relating to human development.

'Which' questions

Answering 'which' questions:

- They range from 1 to 6 marks.
- You must select the correct item or feature from a definite set.
- No detail is required.

Do not spend too much time on questions worth 1 to 2 marks. If you are not sure, give your best guess and move on to a new question.

'Identify' questions

Answering 'identify' questions:

- They range from 3 to 6 marks.
- There is no need to expand to provide more detail.

Worked example

Aarif is 13 months old. He is holding on to the furniture to help him to walk around the room.

Which area of development is Aarif developing? **1 mark**

You need to recall the areas of development and select the correct one to answer this question.

Sample response extract

Physical development

Pie chart: Physical, Intellectual, Emotional, Social

Development needs of a young child

Worked example

Lauren is 8 weeks old and is having her growth measured. The health visitor has measured her head circumference and height.

Which other measurement should be taken to check Lauren's growth? **1 mark**

Sample response extract

Weight

🔗 **Links** You can revise the content needed for the first two questions on pages 1 and 3.

Worked example

Identify three examples of conditions that are a result of a genetic predisposition. **3 marks**

This question would follow a scenario relating to genetic predisposition. You only need to give the names of health conditions in your answer. You do not need to give details of their effects.

Sample response extract

1. Cystic fibrosis
2. Huntington's disease
3. Brittle bones

🔗 **Links** You can revise the content needed for this question on page 21.

Now try this

🔗 **Links** You can revise the content needed for this question on page 14.

Rakeesh is 28 years old. He left school at 16 without qualifications and has worked in the car industry ever since. Recently he applied for promotion. He thought he had done well at the interview but he was not successful.

Identify **three** possible effects of Rakeesh's lack of success on his self-esteem.

'Explain' questions

'Explain' questions range from 1 to 6 marks. You must show that you understand the topic and give reasons to support your answer. You may be told how many features or types of feature you must explain. Here are some examples.

Examples of 'explain' questions

1 Explain the effects of ill health on Tariq's development.

2 Explain **two** possible features of Tariq's social development.

3 Explain **one** positive and **one** negative effect of Tariq's work promotion on his development.

4 With reference to the case study about Tariq, explain, giving **two** examples, how his recent life event may have affected his social and emotional development.

You may need to give a single response or you may need to give a specified number in your answer. You would be expected to give supported reasons for each effect or feature that you identify.

Read the questions carefully to find the command word in the question. The question may not always start with the command word.

Social workers work with individuals to help improve their wellbeing.

Worked example

Rosemary is 79 years old. She recently went into hospital for a cataract operation. Before she was discharged, a social worker visited her to assess whether she would be able to care for herself when she went home.

Explain two possible features of the ageing process which may affect Rosemary's ability to care for herself at home.   **4 marks**

Sample response extract

1. Rosemary may have more difficulty preparing food.
2. Rosemary may have difficulty getting in and out of a bath.

This response gives realistic activities that may affect Rosemary's ability to care for herself at home but does not link them to the features of the ageing process.

Improved response extract

1. Rosemary may have more difficulty preparing food because she has less mobility in the small muscles in her fingers.
2. Rosemary may have lost muscle and strength, therefore she may have difficulty getting in and out of a bath.

You need to give realistic activities that may affect Rosemary's ability to care for herself at home and link them clearly to the features of the ageing process.

In 'explain' questions, you could use words such as 'because', 'due to' or 'therefore' to help you make sure you have given reasons.

Now try this

Mike is 19. Mike's relationship with his father broke down when he was 14, when his father left the family home. Last year, after a row, his mother told Mike to leave home. He lived rough for a few months but is now in a hostel. Mike's friends from college no longer call him.

Using the information given, explain **one** possible effect on Mike's emotional development and **one** possible effect on his social development.

Read the question carefully. You are expected to include **one** explanation relating to Mike's **emotional development** and **one** explanation relating to his **social development**.

Links Look at pages 14 and 17 to help revise for this question.

'Outline' questions

'Outline' questions require a summary or overview of the topic or a brief description.

Answering the question

'Outline' questions range from 1 to 6 marks. The number of marks you are given will indicate how much you need to write. Outline a separate point or feature in each sentence. Imagine that you have to give a brief description of the topic to someone who does not know about it, using a few sentences to outline it.

Examples of 'outline' questions

> Paula is 65 and has just retired.

1 Outline the ways in which retirement may affect Paula's social development.

2 Outline the importance of Paula remaining active when she retires.

The number of examples you need to give is not specified. These are 6-mark questions so you would be expected to outline at least three effects on Paula's emotional development for question 1 and three reasons why remaining active is important for question 2.

Worked example

> Claire is 43 years old. She married Tom last year. They would like to have a baby but Claire is concerned that she has not conceived.

Outline how Claire's physical stage of life may account for her being unable to conceive.　　**6 marks**

It is important that you know the key milestones of physical development for Claire's life stage to be able to answer this question.

This question is worth 6 marks, so it requires you to include **three** features of the perimenopause.

Sample response extract

Claire is over 40 years old so has reached the stage of life when perimenopause may begin. This means that she will be reaching the end of her reproductive period so will not be as fertile. Her oestrogen levels will be starting to decrease, which would affect her ability to produce eggs each month. This will make ovulation less regular and reduce the likelihood of Claire conceiving.

You need to outline the physical features of development, correctly using the terminology used by professionals in the health and social care sector.

Include the key features that are likely to be directly responsible for Claire not being able to conceive.

 **Links** See page 6 to revise the content covered in this question.

Now try this

> Kareem and his partner Angelika have three children under 6 years old. Angelika does not work. Kareem works as a security guard. He enjoys his job but only earns the minimum wage, so the family relies on benefits to pay the bills.

Outline the ways in which Kareem's employment status and income may affect his emotional development.

At first it may appear that there are only negative effects but, looking more closely at the information, there is a clue to more positive aspects of Kareem's situation. He gets satisfaction from his work, which may reduce the likelihood of stress.

 Links You can revise the content for this question on page 14.

'Describe' questions

In 'describe' questions you must give a clear account that shows knowledge of the facts and main features of the topic. 'Describe' questions range from 1 to 6 marks.

Examples of 'describe' questions

1 Describe **three** features of Paula's emotional development at her life stage.

You may be asked to describe a specific number of features. If you are asked to describe three examples, write one or two sentences for each.

2 Describe emotional development in relation to Paula's stage of development.

You may be asked to explore a topic, describing the main features. If there is no indication of how many examples or features you need to describe, make sure you give a full description. Around three to six sentences might be needed.

Worked example

Teddies Nursery has provision for children from 6 months to 3 years old. The staff provide plenty of opportunity for children to develop their play.

Describe three stages of play in infancy and early childhood.   **6 marks**

For this question, you need to recall the three different stages of play using three numbered points. Read the question carefully. It asks for types of play in **infancy** and in **early childhood**. If you gave three types of play in early childhood you would not be answering the full question.

Sample response extract

1. In infancy, babies' play is solitary. They concentrate on their own activity and are not interested in, and do not notice, what other infants or children are doing.

2. By the time children reach 2 years old, they become engaged in ~~social play~~ parallel play. They are still involved in their own activity but watch, and are sometimes influenced by, other children's activities.

3. By the time children reach 3 years old, they begin to engage in co-operative play. This means that they are involved in the same activity as other children. They negotiate with friends, agree rules and roles and share ideas for how the play will develop.

This answer gives three types of play and provides clear descriptions showing understanding of what each type means.

If you make any mistakes, you need to clearly strike through them and enter the correct words.

Links Revise page 15 for the content covered in this question.

Now try this

Padma is 66 years of age. She retired at the age of 64 and since then has been doing voluntary work at a local charity shop. She had lots of friends at work who she misses. She has now joined the Townswomen's Guild, meeting with them regularly and taking part in a range of activities.

Describe Padma's social and emotional development in relation to activity theory.

This case study shows that Padma is coping well with her change of lifestyle.

Links To revise for this question, see page 38 about the theories of ageing.

Extended case study

In the earlier stages of your Unit 1 exam, you will be given small pieces of information about members of the same family. As you continue, you will reach an extended case study. This will give you far more information about one member of the family.

Case study information

The extended case study will give you information about the person's stage of life, their lifestyle, life events and other factors that will have impacted on their development. Following this, you will be asked more questions. At least two may be long-answer questions. It is important that you allow yourself time to read the extended case study carefully.

Worked example

Paul, aged 42, lives with his partner, Clive, and Paul's two children, Sally aged 7 and James aged 11.

Paul's mother Tina is 69 years old. Tina divorced Paul's father 8 years ago and has lived on her own since then. She only worked part-time so has to rely on only a state pension. For two years after retirement she looked after Sally and James after school, which she used to enjoy. She had a car and would drive to visit friends to go out for meals or visit the cinema.

However, Tina began to feel dizzy and went to see her GP. The doctor found problems with Tina's inner ear and gave her medication. Tina was advised that she should not drive, so she could no longer care for the children, and visited her friends far less. She started going out only when she needed to buy food.

Tina was also visited by the community nurse, who advised that she should change her diet to lose weight and give up smoking.

Six months ago Tina had a fall at home and broke her hip. She spent three weeks in hospital. Tina gradually gained some of her mobility and can get around using a walking frame.

When Paul visited his mother recently he noticed that she was not taking personal care of herself. Her clothes and hair looked dirty. In the kitchen he noticed black marks around the stove. When he asked Tina what had happened she said she couldn't remember.

This is an extended case study so it builds on information that would already have been given in an exam, and introduces Paul's mother.

Use underlining to help you remember the key facts about the person.

Paragraph 2 gives some information on ways that Tina replaced her loss of employment with other activities. Paragraph 3 describes how she later became isolated. You could be asked about theories that explain this.

In paragraph 4 you are told something about Tina's lifestyle. Think of ways that this could exacerbate the possible diseases and illnesses linked to ageing that she may experience.

Tina has coped with several life events, some predicted (retirement) and others unpredicted (divorce, illness and her accident). You could be asked about the effects of any of these events.

There are clues in the case study about the effects of ageing on Tina's brain function. You could be asked about the causes and the effects of dementia on a person's life.

The extended case study in your Unit 1 exam will contain a little more information about the person and be longer than this.

Now try this

Identify **three** services that could support Tina.

 You can revise the content for this question on page 39.

Long-answer questions

More than half the marks on your paper will be given for questions worth 10 or 12 marks. Below is an example of a good answer to a question worth 12 marks.

Worked example

> Pearl is 3½. She goes to her local nursery where she loves to take part in role-play, particularly the role-play shop where she likes to dress up as the 'shopkeeper' and make up a story as she sells food to her friends.

To what extent might theories of language and cognitive development explain Pearl's ability to take part in role-play?   **12 marks**

Sample response extract

According to Piaget's theory of stages of cognitive development, Pearl is in the pre-operational stage of cognitive development. She is not yet reasoning or thinking logically but she can explore her ideas symbolically through her role-play. This means she can imagine that one thing is standing for something else, such as using modelling dough as food which she can 'sell' to friends to develop her role as the shopkeeper.

Piaget also believed that children are egocentric at Pearl's stage of development, although his critics suggest that children can empathise with others at an earlier age. Being egocentric would mean she may want to lead the play, make decisions and may not understand if other children do not want to follow her ideas.

According to Chomsky's Language Acquisition Device (LAD) theory, Pearl will have well-developed language skills and be able to construct sentences using correct grammar. She has gone through the critical period for language development so will be able to express her ideas and ask questions as she plays. This will help her to negotiate and socialise and take part fully in the role-play.

Qualities of a good answer

A good answer to a question worth 10 or 12 marks will:

☑ demonstrate **accurate** and **thorough** knowledge

☑ apply knowledge to the **context** of the question

☑ be well structured and balanced, showing **competing viewpoints**

☑ use **specialist language** consistently and fluently

☑ be well structured, with a **supported conclusion**.

 The question says 'theories', so you need to refer to **more than one** theory of development.

 This extract from an answer demonstrates a good understanding of theories of cognitive and language development, and shows how this knowledge links to characteristics of role-play at Pearl's stage of development.

Links You can revise the content for this question on pages 10, 12 and 15.
There is more about applying theories on page 50.

You need to know examples of milestones Lena would be expected to have reached by age 4, and make links to their importance in taking part in school activities, including independent personal care.

Now try this

> Lena is 4 years old. She is meeting the expected milestones for fine motor skills. She will start school in September, where she will need to be independent when dressing, at mealtimes and when taking part in play activities such as writing, art and craft and construction.

Discuss how Lena's fine motor skills will support her independence when she starts school.

 Links The content on page 4 will help you with this question.

Applying theories

Theories help to explain human development. You need to show that you understand the theories that are in Unit 1 and also apply your knowledge to the subject of a case study.

Theories and application

You may study investigations that have been carried out by theorists, such as the Swiss mountain test (Piaget, see page 11) or the Bobo boll experiment (Bandura, see page 19). These help you to understand the theories. Unless you are specifically asked to explain them, you should only refer to the conclusions drawn from them in your answers.

Worked example

Elijah is 27 years old. He worked as an IT consultant but last year he lost his job and is struggling to find work. This affected his ability to pay his mortgage, so he has had to move from his flat into rented accommodation. Elijah's father has not been supportive because, for a number of years, he has been receiving treatment for mental illness. Elijah has now been diagnosed with depression.

Using the information about Elijah, outline the theory that may help to explain his depression.

6 marks

Always read the case study carefully. Here, it gives information about **environmental** and **genetic** factors that may have influenced Elijah's depression. Underlining relevant factors helps you to remember to link the theories to them in your answer.

The names of the theorists or theories may not always be given in the question. You will be expected to know the relevant theories that you need to refer to. You could be asked about 'cognitive learning theories' or 'social learning theory'.

Sample response extract

Elijah may have an underlying biological or genetic predisposition to mental illness passed on by his father. This does not mean that he will definitely develop a mental illness but he may be more susceptible. Losing his job and home will have put additional stress on Elijah. According to the stress–diathesis model, stressful life events can trigger mental illness where there is a predisposition.

This extract outlines the theory, in this case the stress–diathesis theory, which explains the onset of mental illness in terms of genetic and environmental factors.

 Links There is more about theories on page 54.

Now try this

Jack is two and a half years old. He will start nursery soon. He loves books and uses words to describe the pictures. He already knows and uses over 200 words. He is starting to link words together using object and verbs, such as 'me drink it'.

Outline Chomsky's theory of Language Acquisition in relation to Jack's language development.

Take account of Jack's age and the description of his development, and relate this information to Chomsky's Language Acquisition Device (LAD) theory.

Links You can revise the content needed for this question on page 12.

'Discuss' questions

'Discuss' questions require you to explore the topic in detail. The amount of detail will be indicated by the number of marks you are given for your answer.

Qualities of a good answer

To discuss you need to:

☑ show a clear understanding of the topic

☑ consider all aspects of the topic and balance your argument

☑ make connections between different aspects

☑ discuss the extent or importance of features.

'Discuss' questions may require short answers or long answers.

☑ Short-answer questions ranging from 1 to 6 marks require you to discuss straightforward information.

☑ Long-answer questions gaining 10 or 12 marks will require you to discuss more complex topics.

Worked example

Jan is 15 years old. He lives with his parents and older brother. His parents often argue, which can sometimes result in physical violence between them. Jan's brother, Kamil, often picks on Jan and, although he does not physically hurt him, he criticises him in front of others. Jan often gets blamed for things that happen in the home even when they are not his fault.

Discuss the likely negative effects of Jan's family situation on his development and health.   **10 marks**

This case study describes a dysfunctional family, which engages in domestic violence and bullying. The impact on everyone involved can be complex. Although physical violence happens between his parents, it can also have a significant effect on Jan.

You will be expected to explore different aspects of development, including physical, intellectual, emotional and social development.

Sample response extract

Because his parents argue and fight Jan is likely to feel anxious, which will cause stress. This could lead to depression or other mental health problems. Jan could turn to alcohol or drugs to help him cope with his life. He may feel neglected and unloved, which will impact on his feelings of safety and contentment. He could live in fear because of the violence, which may cause him to withdraw and become isolated. Alternatively, Jan may copy the behaviour and become violent, which will get him into trouble with the police. Jan's self-esteem is likely to be low because he is constantly criticised and blamed. It could cause sleep or eating disorders, which would impact on his health in the short and long term.

This extract from a discussion is well balanced and explores a range of possible effects on Jan's health and different areas of development. It considers short- and long-term effects.

It is important to look at different aspects in a discussion, giving alternatives for the possible effects on Jan, for example stating that he could become withdrawn or he could become violent.

Now try this

Add **three** more sentences to the answer above. They should draw a conclusion about the possible effects on Jan's future relationships and the likelihood of him perpetuating negative behaviour if he has children of his own.

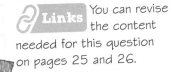

Links You can revise the content needed for this question on pages 25 and 26.

'Evaluate' questions

'Evaluate' questions always require extended answers and are worth 10 to 12 marks.

Worked example

> Meena is 4 years old. She enjoys school and is meeting expected milestones in intellectual development. At school she has opportunities to explore the natural world. She enjoys playing in the pretend home, where she uses playdough to make pretend food to serve to friends. She is developing her mathematical skills through independent exploratory play activities such as water, sand and construction.

Evaluate possible explanations for Meena's cognitive development with reference to Piaget's theories of how children think and learn.

10 marks

Qualities of a good answer

To answer 'evaluate' questions you must consider:

- ✓ strengths and weaknesses
- ✓ advantages/disadvantages
- ✓ relevance or significance, e.g. of a theory, factor or life event.

For this question, you need to show that you understand key features of the theory and relate it to the context of the case study.

Sample response extract

According to Piaget, Meena is in the pre-operational stage of development. At this stage she learns about her environment through hands-on play. Her teachers seem to use Piaget's theory of intellectual development to support Meena's learning by providing experiential learning activities such as water and sand. This has helped her to develop new concepts (schemas). Piaget's theory explains how, when Meena has new experiences, she will question what she already knows (a state of disequilibrium). As she comes to terms with new information she will reach a state of equilibrium and develop a new schema.

This extract from an answer gives examples of how Meena is learning through the activities at school and link Piaget's theory to how she is learning.

According to Piaget, Meena's intellectual development is promoted by being allowed to discover for herself through spontaneous play activities. However, critics believe that support from an adult enables children like Meena to be helped to think more logically.

You need to consider alternative views to help reach a conclusion.

Meena also takes part in pretend play, which Piaget believed was essential for cognitive development as it helps children to apply their linguistic, social and cognitive skills through symbolic behaviour. At school Meena has the opportunity to use symbolic language and objects in her play, such as using playdough as pretend food, which has promoted the development of her imagination and language.

Giving Meena opportunities for hands-on exploration and to take part in pretend play that builds on her knowledge is likely to have supported her to meet her expected intellectual development milestones. However, if she had received more support from an adult during her exploratory play she could possibly have progressed further.

A conclusion is reached by referring back to the question.

Now try this

Read through the answer again and note where it has shown:

1. the significance of Piaget's theory in explaining Meena's development
2. possible weaknesses of Piaget's theory in relation to Meena's development.

 Links You can revise the content for this question on page 10. There is more on applying theory to case studies on page 50.

'Justify' questions

'Justify' questions require you to give valid reasons for your answers and/or prove that something is right or reasonable.

Answering the questions

'Justify' questions can be:

- short-answer questions where the topic is more straightforward
- long-answer questions where information is more complex.

Make sure you give a supported reason for each point you make.

Worked example

> Fatima is <u>married</u> to Mahir. They have two children aged <u>3 years</u> and <u>14 months</u>. They rent a one-bedroomed flat on a <u>large estate</u> next to a <u>motorway</u>. The flat is damp and the <u>heating does not always work</u>. <u>Fatima's health</u> has been <u>deteriorating</u>. She has <u>asthma</u> and <u>high cholesterol</u>. She gets <u>stressed</u> as she is <u>always at home with the children</u>. The family has now been offered a <u>new house</u> with <u>three bedrooms</u> on an estate on the <u>edge of the town</u>. There is a <u>small garden</u> and a <u>playground nearby</u>.

Justify how moving may impact on Fatima's health and wellbeing.   **10 marks**

 Underlining key information in the case study (relating to how Fatima's present housing situation is affecting her health and wellbeing, and the new offer of housing) will help you when comparing and then justifying how her new housing situation will improve her health and wellbeing.

The question asks about the impact on Fatima's health **and** development, so it is important to give several examples of each.

Sample response extract

There will be less pollution on the edge of town, which will reduce the amount of pollutants Fatima breathes in. This should reduce her asthma. A house with adequate heating and without damp will also reduce her respiratory problems. The flat has one bedroom for the whole family, so they are overcrowded. Having three bedrooms will mean that Fatima and Mahir have their own room, which is likely to lead to more contentment and improve sleep, which can lead to better health. The new house has a garden for the children to play in, which will reduce Fatima's stress levels because they can play outside rather than being under her feet. Fatima can visit a park more easily to get more exercise in the fresh air, which is helpful for reducing cardiac and respiratory problems and lowering stress. Better housing conditions are likely to improve how Fatima feels about herself, raising her self-esteem.

 You need to give valid and supported reasons for each point made.

This extract from an answer justifies the points made. For example, it links being near the park with enabling Fatima to get exercise and fresh air. The answer goes on to give supporting information about how this may affect her health.

 Links You can revise the content needed to answer this question on page 23.

Now try this

> Leah has just discovered that she is pregnant. Her midwife has advised her to stop smoking and drinking alcohol to keep the baby healthy.

Justify the midwife's advice.

 This is a short-answer question. To justify you must recall information which shows that the midwife's advice is reasonable.

 Links You can revise the content needed for this question on page 22.

'To what extent' questions

When answering 'to what extent questions' you must provide details and give clear evidence to support your ideas. This type of question is asking about the level or degree of something.

Answering the questions

When answering 'to what extent' questions, remember:

- they may be short-answer or long-answer questions
- the number of marks will depend on the difficulty of the topic
- in long-answer questions you need to show how you have reached your conclusions
- short-answer questions will be more straightforward, for example:

> To what extent might starting nursery affect Naomi's emotional development?   **6 marks**

Worked example

To what extent can theories of ageing help to explain Tina's health and wellbeing?   **12 marks**

Sample response extract

Both Havighurst's activity theory and disengagement theory are relevant in explaining Tina's health and wellbeing. Activity theory is based on observations that the psychological needs of individuals remain the same in older age. When Tina initially retired from work she was filling her time by caring for her grandchildren. She also regularly socialised with her friends. When she remained active and continued to socialise she stayed physically and mentally healthy. Activity helped her to adjust to the effects of ageing at this stage in her life.

When Tina was no longer able to fulfil her psychological needs because of her ear problem, she started to withdraw from activity and meeting people. This problem was exacerbated by a fall, which meant that Tina became more isolated and increasingly reliant on others for her care. Social disengagement theory, based on a belief that older people naturally withdraw from society and social contact, appears to explain this later stage of Tina's life.

Although it is not certain to what extent the different activities, such as child care, fill the void after working, it appears that activity theory goes some way to explaining how Tina's health and wellbeing were promoted initially. However, disengagement theory assumes the inevitability of ageing. Changes to Tina's mental health may be due to her accident rather than a natural ageing process.

 This is a long-answer question that relates to the information in the case study about Tina on page 48. You need to apply your knowledge of theories to different aspects of Tina's life situation and events.

This extract from an answer shows an understanding of the main point of the question, which is the extent to which the theories of ageing can explain the state of Tina's health and wellbeing.

 You need to provide evidence that supports the theories. Initially, this answer shows how activity theory appears to explain Tina's life, but later on, it applies disengagement theory.

 You need to come to a reasoned conclusion about the extent to which each of the theories help to explain Tina's life.

 Links You can find more about linking theories to case studies on page 50.

Now try this

Use the same case study about Tina on page 48 to answer this short-answer question: To what extent might Tina's health have an effect on her self-image?

1. Give a brief overview of self-image.
2. Make links to Tina and the factors given that may affect self-image.
3. Come to a reasoned conclusion about the extent of the impact.

Concise answers

Being concise means answering the question without adding unnecessary information. Make sure you focus on answering the question you have been asked for the marks that are available. You could run out of time if you write answers that are too long. In long-answer questions you could note down a brief plan of key words to help you to keep to the point.

Worked example

> Roger is 64 years old. He lives alone and had a stroke recently, which has caused dementia. This has resulted in mobility and memory problems.

Explain **two** possible reasons why Roger may find difficulty in accessing services. | 4 marks |

 Links You can revise the content needed for this question on pages 24, 35, 39, 40.

Sample response extract

1. Roger may need to get some help from specialist services for people who have dementia caused by a stroke. Service availability could be restricted because of pressure from an increasingly ageing society, so he may have to wait for some time.

2. Roger may not be able to travel to his appointments easily because he has difficulty with mobility. If he cannot get the bus, he may need someone to organise transport provided by the hospital to take him to his appointments.

This answer gives two valid reasons why it may be difficult for Roger to access the services he requires. However, the answer has also taken up time elaborating on the reasons, adding some unnecessary information.

Improved response extract

1. Roger may have to wait for an appointment for dementia services because an increasingly ageing population has put pressures on service availability.

2. As Roger has mobility problems, he may have difficulty in travelling to attend his appointments.

This answer gives two valid reasons why it may be difficult for Roger to access the services he requires. The answer is concise, including only key information. It draws information together from across Unit 1, recalling types of services, and information about strokes, dementia and economic factors.

Now try this

Give a brief outline to show your understanding of genetic susceptibility to disease.

 Being able to summarise factors, features or theories concisely will help you to tackle questions relating to them in your Unit 1 exam.

 **Links** Use page 21 to help you answer this question.

Key roles in healthcare

Healthcare roles are positions in organisations such as hospitals and surgeries. Roles have responsibilities that are carried out by people in their day-to-day duties. Here are six key roles in healthcare.

1 Doctors (GPs) provide medical care for patients. They work mainly in surgeries and local communities. They:

- ✓ diagnose, treat, monitor and prevent illness
- ✓ provide prescriptions for treatment and arrange preventative care, such as flu immunisation
- ✓ refer patients to other health professionals, such as specialist doctors and therapists.

2 Specialist doctors have expert training in particular areas. They work mainly in hospitals and clinics. They:

- ✓ diagnose, treat, monitor and prevent illness in specialist areas, such as cardiology (heart), oncology (cancer), paediatrics (children) and geriatrics (elderly)
- ✓ liaise with other professionals, such as nurses, to carry out treatment in hospital
- ✓ contribute to teams for ongoing patient care.

3 Nurses are trained to carry out medical duties at their level of seniority and specialism, mainly in hospitals, surgeries, clinics and homes. Specialisms include hospital critical care nursing, cardiac nursing, surgical care and oncology nursing. Nurses:

- ✓ monitor and care for the daily chronic and acute medical needs of patients
- ✓ support doctors in giving treatment and prescribed drugs
- ✓ work to restore health and wellbeing.

4 Midwives work mainly in hospital maternity units, clinics and homes. They:

- ✓ monitor the prenatal development and health of mothers and babies
- ✓ help deliver babies
- ✓ provide postnatal care, supporting mothers, babies and families after the birth.

5 Healthcare assistants are trained to help with daily personal care and to support wellbeing. They work mainly in hospitals, clinics, residential care and homes. They:

- ✓ work under the guidance of qualified professionals, such as nurses or doctors
- ✓ meet care needs, such as washing, toileting, making beds, feeding and mobility
- ✓ monitor health by taking temperature, pulse, respiration rate and weight.

6 Occupational therapists facilitate recovery and overcome practical barriers. They work mainly in hospitals, clinics, residential care and homes. They:

- ✓ identify issues people may have in everyday life, such as with dressing, shopping or working
- ✓ help people to work out practical solutions.

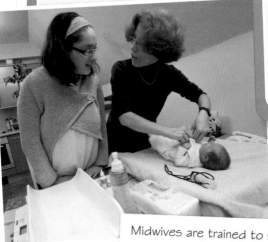

Midwives are trained to support mothers during pregnancy, childbirth and the first 28 days of a baby's life.

Now try this

Describe **two** differences between the role of a healthcare assistant and the role of a nurse.

Consider the level of practical help or specialist care and support that people in these roles are trained to give.

Healthcare settings

Healthcare workers carry out their roles in four main settings.

 GP surgeries and local health centres
- Patients go here first when they need medical advice.
- Doctors diagnose the patient's illness. They may issue a prescription for medication or refer patients to other services.
- Nurses might carry out treatment or health screening, or take blood tests.

 Hospitals
- Patients go here for treatment that a GP cannot give. It is where operations are carried out, and Accident and Emergency (A&E) departments and some walk-in centres are located.
- Patients are referred by their GPs to specialist medical teams.
- Specialist doctors (consultants) may issue a prescription for specialist medication or refer patients to surgeons for operations.

Healthcare settings

 Clinics
- Patients go here to be treated for specific medical conditions.
- Patients are referred by their GPs to specialist clinics based in hospitals and in the community.
- Trained personnel, including doctors and nurses, work in clinics.

 Home
- This is where care is provided for housebound people or those who are recovering from medical treatment such as an operation.
- Most people prefer to recover at home and some who are dying prefer to be nursed at home.
- Care may be provided at home for births.
- Patients are treated at home by community-based nursing and midwifery staff.
- Doctors carry out home visits when necessary.

Settings and treatment

 A patient attends an appointment at their GP surgery to report pains in their chest. The doctor asks questions and might use equipment to help them diagnose the problem.

 The doctor refers the patient to a clinic at the hospital, where the patient is seen by a specialist / consultant.

 The specialist/consultant decides that, at this stage, an operation is not necessary but they prescribe medication to control the heart rate.

 After one month of taking the medication, the patient has an appointment with a nurse at their GP surgery. The nurse checks their progress and the patient might need another appointment with the doctor.

A GP uses a stethoscope to measure the patient's heart rate.

 Now try this

Write an example scenario showing the healthcare settings that might be involved in diagnosis, treatment and recovery of a patient with appendicitis.

You need to know where services and treatment are provided.

 Links Look at page 56 to revise healthcare roles.

Key roles in social care

Social care roles are positions in organisations such as social care services. The roles and training for social care are different from those for healthcare. Here are five key roles in social care.

1 A **care manager** is responsible for the day-to-day running of a residential care setting. Care settings include hospices, supported housing and homes for people who need nursing or help with day-to-day living, who have conditions such as dementia or who are disabled. Care managers:

✓ recruit and manage staff

✓ control the budget

✓ are responsible for ensuring that the services in the care setting meet National Care Standards

✓ put policies and procedures in place and make sure they are adhered to.

2 **Care assistants** are trained to help people of all ages who need care to carry out their day-to-day routines, in homes, day care centres and residential care. They:

✓ meet personal needs, such as washing, toileting, dressing and feeding

✓ assist in monitoring health and wellbeing, by liaising with other professionals

✓ help with transport, household tasks and taking people shopping.

3 **Social workers** are trained to help a wide range of people of all ages to find solutions to their problems. They work mainly in social care centres, homes and clinics. They:

✓ protect vulnerable people from harm or abuse

✓ help people to live independently

✓ support children who live apart from their families, and support their foster carers and adopters

✓ help people with mental health problems, learning disabilities or physical disabilities

✓ support refugees and asylum seekers

✓ help people with alcohol, drug or substance misuse problems, and young offenders.

4 **Youth workers** help the personal, social and educational growth of people aged 11–25, to help them reach their full potential in society. They work mainly in youth centres, schools and colleges. They:

✓ manage and administer youth and community projects and resources

✓ monitor and review the quality of local youth work provision, and work with families and carers

✓ support individuals in other settings, including outreach work relating to drinking, drugs, smoking, violence and relationships.

5 **Support workers** provide care support to a range of service users in homes, centres and residential care, supporting other social care workers. They:

✓ vary their duties depending on the needs and wishes of the individual

✓ support individuals' overall comfort and wellbeing, under supervision of professionals

✓ help people who need care and support to live as independently as possible, also working with families.

One role of support workers is to help people with their day-to-day living. This includes enabling people with learning and physical difficulties to prepare food.

Now try this

Identify **two** different types of people who might receive support from social workers.

You must mention two **different** types of people with **contrasting** needs.

Social care settings

There are three main settings where social care workers carry out their roles.

1 Residential care settings

- These are settings where people who can't be cared for at home, or who feel that they can no longer cope with living on their own, are looked after.
- They may provide full-time or temporary respite care to give a break to carers, or those who struggle living on their own.
- Social care workers provide residents with personal care, such as washing, toileting and dressing.

It is important for the wellbeing of people who live in residential care settings that care workers provide activities to keep residents' minds and bodies stimulated.

Social care settings

2 Domiciliary care

- Social care workers provide care for people in their own home.
- Care workers help people lead their daily lives by supporting their independence.
- Social care workers might help people with shopping, cleaning and transport, such as taking them to a doctor's appointment.
- Social care workers can provide carers with a short break from their duties.

3 Daycare centres

- These are used by older people and those with physical and learning disabilities.
- They provide respite care.
- Social care workers might take part in leisure activities with people attending.

Benefits for people in residential care

👍 Trained staff meet people's needs and support them.

👍 Specialist support is available for those with more complex care needs.

👍 Companionship is provided by other residents and staff.

👍 A range of stimulating activities is offered.

Difficulties for people in residential care

Social care workers have to support people to overcome the difficulties of residential care:

👎 losing some or all of their independence

👎 reluctance to leave their own homes

👎 isolation from friends and relations

👎 cost of care.

Now try this

Alicia is 82, housebound and very frail. Her daughter, Magenta, is 62 and provides some of her care. She is supported by three care assistants who help to provide personal care for Alicia.

Describe **two** ways that **respite care** is provided for people like Magenta who provide care for family members.

 Read the scenario and question carefully. Here, your answer must be about Magenta, not her mother, Alicia.

Responsibilities in healthcare

You need to understand the day-to-day responsibilities of people who work in healthcare settings. One responsibility they all have in common is the need to follow policies and procedures in the healthcare settings in which they work.

Responsibilities of healthcare professionals

Role	Key medical responsibilities	Key non-medical responsibilities
Doctors and specialist doctors	• Diagnosing illness • Prescribing treatment to promote healing and recovery • Referring patients to specialists • Liaising with multidisciplinary teams	• Creating and maintaining relationships of trust with patients • Observing, listening, responding • Maintaining patient records • Maintaining confidentiality • Acting in accordance with legislation
Nurses	• Observing condition of patients • Administering drugs and injections • Carrying out routine investigations • Preparing patients for operations	• Providing care and counselling • Helping with recovery and rehabilitation • Writing patient care plans • Planning patient discharge from hospital • Acting as a patient advocate
Midwives	• Diagnosing, monitoring and examining pregnant women • Providing antenatal care, including screening tests • Assisting during labour • Supervising pain management	• Preparing and reviewing patient care plans • Arranging and/or providing parenting and health education • Providing support and advice on the care of newborn babies • Providing support and advice following miscarriage, termination or neonatal death • Liaising with other agencies to ensure continuity of care

Healthcare assistants	• Monitoring patient conditions by taking
	  • temperature
	  • pulse
	  • respiration rate
	• Taking blood samples
	• Carrying out health checks
	• Weighing patients
		• Washing and dressing patients
		• Helping with patient mobility
		• Supporting day-to-day routines
		• Talking to patients working under the direction of nursing staff
		• Supporting and delivering health education

Occupational therapists	• Being aware of acute medical conditions and how to overcome them in contexts such as Accident and Emergency (A&E) and acute medicine	• Advising on specialist equipment to assist with daily activities • Advising on home and workplace alterations, e.g. wheelchair access • Assisting people to return to work • Coaching people with learning difficulties, e.g. in handling money • Enabling rehabilitation • Organising support and rehabilitation groups for carers and clients

Now try this

Explain how the responsibilities of a nurse and a midwife may differ.

Consider these two roles and the different service users they may care for and support.

Responsibilities in social care

You need to understand the day-to-day responsibilities of people who work in social care settings. They all have to follow policies and procedures in the social care setting in which they work.

Responsibilities of social care professionals

Role	Key responsibilities	Key skills, qualities and tasks
Care managers	• Day-to-day running of residential care settings • Supervising work of care assistants • Ensuring quality of care meets standards and adheres to relevant legislation • Ensuring suitable staff are available	• Creating and maintaining relationships of trust with residents • Maintaining accurate resident records • Observing, listening and responding to resident concerns • Maintaining confidentiality
Care assistants	• Providing appropriate daily personal care • Carrying out general household tasks • Carrying out other routine roles as required by supervisor or service user • Liaising with other health and care professionals	• Working in different care settings • Observing and reporting changes in health and wellbeing of service user • Making service user feel at ease • Maintaining confidentiality
Social workers	• Managing a designated case load • Maintaining professional registration • Working within regulatory guidelines • Keeping informed of changes in policy and procedure • Liaising with other agencies, e.g. the police for vulnerable children	• Preparing and reviewing case files of clients • Taking difficult decisions • Working with a variety of service users of different ages • Ensuring continuity of care
Youth workers	• Demonstrating values which underpin youth work • Completing a background check with the disclosure and barring service • Continuing professional development • Acting as a mentor to young people	• Working across different sectors, including care and criminal justice and in public, private and voluntary sector organisations • Developing projects with schools and other organisations, such as debates about elections or capital punishment • Offering advice on topics such as sexual health using language which is accessible to young people
Support workers	• Following the instructions of health and care professionals • Implementing care plans agreed with social workers • Supporting members of families who provide care with parenting, financial or domestic skills	*People who provide social or personal care often work with people who have had healthcare or who continue to need it.*

Now try this

Explain the skills required by a social worker.

Link your answer to a social worker's knowledge. Consider the decisions that they may need to make in different contexts, and what they may need to do to comply with current legislation and relevant policies and procedures.

Supporting routines

Supporting the day-to-day routines of service users by meeting their needs ensures that their independence remains paramount.

Supporting people with a physical disability

Where?	How?
Home	By ensuring that... ☑ the person has access to all rooms at home, e.g. no stairs or a stair lift ☑ facilities are within reach and not at floor level, e.g. electrical sockets ☑ if necessary, hoists are available in bedrooms and bathrooms.
Educational setting	By ensuring that... ☑ service users can access classrooms and laboratories, e.g. minimum door width requirements accommodate wheelchair users ☑ disabled children have access to play and exercise facilities ☑ the curriculum is adapted to meet their needs, e.g. language used in lessons should respect the dignity of people with disabilities.
Work	By providing... ☑ awareness training for work colleagues ☑ a support worker to help the person in the workplace ☑ extra time, if necessary, to complete work tasks.
Leisure setting	By providing... ☑ accessible changing facilities ☑ suitable signage, e.g. in braille for people with a visual impairment ☑ access to adapted seating and spaces for elevated wheelchair viewing.

Following policies and procedures in work settings

Policies and procedures are in place to:

- ensure the health and safety of service users and health and social care workers
- support the day-to-day routines of service users
- enable the needs and preferences of services users to be met
- promote independence among service users.

Daily responsibilities of workers in health and social care settings

Following policies and procedures in place in their work setting

Providing equipment and adaptations to support people to be more independent

Providing personal care, including washing, feeding, toileting

Healing and supporting recovery

Responsibilities include...

Enabling rehabilitation

Assessment and care and support planning, involving service users and their families

Supporting routines of service users, including daily family life, education, employment and leisure activities

Now try this

Corinne works for an international bank and travels extensively for work. She uses a wheelchair.

Describe **two** ways in which Corinne's employer can ensure that access to her workplace minimises the effects of her disability.

Corinne's employer could provide disability awareness training for her co-workers, so that the effects of her disability are minimised at work. Give two more examples.

Anti-discriminatory practice

It is the responsibility of people who work in health and social care settings to promote anti-discriminatory practice by implementing codes of practice and policies that identify and challenge discrimination. The care needs of all service users must be equally met.

Identifying discrimination

Discrimination is where someone:

- is treated unfairly because of who they are
- is treated unequally because of who they are
- experiences prejudice that has been put into practice.

Accessible signage

Leaflets in many languages

Access to buildings

Examples of anti-discriminatory practice in health and social care

Longer appointments for people with learning disabilities

Policies such as anti-bullying in schools

Types of discrimination

 Direct discrimination: treating someone worse, differently or less favourably because of their characteristics. Examples include **harassment** (e.g. receiving abusive comments) and **victimisation** (e.g. being treated badly because you complained).

 Indirect discrimination: when an organisation's practices, policies or rules have a worse effect on some people than others. An example is **pregnancy and maternity discrimination**, if pregnant women or new mothers are treated unfairly or are disadvantaged.

Action against discrimination

Where people have a protected characteristic, it is possible to do something voluntarily to help them. This is called 'positive action' and may take place if they:

- are at a disadvantage
- have particular needs
- are under-represented in a type of work or activity.

Equality Act 2010

The Equality Act 2010 protects people from discrimination by:

- ✓ employers
- ✓ health and care providers, such as hospitals and care homes
- ✓ schools, colleges and other education providers
- ✓ transport services, such as buses, trains and taxis
- ✓ public bodies such as government departments and local authorities.

All types of discrimination are illegal, although positive action is allowed in certain clearly defined circumstances.

Characteristics protected by the Equality Act 2010

Age

Gender and gender reassignment

Pregnancy and maternity

Sexual orientation

Religion and beliefs

Race

Disability

Marital or civil partnership status

 Now try this

Identify one type of direct discrimination and one type of indirect discrimination.

For example, if a person who uses a wheelchair hears derogatory language about disabled people, this is direct discrimination. If they are unable to access a service because there is no ramp, this is indirect discrimination. Now identify your own examples.

Adapting provision of services

Challenging discrimination is an important part of the work of people in health and social care settings. This includes adapting how services are provided for different types of service users.

Ensuring access

There are different ways to ensure access and adapt services to accommodate user needs, including varying forms of communication and physical adaptations. Here are some examples.

Service user	Examples of anti-discriminatory practices
Traveller	• Enable access to GP services at new locations • Ensure that hostile language is not used
Transgender person	• Use gender terminology which is acceptable to the service user • Recognise any associated mental health issues
Person with hearing impairment	• Provide hearing loops in GP surgeries • Use British Sign Language to communicate
Asylum seeker	• Provide translation services if needed • Recognise cultural preferences
Child with emotional and behavioural difficulties	• Provide peer mediation and mentoring in schools • Provide nurture groups in primary schools as example of early intervention strategy
Person with physical disabilities	• Provide accessible rooms in clinics • Support participation in sport and exercise in schools

Health and social care professionals must challenge discrimination

Professionals should always challenge discrimination, whether it is based on a person's characteristics or background (**direct discrimination**) or caused by an organisation's policies and procedures that do not adapt to meet needs (**indirect discrimination**).

For example:

✓ **Doctors** should consult patient notes to check the patient's preferred language and preferred methods of treatment.

✓ **Nurses** should ask whether the patient prefers a male or female nurse.

✓ **Social workers** should advise on actions the service user can take to address any discrimination they experience.

✓ **Occupational therapists** should help people to live independently by ensuring appropriate kitchen equipment for different cultures (e.g. a wok and chopsticks might be preferred).

Professionals must treat each person with respect and respond appropriately to individual needs.

Now try this

Explain **two** ways a health and social care setting, e.g. a school for people with behavioural, emotional and social difficulties (BESD), should carry out anti-discriminatory practices.

For example, consider anti-bullying policies in schools and equal opportunities.

Empowering individuals

Empowerment is a key value which underpins health and social care services. People who work in health and social care settings must empower the service users they support.

What is empowerment?

Empowerment means giving individuals information and support so they can take informed decisions and make choices about their lives in order to live as independently as possible.

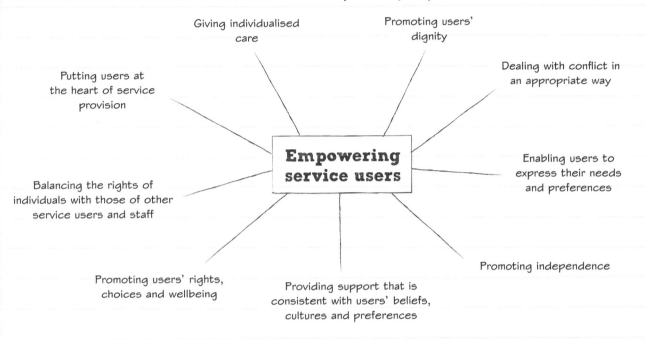

Giving individualised care

Promoting users' dignity

Putting users at the heart of service provision

Dealing with conflict in an appropriate way

Empowering service users

Balancing the rights of individuals with those of other service users and staff

Enabling users to express their needs and preferences

Promoting users' rights, choices and wellbeing

Providing support that is consistent with users' beliefs, cultures and preferences

Promoting independence

Empowering children

Empowering individuals is central to the work of many people who work in health and social care and it requires a wide range of skills. The ways which adults might be empowered are sometimes different to the ways which children and young people are empowered. For example, where a very young child is involved, it will probably not be possible to empower them in the same way as an adult or an adolescent because they might not understand what they are being told or what they might be expected to do.

The skills required by pediatricians (medical staff who work with young children who are ill) are designed to support young children to understand their illness and to explain the treatments available in ways which a young child might understand, e.g. by using language which is appropriate to their age. This is one of the ways in which a young child can be empowered because they gain some insight into their illness/condition and about how they can respond to it.

What are rights?

Rights are entitlements that everyone should receive. People's rights are protected by the laws of the UK such as the Human Rights Act 1998 and the Equality Act 2010.

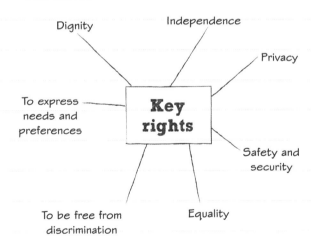

Dignity

Independence

Privacy

To express needs and preferences

Key rights

Safety and security

To be free from discrimination

Equality

Now try this

Explain **two** ways in which elderly people could be empowered by promoting their dignity in a care home.

Empowerment in practice

Empowerment can be put into practice in a variety of ways that place individuals at the heart of service provision. Here are some examples of upholding rights and promoting individualised care.

Rights	Support the right by...	Examples in practice
Dignity	respecting a person's dignity	Providing privacy for a patient who is using the bathroom in hospital
Independence	promoting independence (**autonomy**) through freedom, choice and appropriate support	• Allowing an **older person** to choose where they wish to live, either in their own home or a residential care setting • Supporting a person with **learning difficulties** so they can live independently and safely

Express needs and preferences	providing **active support** to enable choice consistent with **individual beliefs, cultures** and **preferences**	• Providing support with choices about:
		  • food, clothing and religious practice
		  • whether to be treated by male or female practitioners
		• Using methods such as petitions to put forward needs and preferences, and raise concerns with public authorities
		• **Supporting** those who need help to express their needs and preferences

Safety and security	**changing legislation**	The ban on smoking in public places
	dealing with conflict by applying clear policies and training	Applying policies regarding: • residents with dementia who **assault** staff they fail to recognise • what to do if **communication breaks down** between social workers and other agencies
	protecting from risk or harm, by implementing procedures and training	Applying measures to deal with violent behaviour of people attending Accident and Emergency (A&E) who are affected by alcohol or drugs, including provision of security staff in hospitals
	encouraging behaviour change	• Using education and training such as healthy living campaigns • Using language which is accessible to service users
	balancing individual rights with those of other service users and staff	Providing clear training and policies so all are cared for and protected appropriately
Equality	ensuring equal **opportunities** and **access to services**	• Fair **allocation** of budgets for provision of different services • **Accountability** through local authority representation
Freedom from discrimination	**providing clear guidelines for practice** and **complaints procedures**	• Registering complaints, investigating them and receiving feedback • Official recognition of and investigations into abuse • Representing cases where some treatments are available in some areas but not others. This is sometimes called the 'NHS postcode lottery'.

Now try this

For each of the rights above, give one further example of how to empower people who use health and social care services.

Ensuring safety in care

People who work in health and social care need to ensure that service users and staff are safe. Managing risks in settings can help to ensure safety.

Possible risks in care

👎 Abuse by other service users and/or staff.

👎 Inadequate supervision of facilities, such as bathrooms.

👎 Inadequate supervision of support staff, for example when moving patients.

👎 Lack of illness prevention measures, such as clean toilets, hand-washing facilities and safe drinking water.

👎 Infection due to lack of clean facilities and equipment.

👎 Inadequate control of harmful substances.

👎 Lack of properly maintained first-aid facilities.

Managing risks in care

👍 Using risk assessments to identify possible sources of harm, assess the likelihood of them causing harm and to minimise the chance of harm.

👍 Staff training to manage risks.

👍 Clear codes of practice which are familiar to all staff, including safeguarding and control of harmful substances.

👍 Appropriately qualified staff.

👍 Ensuring all staff have Disclosure and Barring Service (DBS) clearance.

👍 Regular and evidenced checks of facilities and provision of safe drinking water.

👍 Availability of protective equipment and knowledge of infection control procedures.

👍 Procedures for reporting and recording accidents, incidents and complaints.

👍 Provision of maintained first-aid facilities.

Mitigating risks in health and social care settings

Example risk	Mitigation
Specialist equipment, e.g. use of hoist to lift immobile patient	Require sufficient staff trained in use of equipment to perform manoeuvre
Adequate supervision and support, e.g. giving hot drink to frail elderly person	Ensure drink is not too hot, use stable cup, supervise if necessary
Infection from accidents and spillage at meal times on wards	Support for meal times, suitable utensils and protection

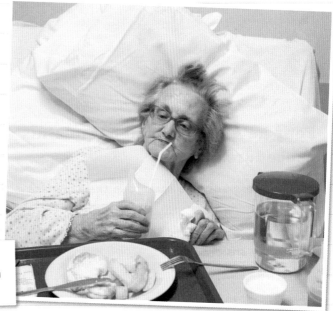

Risks associated with feeding patients in bed include infection and burns from hot food.

Now try this

Explain how a risk assessment could be used to reduce the likelihood of harm arising from an identified risk in a named health or social care setting.

Consider the risks to a person with dementia of leaving a residential care home unsupervised. Measures to reduce the risk might include access controls on external doors and a code of practice setting out the minimum number of carers required to accompany residents on visits, for example, to a hair salon. Now explain your own example.

Reports and complaints procedures

Accidents and incidents which happen in health and social care settings must be reported so that appropriate action can be taken. Complaints procedures must also be followed.

Stages of reporting incidents and accidents

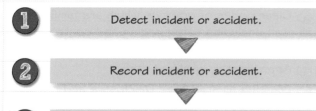
1. Detect incident or accident.

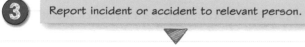
2. Record incident or accident.

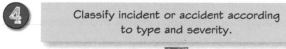
3. Report incident or accident to relevant person.

4. Classify incident or accident according to type and severity.

5. Prioritise issues for appropriate actions.

6. Propose preventative measures.

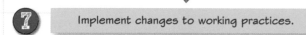
7. Implement changes to working practices.

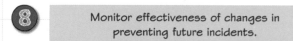
8. Monitor effectiveness of changes in preventing future incidents.

Barriers to incident reporting

- The incident or accident is seen as not important at the time.
- The incident form is too long or requires too much detail.
- Care staff have other, more pressing, duties.
- Staff may not know about reporting procedures.
- It may be difficult to access the person who needs to receive the incident/accident report.
- There may be pressure from managers not to report incidents and accidents.

Problems with evidence

Common problems with evidence in reports include:
- ✓ inconsistent witness statements
- ✓ lack of detail in statements
- ✓ poor recall of events
- ✓ written evidence that conflicts with other types of evidence, e.g. from CCTV or voice recordings
- ✓ low standard of written English.

Four key points about complaints procedures

1. All care settings must have them in place.
2. All care settings must enable service users to access and use them.
3. They are checked when care providers are inspected.
4. They can lead to service improvements.

The right to complain

Service users have the right for:
- complaints to be dealt with within an appropriate time frame
- complaints to be taken seriously
- full and thorough investigations of concerns raised
- information about the outcomes of investigations into their complaints.

Now try this

Marjory slipped and fell on a wet floor at the care home where she works as a care assistant. She didn't report the incident as she wasn't hurt.

Identify two reasons why Marjory may not have reported the incident.

Note that if she experienced back pain the next day, there would be no record of her fall. It might therefore be difficult to prove that the injury occurred at work.

The Data Protection Act 1998

When revising information management and communication, also revise the Data Protection Act 1998. This applies to both staff and service users in all health and social care settings. Staff must protect data about service users, and employers must protect data about staff.

Information about you

The Data Protection Act 1998 controls how personal information is used by organisations, businesses or the government. Data must be:

- used fairly and lawfully
- used for limited, specifically stated purposes
- used in a way that is adequate, relevant and not excessive
- accurate
- kept for no longer than is necessary
- handled according to people's data protection rights
- kept safe and secure.

Protection

There is strong legal protection for information about your:

- ✓ ethnic background
- ✓ political opinions
- ✓ religious beliefs
- ✓ health
- ✓ sexual health and preferences
- ✓ criminal record (if you have one).

Employers and data in health and social care

Data that an employer in health and social care can keep about their employees

- Name
- Address
- Date of birth
- Gender
- Emergency contact details
- Education and qualifications
- Employment history and work experience
- National Insurance number and tax code
- Details of any known disability

Now try this

Describe why the Data Protection Act 1998 is important to:

1 service users in health and social care settings
2 staff in health and social care settings.

The Act sets out the ways in which information about service users and staff can be held and used. You should describe some of the ways in which data is protected and say why this is important to service users and employees.

Ensuring confidentiality

The Data Protection Act 1998 is designed to maintain confidentiality of personal information, including the health and social care histories of individuals.

How is confidentiality ensured?

☑ By applying the requirements of the Data Protection Act 1998

☑ By adhering to legal and workplace requirements specified by codes of practice in health and social care settings

☑ By securely recording, storing and retrieving medical and personal information

☑ By maintaining confidentiality to safeguard service users

☑ By following appropriate procedures where disclosure is legally required

☑ By respecting the rights of service users where they request non-disclosure or limited disclosure of their personal information.

Staff's security responsibilities

Consider what security procedures a domestic care assistant might have to use if they store client information, such as phone numbers and addresses, on their mobile phone.

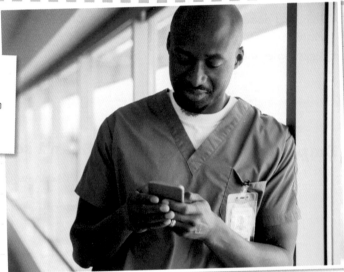

Key term

Confidentiality in health and social care settings means restricting access to information about a service user to individuals who are involved in their care, unless permission to disclose the information is given by the service user.

Data storage

These methods of data storage are covered by the Data Protection Act 1998:

- computers, tablets and mobile phones
- social media
- written, paper records
- photographs.

Safeguarding

Maintaining service-user confidentiality is part of safeguarding practice, so that the clients are protected from harm and abuse and their health and wellbeing is promoted.

Remember: there is more to storing data confidentially than keeping documents under lock and key, and exam questions might ask you to explain. You might like to think, for example, about the use of CCTV cameras in health and social care settings. These are in use to protect people who use services, and people who are working in health and social care settings. Photographs and images collected by CCTV can only be used in particular circumstances and for specific purposes. This is one way in which confidentiality is protected.

Now try this

Discuss how health and social care workers can share information about service users while maintaining their confidentiality.

Think about the kind of information that colleagues share about clients on a 'need-to-know' basis.

Accountability to professional bodies

Professional bodies regulate the people who work in health and social care settings.

Examples of professional bodies

In England

- The Nursing and Midwifery Council (NMC)
- The Royal College of Nursing (RCN)
- The Health and Care Professions Council (HCPC)
- The General Medical Council (GMC)

In Wales (in addition to those in England):

- Care Council for Wales (Social Care)

In Northern Ireland (in addition to those in England):

- The Northern Ireland Social Care Council (NISCC)

The Royal College of Nursing (RCN) sets the standards of professional practice required by its members. In order to continue their registration with the RCN and their ability to practise, nurses have to complete 450 hours of practice every three years.

Accountability

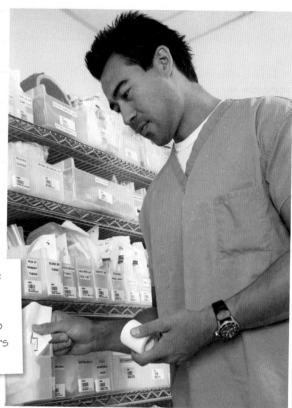

Regulation of workers

People who work in health and social care settings have to follow the regulations set out by the professional bodies which regulate services in their sector. This means that workers must:

- ✓ follow codes of professional conduct
- ✓ be familiar with and able to apply current codes of practice
- ✓ ensure that revalidation procedures are followed, e.g. nurses have to make a health and character declaration in order to be registered
- ✓ follow procedures for raising concerns (whistleblowing).

Workers who do not follow regulations might be disciplined by their employer, e.g. a Foundation Trust, or by a professional organisation, e.g. the RCN, or in some cases by the police when they have committed a crime. When workers are disciplined, this can mean that they have some responsibilities taken away from them or they can lose their professional status, e.g. if a nurse fails to complete enough practice hours, or for serious malpractice, they can lose their job. If health and social care workers are prosecuted, they can be put in prison if the crime is serious enough.

Key terms

A **regulation** is a law which sets the standard of professional conduct required of people who work in health and social care settings.

Regulations are **mandatory**. This means that they **must** be followed by law.

Now try this

Identify **two** ways in which nurses are regulated by the Royal College of Nursing (RCN).

71

Safeguarding regulations

Safeguarding regulations protect service users from harm, abuse and neglect, and promote their health and wellbeing. Safeguarding and prevention of harm takes place in the context of person-centred support and personalised care, with individuals empowered to make choices and supported to manage risks.

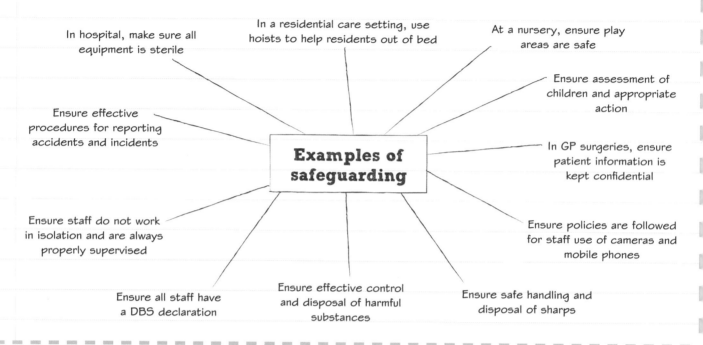

In hospital, make sure all equipment is sterile

In a residential care setting, use hoists to help residents out of bed

At a nursery, ensure play areas are safe

Ensure effective procedures for reporting accidents and incidents

Ensure assessment of children and appropriate action

Examples of safeguarding

In GP surgeries, ensure patient information is kept confidential

Ensure staff do not work in isolation and are always properly supervised

Ensure policies are followed for staff use of cameras and mobile phones

Ensure all staff have a DBS declaration

Ensure effective control and disposal of harmful substances

Ensure safe handling and disposal of sharps

Safeguarding children

Health and social care workers should:

- protect children from maltreatment
- follow their organisation's safeguarding policies for protecting children and the actions to take if a child discloses abuse
- prevent impairment of children's health and development
- protect children from infection
- ensure children grow up in circumstances that are consistent with the provision of safe and effective care
- take action to enable children to have the best outcomes.

Local Safeguarding Children Board

The Children Act 2004 requires every local authority to have a Local Safeguarding Children Board (LSCB). The job of the LSCB is to:

- ✓ make sure everyone understands how important it is to keep children safe
- ✓ make sure that all the agencies that are part of the LSCB are doing the best job
- ✓ report to the Department of Health
- ✓ look into cases where children are badly hurt or have died
- ✓ keep a check on information about child deaths
- ✓ give advice to all agencies
- ✓ listen to children's views and ideas
- ✓ hold discussions to find out what people think about children's issues.

Safeguarding adults

The Care Act 2014 introduced new safeguarding duties for local authorities where they provide care for adults. These include:

- making enquiries where there is a safeguarding concern
- hosting safeguarding adults boards
- carrying out safeguarding adults reviews
- arranging for the provision of independent advocates
- leading a multi-agency local adult safeguarding system.

Now try this

Identify two ways in which children in health and social care settings are protected from maltreatment.

You could consider the work of the LSCB.

Working in partnerships

All services in health and social care function in partnership. This involves multidisciplinary working in order to ensure that service users get the care and support they need.

Why is partnership important?

Partnership working is important because it:

👍 improves the lives of vulnerable adults and children

👍 means service users don't have to give the same information to different health and social care workers

👍 improves information sharing between professionals

👍 improves the efficiency of the care system as a whole (joined-up working)

👍 coordinates the way in which care is provided

👍 helps the service user feel that they are being treated as a whole person (**holistic care**), rather than as a series of unrelated medical issues

👍 improves the planning and commissioning of care, so that health and social care services complement rather than disrupt each other.

Difficulties of partnerships

Problems with partnership working include:

👎 failure to communicate information between services, for example, between social workers and the police in cases where children are in danger

👎 lack of coordination of health and social care services, so people do not receive the care they need or experience duplication

👎 delayed discharges from hospital, mainly of older people; for example, when a patient cannot leave hospital because there is no available support in the community

👎 health and social care providers with different IT systems that cannot communicate with each other

👎 cuts in funding that prevent effective partnership working.

Partnership with families

Working in partnership in health and social care may include working with a service user's informal carers, friends and family to plan, aid decision-making and enable support with other service providers.

It is important to be willing to work with different people, both professionals and non-professionals, showing respect for all expertise and opinions, and accepting help when you need it. For example, a family member may know a service user better than anyone else and may be in the best position to be their **advocate**, helping them express their needs and wishes.

 Links Look at pages 74 and 86 to revise advocacy.

Look at pages 74 and 86 to revise advocacy.

Now try this

'Partnership working provides the best outcomes for people who use health and social care services.' Discuss this view.

Your answer should include benefits **and** disadvantages to the service user of partnership working. For example, in effective partnership working, a service user may only have to explain their history once and may experience holistic care. However, they may perceive non-continuity in care and be confused by interacting with lots of different people.

Holistic approaches

A holistic approach takes account of a person's wider needs (physical, intellectual, emotional, social, cultural and spiritual) and seeks to meet these needs to promote health and wellbeing.

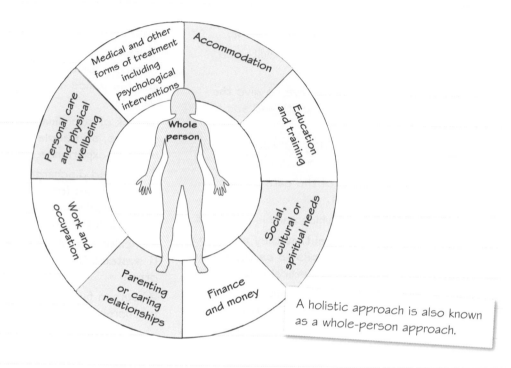

A holistic approach is also known as a whole-person approach.

Advantages

Benefits of a holistic approach are that:

👍 care is more personalised

👍 other issues which contribute to the individual's ill health, such as stress or poor housing, may be identified and addressed

👍 being viewed as a 'whole person' and not a medical problem can improve an individual's general health and wellbeing.

Disadvantages

Disadvantages of a holistic approach are that:

👎 most people only want their particular illness or symptom treated

👎 generally, doctors do not look for other issues during diagnosis

👎 health and social care workers are not employed or skilled to manage all aspects of an individual's needs.

Advocacy

Service users, their carers and other advocates should be involved in decision-making and planning support with service providers, working in partnership. Advocacy allows people to:

✓ express their views and concerns, so that they are taken seriously

✓ access information and services

✓ defend and promote their rights and responsibilities

✓ explore choices and options.

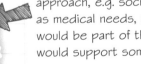

Describe a holistic approach that might be used to support someone who has bipolar disorder.

Consider the different aspects of a holistic approach, e.g. social and cultural needs as well as medical needs, and the professionals who would be part of the multidisciplinary team that would support someone with bipolar disorder.

 Links Look at pages 56–61 to revise roles and responsibilities in health and social care.

Monitoring care internally

The professional standards of workers in health and social care settings are monitored both internally and externally. Internal monitoring is a key part of line management, where staff have responsibility for other colleagues and for ensuring they deliver quality care.

Internal monitors

Health and social care workers must follow the codes of practice and policies in the settings where they work.

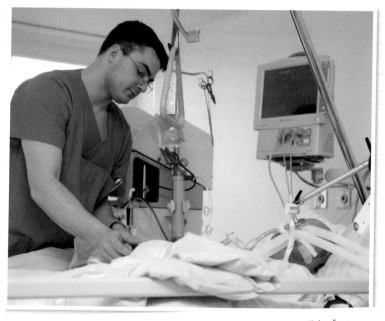

People who work on hospital wards are responsible for monitoring the care which patients receive. Because they work in hospitals, they are called the internal monitors. Staff with responsibility for other colleagues are line managers.

Internal monitor roles

- **Lead nurses** or **senior nurses** are in charge of a group of wards and can deal with a problem if the ward staff are unable to do so.
- **Doctors** are medical consultants who oversee diagnosis, investigations and treatment.
- **Matrons** are in charge of a group of wards and take responsibility for ensuring excellent patient experience and safety.
- The **ward sister** or **charge nurse** manages the whole ward.
- **Nurse specialists** offer expert and specialist advice on a range of treatments.
- **Healthcare assistants** help qualified nurses to meet care needs.

Whistleblowing

Whistleblowing can take place in both social care and health settings. In a health setting, for example, a member of staff might raise concerns about patient care, such as when the health and safety of a patient is put at risk. The concerns are reported to the relevant staff in the hospital, such as a senior nurse, a doctor or one of the hospital managers.

Whistleblowing helps to maintain best practice. When whistleblowing policies are **not** followed:

👎 bad practice could continue, harming individuals

👎 there will be more complaints from service users or their representatives

👎 staff may leave or perform less well

👎 the service provider may receive more negative reports.

Whistleblowers are protected by law and should not be treated unfairly or lose their job.

Now try this

Explain **two** ways in which the work of healthcare assistants is **internally** monitored to ensure that they are providing the best care for patients on a hospital ward.

 Think about who a healthcare assistant would report to within the hospital and refer to the policies and procedures that would inform their work.

Monitoring care externally

Organisations that are external to care settings use codes of practice and regulations to govern how health and social care workers carry out their roles.

Inspections

External bodies monitor services, including through inspections. These cover:

- analysis of internal data and trends, for example on health outcomes
- investigation of complaints
- observation of service delivery
- collection of service-user feedback
- interviews with staff.

> **Links** Revise regulation and inspection in England, Wales and Northern Ireland (pages 88–90) and the regulation of professions (page 91).

Criminal investigations

Criminal investigations in care settings:

- are pursued where sexual, physical, financial or emotional abuse is suspected
- have to take account of safeguarding
- follow referrals to the police from care providers, Clinical Commissioning Groups (CCGs) and specialised care settings such as prisons
- follow referrals from individuals who suspect that a crime has been committed
- may lead to the suspension or dismissal of care workers following an investigation.

Examples of external monitoring

External agencies may inspect care settings by visiting and observing practice. Service-user feedback takes place as part of the inspection process and can also be used informally to monitor care through everyday feedback from individuals receiving care and their family and friends.

Now try this

Explain how external monitoring of the work of people in health and social care settings is important for ensuring best practice and delivery of quality care.

76

Public sector services

Many health and social care services are provided by the public sector. This is the part of the economy that provides essential government services.

Health public bodies

NHS Foundation Trusts and **GP services** are public sector organisations which provide NHS services for **adults** and **children**.

For example, Great Ormond Street Hospital in London is part of the Great Ormond Street Hospital for Children NHS Foundation Trust.

Social care public bodies

Local authorities (councils) are public sector organisations which provide social care services for **adults** and **children**. These include:

- help in the home
- support for carers
- financial support
- equipment to enhance independence.

Partnership working

Health and social care organisations often work together to provide services which people need.

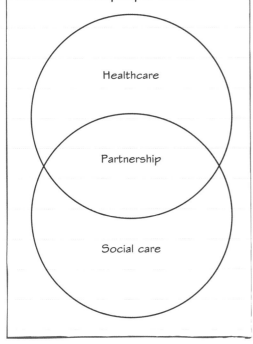

Commissioning

Commissioning of services means:

- **planning** service specification – e.g. what services will consist of
- **agreeing** service procurement – e.g. the process of obtaining the necessary services
- **monitoring delivery** – continuous quality assessment, e.g. checking that the services provided meet the needs of service users.

An example of commissioning is where the NHS commissions primary healthcare services that deal with a range of physical, psychological and social issues.

Primary care

Primary health care provides the first point of contact, such as a GP, who gives access to day-to-day services for patients and refers them to relevant specialists where needed. Other examples of primary care in the community include:

- dental practices
- high street pharmacies
- optometrists.

What NHS Foundation Trusts do

- Run hospitals.
- Provide mental health services.
- Provide community health services.
- Provide children's health services.
- Work in partnership with other organisations.

What local authorities do

- They commission organisations to provide social care services. These include daycare and domiciliary care (care in a person's own home).
- Commissioned organisations can be in the public, private or voluntary sector.
- Commissioned services for adult social care include residential care homes and nursing homes.

Now try this

Identify **two** ways in which the public sector provides **health** services.

Read questions carefully. You are being asked about **health** services, so don't include social care services in your answer.

Private and voluntary services

Health and social care services are also provided by the **private** and **voluntary** sectors, as well as by the public sector (see page 77).

Types of private and voluntary providers

Sector	Description	Examples of healthcare providers	Examples of social care providers
Private	• Services are provided by businesses, which are usually run for profit. • Services are often paid for by the person who uses them.	• Boots • BUPA • Virgin Healthcare • Private sector doctors	• Residential care homes • Nursing homes • Counselling services • Some home-help services
Voluntary/ Third	• Non-profit making organisations which provide services alongside those provided by public and private sector organisations. • Usually charities with paid staff as well as volunteers.	• Hospices • Macmillan Cancer Support nurses • Marie Curie nurses • Marie Stopes • Sexual health services	• Age UK • Mind • Barnardo's • The Children's Society • Mencap

Support services

Two examples of how service users are supported by private and voluntary services:

 How sexual health services support service users

- Sexual health services are provided by GPs, GUM clinics and young people's services (examples of primary care).
- They provide advice about sexually transmitted infections (STIs), contraception, pregnancy, sexual assault and abortion.
- They provide contraceptives and medication.
- They are free and available to everyone.
- They target specific groups, e.g. those at high risk of infection or pregnancy.

 How Mencap supports people with learning disabilities

- Mencap provides residential care for people with a learning disability.
- It provides education services.
- It trains people to work with those who have a learning disability.
- It promotes awareness of learning disability.
- It challenges prejudice, discrimination and stigma.

Organisations such as Mencap value and support people with a learning disability, their carers and their families. They allow people with learning disabilities to participate in activities like everyone else. Each person is included, listened to and valued equally.

Now try this

Explain what services are available in the private and voluntary sectors for a person with a learning disability.

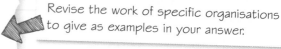 Revise the work of specific organisations to give as examples in your answer.

Hospitals and daycare units

You need to understand the **types of services** which are provided in hospitals and daycare units and the **reasons** why they are provided there.

Hospitals

A **hospital** is a healthcare setting where patients receive treatment from **specialised staff and equipment**.

- People with specialised health needs are **referred** to hospitals by their GPs.
- Hospitals provide **emergency care** via Accident and Emergency (A&E) Departments.
- People who need health services have a right to **choose** which hospital they attend, which team of specialist doctors they see (they can't choose a particular individual) and to be involved in decisions about their treatment.

Daycare units

Staff in **daycare units** may provide patients with an **assessment** of their health needs.

- Surgery and other medical procedures may be carried out in daycare units.
- They usually provide services which meet the health needs of **older people**, people with **mental ill health** or people with **learning disabilities**, and can also provide respite care.
- Daycare units can be part of the NHS but some are privately run or are provided by charities.

Secondary care and specialists

Secondary care services are usually provided to referred patients by medical **specialists**. Secondary care is centralised and usually takes place in **hospitals**.

Here are some examples of specialists who provide secondary care:

- **Cardiologists**: treat diseases and illnesses of the heart and blood vessels.
- **Urologists**: treat diseases and illnesses of the urinary tract.
- **Orthopaedic surgeons**: treat injuries to, and disorders of, the skeletal system.
- **Radiologists**: treat illness using x-rays, MRI scans and other medical imaging techniques.

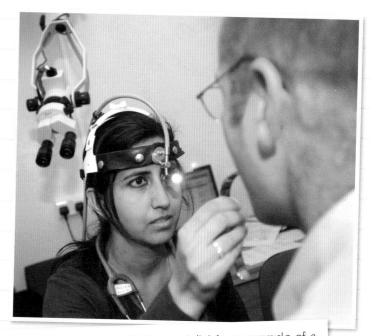

An ear, nose and throat (ENT) specialist is an example of a secondary care provider. If you needed ENT services, you would receive a **referral** from your GP. In this case, the GP, who provides the **primary care**, is the **first contact**.

Now try this

Identify **two** services that are provided in hospitals.

 Think about the different types of specialist doctors who work in hospitals, for example, ENT and paediatric specialists.

Hospice care

Hospice care is provided in a range of settings, not just in hospice buildings. These settings include day services, care homes and, most often, people's own homes.

What hospice staff do

The aim of hospice care is to improve the lives of people who have a **terminal** illness that cannot be cured. Staff in hospices:

- take care of people's **physical, intellectual, emotional** and **social** needs **(PIES)**
- aim to control the pain and other symptoms experienced by the patient through **palliative care**
- support carers, family members and close friends, both during a person's **illness** and during **bereavement**, after the person has died and family and friends are grieving.

Palliative care

Palliative care is offered to people towards the end of their lives. It:

- is a **multidisciplinary** approach to specialised medical care for people with serious illnesses
- is **active** and **holistic**
- focuses on providing patients with **relief** from symptoms and pain, and the physical and mental stress of a serious illness
- regards as **paramount** the **management of pain** and other symptoms, and provision of psychological, social and spiritual support.

Anyone could need palliative care

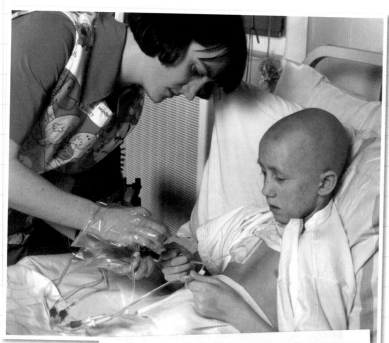

People of any age may require palliative care in a hospice or at home. Do not assume that this type of care is only for older people.

Quality of life

The goal of palliative care is to achieve the best quality of life for patients and their families.

Palliative care aims to:

- ✓ affirm life and help people to regard dying as a normal process
- ✓ offer support to help patients live as actively as possible until their death
- ✓ help relatives cope during the patient's illness and their own bereavement.

Now try this

Jenna is 7 years old. She has terminal leukaemia. She is being cared for at home by staff from a local hospice. She receives medication and help with her day-to-day routines. Her parents are supported to manage her physical and emotional needs.

Identify **two** reasons why Jenna might be cared for in her own home.

Consider Jenna's physical, intellectual, emotional and social needs, and how far a familiar environment might be suitable. You could think also of Jenna's parents' wellbeing, as one of the aims of palliative care is to support relatives and carers.

Residential care

Residential care settings offer a service to people who are unable to look after themselves and who don't have family members to look after them at home. Most people in residential care receive personal care but some also need healthcare.

Personal care

People who live in residential care homes receive social care or personal care from care assistants or support workers.

A care home that provides only personal care can assist residents with meeting their day-to-day needs, such as meals, bathing, going to the toilet and taking medication.

🔗 **Links**   Look at page 88 to revise how Care homes have to register with the care Quality Commission (CQC).

Nursing care

People in nursing homes receive healthcare from trained medical staff such as nurses.

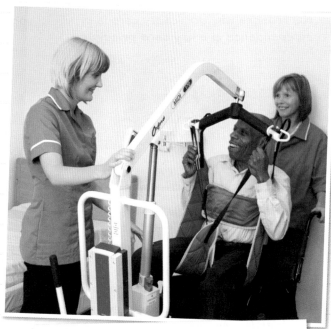

When residents need medical care they are cared for in homes registered to provide it. These are often known as nursing homes.

Other residential care settings

- **Care homes for adults aged 18 to 65** provide care and support for younger adults with, for example, severe physical disabilities, learning disabilities, brain injury resulting from an accident, or mental health problems. Other settings support people who are alcohol or drug dependent.
- **Residential care settings for children and adolescents** specialise in providing support for children with physical disabilities, learning disabilities or emotional problems.

Now try this

Aquilina is 83 and very frail. She lives in a residential care home. She can't walk unaided and, most of the time, she moves around in a wheelchair. She needs personal care, which is provided by care assistants who help her with eating, washing and toileting. Despite her physical frailty, she has an active mind. She enjoys watching TV, including *The Big Bang Theory*, *Game of Thrones* and *Strictly Come Dancing*. She uses her iPad to FaceTime her friends. The staff think she is cool!

What type of services does Aquilina **not** need?

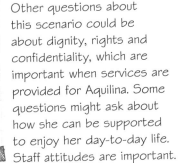

Other questions about this scenario could be about dignity, rights and confidentiality, which are important when services are provided for Aquilina. Some questions might ask about how she can be supported to enjoy her day-to-day life. Staff attitudes are important.

Domiciliary and workplace care

A high proportion of care takes place at home. Care at home is called domiciliary care. Some care might also be provided in the workplace. You need to remember that carers must be safe at work, wherever they work.

Independence

People who are able to live independently at home are usually happier and healthier than people who need hospital or residential care. This is one of the reasons why domiciliary care is provided and independence is a **key care principle**.

Workplace care

Codes of practice and health and safety regulations are designed to ensure the safety of all people in health and social care settings. People who use services need to be safe and so do the people who work there.

Some places of work support employees with specific needs, for example limited mobility capabilities or hearing impairments. There may also be provision of services such as counselling. A health and safety officer might give advice on safety at work.

In the workplace, employers must make reasonable adjustments so that employees with specific needs are not disadvantaged when doing their jobs.

Types of domiciliary care

Formal care is provided by paid staff. They are referred to as home helps, care assistants or carers. They have qualifications and undergo training to carry out their roles.

Informal care is provided by family members, relatives and friends, who are not paid. Sometimes informal care is provided by children.

Voluntary sector: both formal and informal care is often provided by people and services within the voluntary sector.

Young carers

Young carers often have to grow up fast as they take on adult roles within the family. They may suffer from stress and isolation, and the effects of poverty. They often miss out on schooling and other opportunities, which limits their long-term life chances.

Respite care

Respite care gives an informal carer a short break away from caring for a particular individual. The Care Act 2014 sets out the rights of adults who provide care. One of these rights is an assessment of their needs as a carer, which might include respite care.

Respite care might include homecare services or residential or nursing care. For example, a carer might receive a break from providing overnight care with a replacement carer provided in the home, so they can catch up on their sleep. Some hospices provide high-level respite care in the home to give the carer a break. Alternatively, the person being cared for might move into residential or nursing care for a short stay while the carer has a break, or attend some day care activities away from home. Supported holidays for the carer and person being cared for might also be arranged.

Now try this

Manfred and Jurgen are 12 years old. They live with their father, Siegmund, who is unable to work because he has mental health problems. When the twins are at school, a support worker sometimes comes to their home and Siegmund attends events at Local Mind, a day centre which is run by the charity Mind. During the evenings and at weekends, the twins, who do some of the cooking, cleaning, food shopping and laundry, also care for their father. A social worker is supporting the family.

Describe one impact on the twins of providing care for Siegmund.

You could think about how the twins are supported to cope with an adult with mental illness. For example, consider the sorts of problems they might face when they carry out day-to-day routines such as cooking and cleaning, or if there is a problem while they are at school. You could also consider the impact on their schoolwork.

Access to services

Adults and children who need health and social care services may encounter issues that prevent access to services. There is a process in place to define what services are suitable and what can be offered. Three criteria are used to decide which services, if any, individuals receive: referral, assessment and eligibility criteria.

① Referral

People who need healthcare usually make an appointment with their GP, where their healthcare needs are assessed. The GP may refer them to a specialist doctor in a hospital or to medical staff at a clinic.

 Look at page 79 to revise specialist doctors.

Types of clinic

Clinics provide outpatient care. They are usually located in hospitals and support many types of health need. Examples of clinic support are specialised baby care, ear, nose and throat issues, asthma/allergy issues, genitourinary problems, sleep issues, glaucoma, diabetes, dermatology and cardiac issues. Outpatients do not stay in hospital overnight and are usually treated in day clinics.

② Assessment

People who may require personal care will have a **needs assessment** which will be carried out by social services. It will consider:

- their needs and how these impact on their care
- the things that matter to them, for example, help with getting dressed
- their choices and goals, for example, if they wish to take up a new activity
- the types of services, information, advice, facilities and resources which will prevent or delay further needs from developing, helping the person to stay well for longer
- the needs of their family
- the limitation of cost and service provision.

③ Eligibility criteria

Local authorities use needs assessments to assess whether people meet the eligibility criteria for personal care. They consider whether the person's needs:

- arise from, or are related to, a physical or mental impairment or illness
- make them unable to achieve two or more of the **specified outcomes**
- impact significantly on wellbeing as a result of being unable to meet these outcomes.

An adult is only eligible for personal care if they meet **all three** of these conditions.

Now try this

Quentin has a profound learning disability. He is unable to carry out basic daily tasks without help, some of which is given by his family. Quentin gets distressed when he is unable to dress himself as he feels he should be able to do so by himself.

Apart from being unable to dress himself, identify **two** other **specified outcomes** which Quentin will be unable to achieve, therefore making him eligible for personal care.

Consider the eligibility criteria. The two specified outcomes must have a significant impact on his wellbeing.

Barriers to services

Reasons why people do not get access to health and social care services include barriers such as specific needs, individual preferences and financial, geographical, social and cultural factors.

Specific needs

People with specific needs that cause difficulties in accessing services include:

- people with learning and physical disabilities
- people with mental ill health
- older people
- children
- refugees
- people transitioning from one sex to another.

For example, people with mental ill health might not be able to ask for help, or they might need an advocate or miss appointments. A person who is unable to read would have difficulty completing forms.

Individual preferences

These can affect access to health and social care services and include, for example:

- people with religious and/or cultural beliefs who reject certain medicines
- people who exercise their right to be treated in a local hospital
- women who prefer to receive care from women
- people with a terminal illness who choose not to have treatment
- people with mental ill health who may be unable to make decisions for themselves at a particular point in time
- an older person who wants to remain independent.

 Links Look at page 82 to revise the key principle of independence.

Professionals and individuals can work together to overcome barriers to health and social care services.

Other barriers to accessing health and social care services

Financial, e.g. some richer people have to pay for personal care

Social, e.g. rough sleepers are unlikely to get the health and social care they need

Other factors affecting access

Cultural, e.g. if English is not the patient's first language

Geographical, e.g. people who live in certain areas may not get the same level of service as others, for example fertility treatments are less available

Now try this

Identify **two** barriers that a person with a serious mental health problem would need to overcome to access the services they might need.

 Consider the specific needs of mental ill health and any additional barriers, such as the possibility of rough sleeping or language difficulties.

Representing service-user interests

Two important ways that the interests of service users are represented are through **charities** and **patient groups**.

Charities

A charity is an organisation set up to represent people with specific needs and provide help and support, often voluntarily. Health and social care charities include, for example:

- **NSPCC:** works to prevent and end child abuse in the UK and offers advice on safeguarding and preventing neglect.

- **Mental Health Foundation:** works to improve the lives of those with mental illness. It carries out research, promotes service development and seeks to achieve good mental health for all.

- **Shelter:** works to reduce homelessness, provides advice about tenancy and renting properties, promotes the need for safe, secure and affordable homes.

- **Stonewall:** works to promote awareness of lesbian, gay, bisexual and trans (LGBT) issues to reduce prejudice and discrimination, and provides advice about sexual orientation.

What charities do

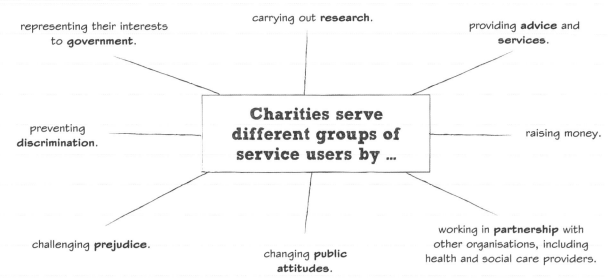

representing their interests to **government**.

carrying out **research**.

providing **advice** and **services**.

preventing **discrimination**.

Charities serve different groups of service users by ...

raising money.

challenging **prejudice**.

changing **public attitudes**.

working in **partnership** with other organisations, including health and social care providers.

Patient groups

All NHS organisations have a legal duty to involve the public in decisions about running local health services. Some **Clinical Commissioning Groups** (CCGs) have patient groups. Patients should be listened to and actions taken to meet their concerns.

Some other ways that the interests of service-users are represented are:

- by governors of NHS trusts
- by MPs
- by advocates
- through comments/feedback on proposed changes to legislation or government policy.

What patient groups do

☑ Represent the interests of people with particular health needs.

☑ Provide feedback on NHS services.

☑ Provide volunteers.

☑ Take part in research carried out by the NHS.

When answering a question like this, it is helpful to refer to a named charity, such as the NSPCC, which campaigns about child protection, and offers services to children who have been abused and their families. The 'what we do' tab on charity websites gives relevant information.

Now try this

Describe **one** way in which a charity represents the interests of service users.

Advocacy

Advocacy means speaking on behalf of someone else, to represent their interests. It is a very important aspect of the way that health and social care services are provided.

What does an advocate do?

An advocate is a person who enables a service user to:

- ✓ express their views and concerns so that they are taken seriously
- ✓ access information and services
- ✓ defend and promote their rights and responsibilities
- ✓ explore choices and options.

An advocate can enable people to **challenge discrimination** and avoid the effects of being labelled (**stigmatised**).

Why is advocacy important?

Who can be an advocate?

This depends on the kind of support a service user wants in each situation.

- Some organisations and charities have professional advocacy services.
- Friends, family members and carers can act as advocates.
- An individual can be an advocate on their own behalf (called **self-advocacy**).

Who might need an advocate?

People with mental ill health

People with a learning disability

Advocates represent the interests of individuals with communication issues

Children

People whose first language is not English

People with speech difficulties or confidence issues

Two other types of advocacy

1 **Peer advocacy:** where people with, for example, mental ill health can support someone with similar problems.

2 **Statutory advocacy:** where an individual is entitled to advocacy under the law.

Representing interests of service users

Complaints and **whistleblowing** policies also represent the interests of service users.

- ✓ All care settings must provide access to complaints procedures, which are checked in an inspection and can lead to service improvements.
- ✓ Whistleblowing helps maintain best practice if a member of staff raises concern about the quality of care.

Links See page 68 to revise complaints procedures and pages 75 and 94 to revise whistleblowing.

Now try this

Describe **one** problem which might occur when using an advocate.

Consider the types of people who might not be able to speak for themselves. How will the advocate find out their views? How might consent to use an advocate be obtained?

Regulation and inspection process

When a service provider registers with an external regulatory organisation, it is inspected to ensure that it meets the required standards in resourcing and staffing for high-quality care. The regulatory organisations are different in England, Wales and Northern Ireland (see pages 88–90).

Regulation and inspection

Inspectors carry out inspections, using experts to help reach judgements on quality. They need to know that the services are safe, caring, effective and well led.

How inspectors carry out inspections

1. Identify the scope and purpose of the inspection
2. Gather views of service users
3. Gather information from staff
4. Observe service delivery
5. Review records
6. Look at documents and policies
7. Feed back at a meeting with the inspection team and senior staff
8. Publish findings
9. Take action to improve services where needed

After the inspection

- The service provider is graded – this may reflect a range from outstanding or fully met to inadequate or not met.
- Requirements or warning notices may be given, setting out improvements required and a timescale.
- Organisations and individuals may be asked to implement policy and/or practice changes.
- In some instances, a provider might be required to limit the range of services or to face criminal prosecution.

Actions in response to inspection

Providers may need to:

- write and implement an improvement action plan
- implement enhanced staff training, for example to ensure familiarity with policies and codes of practice
- improve partnership working, such as when services have failed to protect vulnerable children
- ensure changes to working practices, for example, changes to hand hygiene procedures.

Examples of service improvement through changes in working practices

Improvements at a hospital

- Monitor compliance with hand hygiene procedures.
- Store cleaning equipment correctly to avoid cross contamination.
- Replace damaged theatre equipment.
- Provide better nutrition for patients.
- Complete documents accurately.
- Reduce delays in patient referral.

Improvements at an early years setting

- Replace unsafe equipment.
- Promote individual development and meet individual needs.
- Improve record keeping.
- Improve partnership with parents.
- Provide a rich learning environment that challenges and stimulates.
- Improve leadership and motivate staff.

Now try this

Identify **two** changes in working practices that might affect a nurse on a hospital ward.

After an inspection there may be changes in ways of working, e.g. a nurse might use a new record keeping system or improve the way he seeks patient views.

Regulation and inspection in England

You need to know about the agencies that regulate and inspect care providers to ensure high-quality and safe care **in the area that is relevant to you**. For Wales, see page 89 and for Northern Ireland, see page 90.

The Care Quality Commission (CQC)

What it is: the independent regulator of health and social care in England.

Its role is to:

- register care providers
- **monitor, inspect and rate** services, e.g. NHS trusts, independent hospitals, GP practices and residential care settings, including nursing homes
- take action, including legal action, to **protect service users**
- **be an independent voice**, publishing regional and national views of quality issues in health and social care.

CQC inspections

The CQC asks five questions of each service it inspects.

1. Is it **safe**? The service should protect service users from harm.
2. Is it **effective**? There should be evidence of good outcomes and quality of life.
3. Is it **caring**? It should treat everyone with dignity and respect.
4. Is it **responsive** to people's needs? Care should be of high quality, based on individual needs.
5. Is it **well led**? The service should be organised to meet needs.

The National Institute for Health and Care Excellence (NICE)

What it is: NICE provides national guidance and advice to improve health and social care.

Its role is to:

- **produce** evidence-based guidance and advice for service providers
- **develop** quality standards and performance measurements for organisations which provide and commission health, public health and social care services
- **provide** a range of information services.

Ways that NICE provides guidance

NICE provides guidance about standards in care. It also advises on safety and effectiveness of medications, treatments and services, covering:

- ✓ conditions and diseases, e.g. cancer, diabetes
- ✓ lifestyle and wellbeing, e.g. sexual health
- ✓ population groups, e.g. prison population and offenders
- ✓ service delivery, organisation and staffing, e.g. patient experiences in adult NHS services
- ✓ settings, such as when patients move from hospitals to community care settings.

Office for Standards in Education, Children's Services and Skills (OFSTED)

What it is: an independent, impartial public body that reports directly to Parliament.

Its role is to: achieve excellence by inspecting childcare, adoption and fostering agencies, and initial teacher training. It publishes reports of its findings to help improve quality and inform policy. It also regulates early years and children's social care services, so they are suitable for children and vulnerable young people.

Public Health England (PHE)

What it is: a government body that protects and improves England's health and wellbeing.

Its role is to:

- work as part of regional and local health systems to reduce health inequalities
- **protect** the health of people in England
- **share information** and expertise to make improvements in the public's health
- carry out **research**.

Now try this

Explain the role of the Care Quality Commission (CQC).

 First state the role of the organisation and then explain how its role is carried out.

Regulation and inspection in Wales

You need to know about the agencies that regulate and inspect care providers to ensure high quality and safe care **in the area that is relevant to you**. For England, see page 88 and for Northern Ireland, see page 90.

The Care and Social Services Inspectorate Wales (CSSIW)

What it is: the regulator for adult and childcare and social services in Wales.

Its role is to: inspect social care services to make sure they are safe for the people who use them.

What it does

☑ Provides independent advice about the quality and availability of social care in Wales.

☑ Safeguards adults and children, making sure that their rights are protected.

☑ Improves care by encouraging and promoting improvements in the safety, quality and availability of social care.

☑ Provides advice to the people developing policy in the public and social care sectors.

Healthcare Inspectorate Wales (HIW)

What it is: the independent inspectorate and regulator of all healthcare in Wales.

Its role is to: inspect NHS and independent healthcare organisations in Wales.

What it does

It carries out inspections by:

☑ focusing on how well those who may be in vulnerable situations are safeguarded

☑ identifying which services are effective and highlighting where services need to improve

☑ investigating systemic failures in delivering healthcare

☑ taking immediate action if the safety and quality of healthcare do not meet required standards

☑ informing patients, service users and the public about the standards of healthcare in Wales.

The National Institute for Health and Care Excellence (NICE)

What it is: an independent organisation which provides national guidance and advice to improve health and social care.

What it does

☑ Improves outcomes for people using the NHS and other public health and social care services.

☑ Produces evidence-based guidance and advice for health, public health and social care practitioners.

☑ Develops quality standards and performance measurements for organisations which provide and commission health, public health and social care services.

☑ Provides a range of information about the health and social care system.

Her Majesty's Inspectorate for Education and Training in Wales (Estyn)

What it is: a Crown body, independent of but funded by the Welsh Government, that inspects education providers in Wales.

What it does

☑ Inspects all maintained schools in Wales, non-maintained nurseries, regional education consortia and post-16 education providers.

☑ Provides advice on quality and standards in education and training in Wales to the National Assembly for Wales and others.

☑ Makes public good practice based on inspection evidence.

It carries out inspections by:

☑ observing practitioners

☑ measuring the performance of organisations and personnel against national standards

☑ providing evidence-based judgements.

Now try this

Explain one role of the Care and Social Services Inspectorate Wales (CSSIW).

> First state the role of the organisation and then explain how its role is carried out.

Regulation and inspection in Northern Ireland

You need to know about the agencies that regulate and inspect care providers to ensure high-quality and safe care **in the area that is relevant to you**. For England, see page 88 and for Wales, see page 89.

The Regulation and Quality Improvement Authority (RQIA)

What it is: Northern Ireland's independent health and social care regulator.

RQIA's role is to:

✓ register and inspect a wide range of independent and statutory health and social care services including care homes, domiciliary care agencies, day care settings, and private dental services

✓ assure the quality of services provided by Northern Ireland's HSC Board, HSC trusts and agencies – through a programme of reviews

✓ undertake a range of responsibilities for people with mental ill health and those with a learning disability.

Public Health Agency (PHA)

What it is: the organisation for health protection and improving health and social wellbeing in Northern Ireland.

PHA's role is to:

✓ promote health and social wellbeing

✓ promote health protection

✓ give support to commissioning agencies

✓ lead policy development

✓ carry out research and development.

How it carries out its role

- In 2014, it published a 10-year strategy for improving public health called Making Life Better, including key indicators and baseline measures for improvements.
- It implemented the strategy through partnership working.
- It monitors the implementation of the strategy.

The National Institute for Health and Care Excellence (NICE)

What it is: An independent organisation which provides national guidance and advice to improve health and social care

What it does

✓ Improves outcomes for people using the NHS and other public health and social care services.

✓ Produces evidence-based guidance and advice for health, public health and social care practitioners.

✓ Develops quality standards and performance measurements for organisations which provide and commission health, public health and social care services.

✓ Provides a range of information about the health and social care system.

Education and Training Inspectorate (ETI)

What it is: An independent organisation which inspects education providers in Northern Ireland

What it does

✓ Inspects all schools, nursery schools, special schools and education outside school provision centres.

✓ Provides information about the quality of education to the Northern Ireland government.

✓ Promotes best practice.

It carries out inspections by:

- insisting that its inspectors follow its code of conduct
- observing practitioners
- assessing the quality of teaching and learning
- assessing the standards achieved by learners
- providing reports which are publicly available.

Now try this

Explain one role of the Regulation and Quality Improvement Authority (RQIA).

 First state the role of the organisation and then explain how its role is carried out.

Regulation of professions

Professionals who work in health and social care are regulated by external organisations to ensure they maintain high standards and provide safe care. The four agencies used in England also apply to Wales and Northern Ireland, which also have an additional agency each.

The Nursing and Midwifery Council (NMC)

The NMC regulates nurses and midwives in the UK by:

✓ ensuring nurses and midwives have the right qualifications and skills

✓ setting standards of practice and behaviour

✓ requiring nurses and midwives to challenge discrimination, and review practice yearly.

The Royal College of Nursing (RCN)

The RCN represents nurses, midwives and healthcare assistants in the UK by:

✓ setting out the principles of nursing practice, and nurses' roles and responsibilities in safeguarding

✓ ensuring accountability of practitioners, promoting continuing professional development (CPD)

✓ supporting diversity in nursing.

The Health and Care Professions Council (HCPC)

The HCPC protects the public by keeping a register of health and care professionals who meet their standards for training, professional skills, behaviour and health. It sets standards for health and care professionals in:

✓ conduct and ethics

✓ performance and efficiency

✓ character and health

✓ education and training.

The General Medical Council (GMC)

The GMC is an independent organisation that helps to protect patients and improve medical education and practice across the UK. It:

✓ decides which doctors are qualified to work here, and oversees UK medical education and training

✓ sets the standards that doctors need to follow, and makes sure that they continue to meet these standards throughout their careers

✓ takes action to prevent doctors from putting the safety of patients, or the public's confidence in doctors, at risk.

Care Council for Wales (CCW/Social Care)

The CCW regulates the social care profession. It works with partners to make sure social services and childcare in Wales are of a high standard by:

✓ identifying roles relevant to the care sector

✓ requiring registration of care workers

✓ setting a code of professional practice

✓ carrying out inspections to ensure that professionals are following regulations and meeting the required standards

✓ recommending removal of people or roles if they fail to meet the standards.

The Northern Ireland Social Care Council (NISCC)

The NISCC is the regulatory body for the social care workforce in Northern Ireland. It:

✓ requires registration of care workers

✓ sets out a code of practice

✓ requires employers to ensure that care workers follow the code of practice

✓ monitors and approves training and qualifications for care workers

✓ provides workforce development to ensure that workers follow regulations and meet required standards.

Responding to regulation

Organisations and individuals must respond to regulation and inspection with changes in working practices where required, and improvement of services.

Now try this

You could give two ways for one setting, or one way for each of two settings.

Identify **two** ways that people who work in health and social care professions are regulated.

Links Look at pages 87–90 to revise regulation and inspection.

Links Look at page 71 to revise accountability to professional bodies.

Meeting standards

Every organisation that provides health and social care services is responsible for ensuring that employees implement the **organisation's codes of practice** and meet the **standards** for their work. You need to know how people working in health and social care can meet the standards.

Occupational standards

According to the UK Commission for Employment and Skills:

'National Occupational Standards (NOS) are statements of the standards of performance individuals must achieve when carrying out functions in the workplace, together with specifications of the underpinning knowledge and understanding.'

NOS:

- describe **best practice** to apply in all settings
- underpin **codes of practice**.

Examples of standards

✓ Receiving visitors in health and social care settings.

✓ Providing advice and information to people who ask about health and social care services.

✓ Contributing to social care during emergency situations.

✓ Supporting individuals to use medication in social care settings.

✓ Monitoring and maintaining health, safety and security of self and others.

✓ Minimising the risk of spreading infection by cleaning, disinfection and storing care equipment.

Performance criteria examples

One of the standards for people who work in health and social care, and for which organisations provide a code of practice, is how to receive visitors. Here are some examples of the performance criteria which employees must demonstrate when they receive visitors.

Ensure the visiting area is safe

Talk to the visitor to find out why they are visiting

Provide support to the visitor according to their needs

Performance criteria for meeting visitors

Seek help if unable to deal with a situation

Maintain confidentiality

Ensure that any information given to the visitor is accurate

When receiving visitors, organisations should ensure a safe environment and good communication and listening skills to meet the needs of the visitor.

Now try this

Identify **two** ways in which a support worker in a residential care home for older people would be able to show that they meet the standard for receiving visitors.

Think about what happens in the reception area of a residential care setting. One way might be that a support worker would find out the purpose of a visit.

Training for health and social care workers

Those who work in health and social care settings are expected to undertake continuing professional development (CPD), which includes training to ensure that they understand and know how to implement codes of practice and keep their skills up to date.

What is a code of practice?

It is a set of guidelines, sometimes based on legal regulations, which explains the way members of a profession have to behave.

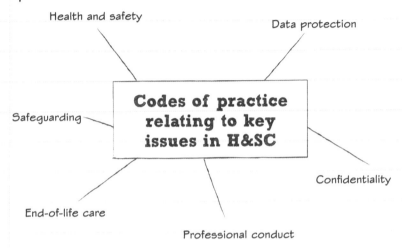

Health and safety

Data protection

Codes of practice relating to key issues in H&SC

Safeguarding

Confidentiality

End-of-life care

Professional conduct

Why do we need codes of practice?

Codes of practice are central to work in health and social care. They:

- ✓ are essential guides to **best practice**
- ✓ inform practitioners of their rights and responsibilities
- ✓ outline the behaviours and attitudes that service users can expect from service providers
- ✓ help to achieve high-quality, safe, compassionate care and support
- ✓ enable safety for the people who use health and social care services and for the people who work in them.

Training

Health and social care workers can access different forms of continuing professional development and training at different points in their careers.

- Before they become employees, workers have to gain qualifications.
- Workers undertake induction before starting their jobs.
- Workers undertake training while in post.
- Workers are trained by other, more experienced professionals.
- Workers can access training provided by their regulatory bodies.
- Nurses have to be revalidated every three years. As part of this, they have to complete 35 hours of CPD.
- CPD is mandatory for social workers who wish to renew their registration.

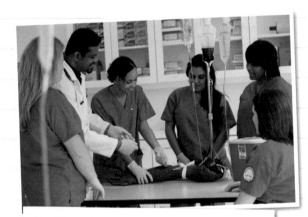

Health and social care workers undertake continuing professional development and training throughout their careers.

Now try this

1 Identify **two** areas of care which are covered by a code of practice.
2 Explain how codes of practice and training are related.

If you are asked to 'identify', you do not need to explain – just state the two areas.

Codes of practice are guidelines for best practice. Think about these in relation to both pre- and post-qualification training.

Safeguarding employees

Organisations that provide and deliver health and social care services must ensure that their employees are safeguarded in their day-to-day routines. Here are some examples.

Safeguarding employees

Following the protocols of regulatory bodies should safeguard employees day to day. In addition, membership of trades unions helps to safeguard their interests.

- The **British Medical Association (BMA)** is the trades union and professional association for doctors and medical students.
- The trades union and professional association for nurses is the **Royal College of Nurses** and for midwives is **the Royal College of Midwives**.
- The unions **Unite** and **Unison** protect people who work in all occupations across healthcare.

Trades unions and professional associations

Trades unions are organised associations of workers in a trade, group of trades, or profession. They protect and promote the rights and interests of their members. Trades unions may be involved when employees make complaints about how they are safeguarded. They offer advice and legal support to protect members who work in health and social care.

Professional associations carry out similar roles to trades unions but usually represent one group or type of worker, such as doctors or teachers. In addition, they also represent and protect the interests of the general public.

Employees are safeguarded when internal and external complaints are dealt with properly

> Complaint is made against health and social care employee.
>
> ▼
>
> Employee has the right to be accompanied by a trades union representative or work colleague.
>
> ▼
>
> Where feasible, employee continues to work whilst complaint is investigated.
>
> ▼
>
> Employee should not experience direct or indirect discrimination.
>
> ▼
>
> Informal resolution, e.g. with line manager.
>
> ▼
>
> Formal resolution, e.g. through human resources department.

Regulatory bodies

Following the protocols of regulatory bodies safeguards employees. Some complaints may be dealt with using the organisation's internal procedures. More serious breaches may involve external agencies such as regulatory bodies or the police.

Whistleblowing

If an employee is concerned about unsafe work practices or lack of care by other professionals, they have a professional duty to promptly raise concerns if they believe patients' or clients' safety is at risk, or that service users' care or dignity is being compromised. Whistleblowers are protected by law as they are acting in the public interest.

Now try this

You work as a care worker in a supported housing project for people with learning disabilities. You become aware that your colleague uses the same pair of gloves throughout her shift and doesn't wash her hands between tasks. For example, she prepares breakfast, delivers personal care and writes in the handover book without taking the gloves off. This is putting clients' safety at risk and you have a professional duty to raise your concerns.

To whom would you report your concerns initially? What would you say? Would you take it further? What would you expect to happen next?

With reference to the scenario, describe how you would report your concerns.

Ill health and specific needs

Treatment and care for people with specific needs and ill health take place in a range of settings and are carried out by a range of different people, including those who have had no training, such as family members.

Where care is given

Care for people with specific needs and ill health is given in six key settings:

- hospitals/daycare units/clinics
- GP surgeries
- hospices
- residential and nursing homes
- at home (domiciliary care)
- the workplace.

The people who provide care in different settings have different roles. For example, a nurse may specialise in early years or later adulthood care, and be part of a team in a hospital ward, a clinic, home care or hospice care. A health and safety officer may give advice on safety at work for a person with specific needs and ill health who needs particular forms of access or safeguarding.

Who provides the care?

Care is provided through four key roles:

- doctors
- nurses
- midwives
- healthcare assistants.

These medical staff help people who are ill to get better or learn to manage their conditions. A midwife might work with a family where a baby has inherited an illness. People in later adulthood might have a range of ill health issues, with multidisciplinary teams meeting to discuss the best overall options.

 Links Look at pages 77–84 to revise settings and access for service users with different needs.

Look at page 96 to revise caring for mental ill health, and pages 99–100 for early years and later adulthood care.

The nurse's role

When caring for people with specific needs who are ill, nurses should follow the correct procedures in the context of multidisciplinary teams and in communication with the family.

Nurses should follow correct procedures.

1. Follow correct admission procedures, assessing specific needs.
⬇
2. Provide correct information when answering questions from patient and family members.
⬇
3. Use appropriate language when discussing illness with patient and family members.
⬇
4. Ensure that patient preferences are respected and specific needs catered for.
⬇
5. Provide and administer correct dosages of medication.
⬇
6. Ensure notes are complete and accurate.
⬇
7. Prepare patient for surgery where needed.
⬇
8. Monitor recovery.
⬇
9. Prepare care plans that are appropriate for specific needs, with clear support in place.
⬇
10. Ensure patient discharge forms are correctly completed.

Now try this

Describe ways that patients with specific needs are cared for by nursing staff in hospitals before an operation.

Consider how professionals need to vary their support to meet specific needs of all people, of all ages, especially in early years and later adulthood.

Caring for people with mental ill health

Care for people with mental ill health is provided by GPs and specialist mental health services.

Types of mental health problems

- Alzheimer's disease
- Anorexia nervosa
- Bipolar disorder
- Dementia
- Obsessive compulsive disorder
- Post-traumatic stress disorder
- Postnatal depression
- Psychosis
- Schizophrenia
- Self-harm

Care is through four main providers

1. Family and friends
2. NHS
3. Charities such as Rethink or Mind
4. Private sector organisations, e.g. the Priory Group

Professionals in mental health include psychologists and psychiatrists, and specialists in, for example, mental health related to drugs, domestic abuse or trauma from the impact and settings of war.

Links See page 78 for how the NHS commissions private sector organisations and charities to provide mental health services.

Legislation

In the most serious cases of mental ill health, people can be detained under the Mental Health Act 1983 (Amended 2007). They can be admitted to hospital, detained and treated without their consent, either for their own health and safety or for the protection of other people. Usually, doctors or other mental health professionals make the decision to detain someone and the police may be involved.

Preventing mental ill health

Prevention is an important part of the process of caring for people with mental ill health. People can help themselves to maintain good mental health by:

- talking about their feelings
- keeping active
- eating well
- drinking sensibly
- keeping in touch with friends and loved ones
- asking for help when needed
- taking a break
- doing something they are good at and enjoy
- accepting who they are
- caring for others.

Now try this

Identify **two** ways that people can help themselves to maintain good mental health.

 You could think about professional help and day-to-day practical approaches.

Caring for people with a learning disability

Care for people who have a learning disability is very specialised. People with profound learning disabilities need to be cared for by highly trained staff.

The four key care priorities

1 **Choices** for people and their families, so they have a say in their care.

2 **Care in the community**, with **personalised support** provided by multidisciplinary teams.

3 **Innovative services** that offer a range of care options, within personal budgets, so that care meets individual needs.

4 Providing **early, intensive support** for people who need it so they can stay **independent** in the community, near home.

Care is through four main providers

1 Family and friends   **3** Psychologists

2 Support workers   **4** Social workers

Focus on people

Professionals may refer to some people with learning disabilities as 'people with behaviour which challenges'. It is important to recognise that they are people first and their condition is not the main way that they should be recognised, labelled or treated.

The carer's role

When caring for people with learning disabilities, carers should follow the correct procedures.

- Preserve independence.
- Use language the person can understand.
- Make sure care meets the person's needs.
- Ensure that the person's preferences are respected.
- Report risk.
- **Caring for people with learning disabilities of all ages**
- Empathise.
- Support the person to access appropriate healthcare.
- Treat the person with dignity.
- Facilitate social activities.
- Ensure information about the person remains confidential.

Family members are important providers of care, as well as professionals.

Now try this

Identify **two** concerns when providing care for someone with a learning disability.

For example, there may be a conflict between trying to preserve the person's independence and the obligation to report risk.

Caring for people with physical and sensory disability

Physical and sensory disability covers a wide range of impairments that may affect people in different ways. The type of disability will determine the type of care and amount of support that a person needs.

Types of physical and sensory disability

Some people are born with a physical or sensory disability and others acquire a disability as a result of injury, illness or disease. There are four main types of disability.

1 **Sensory**, e.g. hearing or visual impairment.

2 **Neurological**, e.g. motor neurone disease; multiple sclerosis.

3 **Spinal cord injury**, e.g. spina bifida.

4 **Amputation**, e.g. a limb is removed by surgery.

Care is through four main providers

1 Family members and friends

2 Support workers

3 Physiotherapists

4 Specialist medical teams

The carer's role

When caring for people with physical or sensory disabilities, such as multiple sclerosis or hearing impairment, carers should follow the correct procedures.

Family and friends can support people with sensory impairment to use specialised equipment and cope with adjustments to normal living.

Help the person to deal with the diagnosis.
▼
Support family members and relatives when they are told about the diagnosis.
▼
Ensure that care reflects the service user's needs and preferences.
▼
Enable the person to access the health and social care they need.
▼
Help the person to obtain suitable equipment, e.g. motorised wheelchair, hearing aids.
▼
Arrange for necessary adaptations to settings, e.g. adapted shower.
▼
Support the person with self-care programmes and care of specialised equipment.
▼
Help with access to benefits.
▼
Ensure that respite care is available.
▼
Help the person's family to cope with adjustments to normal living.

Now try this

Molly is 35. She was injured while serving in the armed forces and had her leg amputated. After her discharge from hospital she completed a care assessment and is now entitled to support from a care worker to help her adjust to her disability. In addition to medical care, she also receives support from the charities Help for Heroes and Army of Angels.

Explain how a support worker might help Molly and her family cope with living with her physical disability.

Look at the information in the flow chart. The question is asking about the support worker's role in supporting Molly's family, as well as their role in supporting Molly herself.

Early years care

Early years care for specific needs is provided in a range of settings, including homes, schools, hospitals and also in special units for children with severe physical and learning disabilities.

Children's specific needs

Some children have very specific care needs. These include children who:

- have a learning disability
- have a physical disability
- exhibit behaviour which challenges
- have severe illnesses
- have been victims of abuse or neglect.

Care is through five main providers

1 Parents

2 Other family members and friends

3 Teachers/teaching assistants/support in nursery or playgroup from qualified nursery assistants

4 Specialist support workers, e.g. for children with learning or physical disabilities

5 Specialist medical staff who treat children (**paediatricians**). They work in settings such as hospitals like Great Ormond Street, which provides specialised care for very ill children

The carer's role

When caring for children, carers should follow the correct procedures.

☑ Keeping children safe.

☑ Ensuring a healthy environment.

☑ Providing an accessible learning environment.

☑ Encouraging children's learning and development, including play.

☑ Enabling children to make a positive contribution.

☑ Ensuring the welfare of the child is paramount.

☑ Ensuring that information about a child remains confidential.

☑ Working in partnership with the parents of the child.

☑ Ensuring that children do not experience discrimination.

☑ Not being judgemental.

☑ Promoting children's rights.

Children's entitlement

According to the Early Years Foundation Stage curriculum, all children are entitled to learning and development in **three prime areas** and **four specific core areas**:

Prime areas

1 Communication and language

2 Physical development

3 Personal, social and emotional development

Core areas

1 Literacy

2 Mathematics

3 Understanding the world

4 Expressive arts and design.

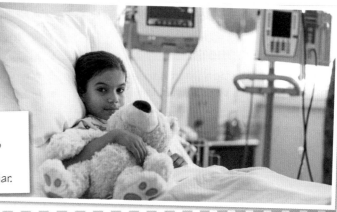

Providing toys and teddies helps children in hospital to feel comfortable and that their surroundings are familiar.

Now try this

Identify **two** factors which must be considered when providing care in early years.

You could think of one factor that is particular to care in the early years (e.g. play) and a further factor that is common to care in other areas (e.g. confidentiality).

Later adulthood care

Some older people have specific needs for care and support. Whatever a person's age, their care should meet their needs.

Rights

Adults with specific care needs have the right to:

- choose their own GP
- have equal and fair treatment
- be consulted about the care they need
- be consulted about their preferences
- be protected from harm and risk
- have access to complaints procedures
- have access to advocacy and empowerment.

Specialists who promote health and prevent and treat disease for people in later adulthood are involved in **geriatrics** or **geriatric medicine**.

 Links See page 66 to revise the rights of people who use care services.

Safeguarding from risk

Some adults are vulnerable, which means that they are more likely to come to harm and must be safeguarded from risk.

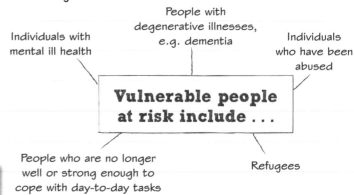

People with degenerative illnesses, e.g. dementia

Individuals with mental ill health

Individuals who have been abused

Vulnerable people at risk include . . .

People who are no longer well or strong enough to cope with day-to-day tasks

Refugees

The carer's role

When caring for older people with specific needs, carers should follow the correct procedures.

☑ Keep people safe by supporting them to manage risks.

☑ Enable people to live independently.

☑ Ensure that they can access the benefits they need, e.g. personal budgets.

☑ Ensure that information about them remains confidential.

☑ Work in partnership with different personal care providers, e.g. where help with dressing is provided by a private agency and where meals are delivered by a local authority service.

☑ Ensure that they do not experience discrimination.

☑ Promote their rights.

☑ Provide mediation when necessary, e.g. between the person and family members over financial matters.

☑ Prevent self-neglect.

☑ Prevent abuse, e.g. financial.

Examples of specific needs

Specific health and social care needs in later adulthood can vary. Here are some examples.

1 Development or progression of physical and mental conditions

- Treatment and medication to help manage conditions such as arthritis, osteoporosis, heart disease, respiratory diseases, cancer
- Treatment and medication to help manage mental conditions such as dementia or Alzheimer's
- Treatment and support for sensory impairment such as hearing loss or cataracts
- Treatment involving surgical intervention and physiotherapy, for example if there has been a fall or break to the hip, leg or arm, or joint replacement
- Provision of support in the home such as appliances, help with daily tasks and meals; or at a care or nursing home

2 Involvement of family or friends

- Advice from specialist staff in this area (geriatrics) on ways to support the person and themselves
- In cases of dementia or Alzheimer's, the person can be supported if they are unable to express needs and preferences

3 Interventions to maintain physical and mental health

- Support such as exercise programmes and guidance to prevent osteoporosis and falls
- Guidance on nutrition such as avoiding obesity and ensuring a healthy diet
- Ensuring oral health; regular sight and hearing tests
- Provision of healthy ageing advice, screening and assessments for early diagnosis of conditions

Now try this

Identify **two** factors that must be considered when providing care in later adulthood.

Policies, procedures and regulations

Policies and procedures for specific needs are designed to protect service users with specific needs from risk, ensuring they are cared for by people who are qualified to meet their needs and are informed about the best ways to do this safely. The policies and procedures are also designed to help protect the staff who provide the services.

Purpose of policies and procedures

✓ The needs and interests of at-risk adults and children are always respected and upheld.

✓ The human rights of people at risk are respected and upheld.

✓ Interventions and responses are appropriate, timely, professional and ethical.

✓ All decisions and actions are taken in line with legislation which is active at the time.

Key terms

Regulations: laws issued by the government.

Codes of practice: guidelines, sometimes based on legal regulations, which explain how members of a profession have to behave.

Guidelines: advice from regulatory bodies about how to follow codes of practice in the workplace.

Policies: a service provider's statements of intent followed by a description of procedures to be followed to ensure that codes of practice and regulations are adhered to.

Procedures: step-by-step instructions that employees must follow when completing a particular task to the standard required by an organisation.

Protecting service users

Regulation requires staff to follow codes of practice, guidelines, policies and procedures which are designed to ensure that service users are protected and safe. Effective implementation of these documents ensures that staff:

✓ work together to prevent, and protect service users from, abuse

✓ empower and support people to make their own choices

✓ investigate actual or suspected abuse and neglect

✓ provide services to people who are experiencing abuse, neglect and exploitation.

Protecting staff

Policies and procedures protect managers, professionals, volunteers and staff working in public, voluntary and private sector organisations. When health and social care workers follow policies and procedures, they are:

✓ implementing best practice to meet needs

✓ using the relevant skills required to work in their area

✓ working effectively with colleagues

✓ working within the law

✓ adhering to guidelines that are designed to keep them safe at work, for example using safe lifting techniques and infection control

✓ minimising risk, both to themselves and to the service user

✓ more protected if something goes wrong.

Now try this

Describe **one** way that regulation ensures that people with specific needs who use health and social care services are protected and safe.

🔗 **Links** See pages 88–90 for organisations that regulate health and social care services and pages 95–100 for care for people with specific needs.

Working practices in healthcare

Working practices for people with specific needs are set out by organisations which regulate healthcare services, to promote best practice and avoid failure.

The five goals of the NHS Outcomes Framework (2015)

1 Preventing people from dying prematurely.

2 Enhancing quality of life for people with long-term conditions.

3 Helping people to recover from episodes of illness or following injury.

4 Ensuring that people have a positive experience of care.

5 Treating and caring for people in a safe environment and protecting them from avoidable harm.

Excellent working practices help to achieve these goals. Progress is monitored against measures called **performance indicators**.

Principles of nursing practice

These principles, devised by the Royal College of Nursing (RCN), are an example of what constitutes safe and effective nursing care.

Principle A: Nurses and nursing staff treat everyone in their care with dignity and humanity – they understand their individual needs, show compassion and sensitivity, and provide care in a way that respects all people equally.

Principle B: Nurses and nursing staff take responsibility for the care they provide and answer for their own judgements and actions – they carry out these actions in a way that is agreed with their patients, and the families and carers of their patients, and in a way that meets the requirements of their professional bodies and the law.

Principle C: Nurses and nursing staff manage risk, are vigilant about risk, and help to keep everyone safe in the places they receive healthcare.

Principle D: Nurses and nursing staff provide and promote care that puts people at the centre, involves patients, service users, their families and their carers in decisions, and helps them make informed choices about their treatment and care.

Principle E: Nurses and nursing staff are at the heart of the communication process: they assess, record and report on treatment and care, handle information sensitively and confidentially, deal with complaints effectively, and are conscientious in reporting the things they are concerned about.

Principle F: Nurses and nursing staff have up-to-date knowledge and skills, and use these with intelligence, insight and understanding in line with the needs of each individual in their care.

Principle G: Nurses and nursing staff work closely with their own team and with other professionals, making sure patients' care and treatment is coordinated, is of a high standard and has the best possible outcome.

Principle H: Nurses and nursing staff lead by example, develop themselves and other staff, and influence the way care is given in a manner that is open and responds to individual needs.

Failures

Poor working practices have led to some high-profile cases, such as the failings in the standards of care and apparently high death rates noted by the Care Commission at the Mid Staffordshire NHS Trust. The Francis Enquiry identified widespread problems at the Trust. Subsequently, the Cavendish Report looked generally at the quality of recruitment, training and support for non-registered staff in hospitals and other care settings. As a result, a new training regime for health care assistants was introduced in 2015.

Now try this

Describe **one** way that a nurse might take responsibility for the care they provide.

Working practices in social care

Working practices for people with specific needs affect the people who give and receive care in different ways, such as the examples below in relationship to later adulthood and children.

Working practices for people in later adulthood

The principles for good working practices in nursing and care homes shown here are adapted from the Centre for Policy on Ageing's *A Better Home Life*. They describe **four** aspects of rights that should be given to everyone with specific needs who is in the care of others.

1 Privacy, dignity and self-esteem

Staff should value the contribution that individuals can make to the life of the home. Residents' self-esteem is enhanced when they feel valued. Residents should:

- have their own private space
- the opportunity to choose how they dress, what they eat, when they go to bed and how they spend their day
- decide how they want to be addressed by staff, other residents and visitors, e.g. by their first name or by a title such as Mrs Smith.

2 Independence, choice and control

Staff should allow residents time to do things themselves when they can and not take over or make them unnecessarily dependent.

Residents should be able to:

- choose how they spend their time
- decide how far they participate in the life of the home
- decide how they maintain relationships with family, friends and the local community
- have opportunities for emotional and sexual expression, and for intimate and personal relationships within and outside the home
- have access to external advice, representation and advocacy.

3 Diversity and individuality

Even though residents are living in a home with other people, they remain individuals with their own likes and dislikes. Ethnic, cultural, social and religious diversity should be recognised. Residents should:

- feel that their needs will be responded to by staff, who understand the value of maintaining a sense of continuity and identity based on past traditions and practices
- have opportunities to express and pursue religious and political beliefs, for example observing dietary and dress requirements, and having space for prayer
- be able to attend places of worship.

4 Balancing safety and risk

The balance between risk and safety should be carefully maintained. Anxieties raised by staff and relatives should be discussed, where possible, with the individual resident concerned. An agreement should be reached which balances the risks against the individual's rights. Residents should:

- not be discouraged from undertaking certain activities solely on the grounds that there is an element of risk
- live in a context where responsible risk-taking is regarded as normal and important in maintaining autonomy and independence.

Working practices and children

Failures in the care system, particularly in relation to cases in which children have been killed or harmed, have led to inquiries and subsequent changes in working practices. In 2002, criminal record and other background checks became mandatory for all people working with children and other vulnerable people. The Children Act (2004) has created roles and organisations with specific responsibility for child welfare, and demands improved co-working between agencies.

Now try this

Identify **two** ways in which a resident in a care home might have choice and control.

 You don't need to explain choice and control. You could focus on how residents dress, what they eat and activities they take part in, for example.

Your Unit 2 exam

You will have 1 hour and 30 minutes to complete the Unit 2 exam paper. You must answer every question.

Structure of the exam

The paper is divided into **four sections**, A–D.

Each section is based on a **scenario** that briefly explains the situation of a person with health and social care needs. The scenarios may describe people with ill health, learning disabilities, physical/sensory disabilities, age-related needs. Each section is worth 20 marks. You are asked four questions in each section.

Types of question

The four questions in each section are in the following order each time:

1 **Identify/Outline** – 2 marks (see page 106)

2 **Describe** – 4 marks (see page 107)

3 **Explain** – 6 marks (see page 108)

4 **Discuss** – 8 marks (see page 109)

Number of marks

The paper is worth **80 marks in total**.

The marks are shown at the end of each question. The number of marks reflects the amount of **time you should spend** on each question.

The amount of writing space available will give you an idea of how much detail is needed.

You will be expected to write more for a question with higher marks.

Remember to take a **black** ballpoint or ink pen into your exam. It's a good idea to have a spare one.

Spelling, punctuation and grammar

Make sure that your answers are clear, using accurate spelling, punctuation and grammar.

✓ **Spelling:** know how to spell key technical terms, such as **domiciliary** care.

✓ **Grammar:** use paragraphs in longer answers to help structure your points.

✓ **Punctuation:** when writing in full sentences, use commas and full stops to make your meaning clear.

Worked example

Identify **two** responsibilities of midwives.   2 marks

Sample response extract

1. They support women during their pregnancy.
2. They help deliver the baby.

This question would follow a scenario involving midwives. It is worth 2 marks so you should spend only a couple of minutes on it.

This is an '**identify**' question. You need to recall your knowledge. You could identify responsibilities from what midwives do at different stages of pregnancy, how they follow codes of practice or how they meet the needs of their service users.

🔗 **Links** See pages 56 and 60 to revise the responsibilities of midwives and page 106 for more on 'identify' questions.

Now try this

Fred is 81 and lives alone. He injured his arm badly in a fall in his garden. Following treatment, he is recovering at home.

Describe **two** responsibilities of the healthcare assistants who provide care for Fred in his home.

This question would follow a scenario involving domiciliary care of an elderly person. An extract from the scenario is given here. For a '**describe**' question you need to show your knowledge of facts and other information, and **apply your knowledge to the situation** given in the scenario.

🔗 **Links** See pages 56 and 60 to revise the responsibilities of healthcare assistants and page 107 for more on 'describe' questions.

Responding to scenarios

Each of the four sections in your exam starts with a different health and social care scenario. Four questions then ask you to identify, describe, explain and discuss aspects of each scenario.

Why scenarios are important

Scenarios let you apply your knowledge and understanding of this unit to **realistic situations** and **contexts**. You will need to apply knowledge and understanding about:

- the **care focus** of each of the four scenarios, for example, ill health, learning disability, physical and sensory disability or age-related needs.
- the **service user(s)** with needs in the scenario. Take note of the **individual(s)** described. Are they male or female? Young or old? What is their background or culture? These details will be relevant to their needs, and the care and support they receive.
- the **specific health and/or social care needs** of the service user. In some scenarios the individuals might have health needs; in others they might have personal care needs. Some may have both. Make connections between the needs and how the people are supported.
- the **health and social care workers** who provide the care and support. You need to know their day-to-day routines, and how these help and support people with specific needs.

Worked example

Physical and sensory disabilities

Raj is 40 and has been diagnosed with motor neurone disease, a progressive degenerative condition that causes physical disability through muscle weakness and wastage. The Motor Neurone Disease Association has given Raj information about how he can manage his condition and how his family can support him. Raj will need a mobility chair, his home will be adapted and he will be able to access respite care. He will also need medication to manage his pain, and exercises to ease his breathing difficulties. Following his care assessment, Raj will have a support worker for five mornings a week.

Identify two day-to-day needs of an individual with a physical disability caused by a condition such as motor neurone disease.   2 marks

In your Unit 2 exam you will be given scenarios in rectangular boxes like this. Each scenario will have a heading that states the focus of the scenario. Always take the time to read the scenarios carefully and refer to relevant details as you answer each question.

Some of the needs of the individual and their symptoms will be stated. You must notice these when you read through it.

The first question after a scenario is an 'identify' or 'outline' question.

Sample response extract

1. Help getting in and out of their mobility chair.
2. Help with washing and bathing.

 Links See page 98 to revise caring for people with physical disabilities and page 106 to revise 'identify' questions.

Now try this

Describe **two** ways in which an individual with a physical disability such as motor neurone disease will be supported with their healthcare needs.

The second question after a scenario is a '**describe**' question. In the question given here, you are asked to focus on healthcare needs, such as taking medication correctly. Do not describe personal care needs.

 Links See page 107 to revise 'describe' questions.

'Identify' and 'Outline' questions

'Identify' or 'outline' questions are the first question after the scenario and will usually be based closely on it. Here are some examples based on extracts from the scenarios.

Answering 'identify' questions

✓ **Two marks** will be allocated.

✓ You will have to **recall knowledge** that you have learned.

✓ Your answers should **stick to the facts** and be **brief** – no explanatory detail is required.

'Outline' questions

Here is an example of an 'outline' question:

> Outline the role of external agencies in inspecting health and social care services. **2 marks**

You will need to give an overview where you give a brief outline of the topic and may give a linked response. For example: Inspection to monitor and grade against national standards and benchmarks.

Worked example

> Alan is 16 and has just started at college. He is alcohol dependent. Alan's curriculum leader has told him he must seek help. His GP has referred Alan to a local community alcohol service that can provide him with counselling.

Apart from his curriculum leader, **identify** two people who work in health and social care who might support Alan to recover from his alcohol dependency. **2 marks**

Sample response extract

1. His GP.
2. A support worker at the local community alcohol service.

Links See pages 56, 58, 60 and 61 to revise roles and responsibilities in health and social care.

Your answers to identify questions should show your knowledge, and be brief and factual.

Here you need to recall your knowledge about access to community services and supportive organisations to meet the different needs of individuals.

Worked example

> Alan decides to attend his local community alcohol service, provided by the charity Addaction. Before he goes, he looks at the information which they provide online at youngaddaction.org.uk. He identifies with the stories other young people tell about their alcohol dependency.

Identify two ways that online support might help people like Alan. **2 marks**

Sample response extract

1. It enables him to access services he needs.
2. It enables him to maintain privacy.

You need to make two different points. An alternative second point could be that the level of language of the stories helps him to understand his dependency.

Now try this

> Alan does not take the advice of his GP, or the advice he found online. He continues to drink heavily and is involved in a serious accident after a night out with his friends. He sustains multiple fractures and is taken to hospital in an ambulance. The paramedic in the ambulance finds it difficult to make him stable and Alan is admitted to hospital.

Identify **two** types of healthcare Alan might receive.

Look at the scenario. Which medical staff are involved in Alan's care? One is named. Two others might be a doctor and a nurse. This should help you to work out the answer.

Links See pages 56 and 60 to revise roles and responsibilities in healthcare.

'Describe' questions

'Describe' questions are the second question following a scenario. Here are some examples based on extracts from scenarios.

Answering 'describe' questions

✓ **Four marks** will be allocated so keep your answers brief.

✓ You will be asked to **recall** a point or fact from your **knowledge** and state it.

✓ You then **apply your knowledge** in relation to the scenario.

Worked example

> Shazia is 45 and is expecting her first child. She has had regular contact with a midwife. They have discussed issues that affect pregnant women of Shazia's age. The midwife has monitored Shazia's health and that of her unborn child. Shazia has told the midwife that she prefers to have her baby at home. The midwife has carefully explained the risks involved.

Describe two ways that the midwife will support Shazia to have her baby at home.

`4 marks`

Sample response extract

1. Prior to the birth, the midwife will continue to monitor Shazia's health and that of her baby to assess whether a normal delivery is expected and if a home delivery would be considered safe.

2. The midwife will ensure that all the necessary equipment is available. This will limit the risks when the birth takes place at home.

Links See pages 56 and 60 to revise roles and responsibilities in healthcare.

'Describe' questions may ask you for things, e.g. 'two ways that…' or 'two activities that…'. There are two marks for each way and four marks in total.

For each of the two ways you describe, you should state a fact and then apply your knowledge to the situation.

Worked example

> Walter is 35 and lives with his husband, Jack. They would like to adopt a child and have contacted a local adoption agency. Following discussions with agency staff, if they decide to apply to adopt a child, they will be assessed by a social worker to see if they are suitable adopters.

1 **Describe** one factor that staff at the adoption agency must consider when discussing adoption with Walter and Jack.

`2 marks`

Sample response extract

The staff at the adoption agency must ask Walter and Jack about their family support network, for example, whether they live close to family members who could support them looking after their child if one or both of them were ill.

2 **Describe** one factor that the social worker must consider when assessing Walter and Jack as suitable adopters.

`2 marks`

Sample response extract

The social worker must consider the stability of their relationship and not discriminate against them as she is required by law to prevent discrimination against same-sex couples.

In each of your two answers state a fact and then apply knowledge by saying more about it.

Links See pages 58 and 61 to revise roles and responsibilities in social care, and pages 63 and 64 to revise anti-discriminatory practice.

You may be asked two separate describe questions. There are two marks for each answer and four marks in total.

Now try this

Read Shazia's case study again. Describe another way that the midwife will support Shazia to have her baby at home.

Remember to state a fact and then apply your knowledge to the situation. How might the midwife involve Shazia in planning support at the time of birth?

'Explain' questions

'Explain' questions are the third question following a scenario. Here are some examples based on extracts from scenarios.

Answering 'explain' questions

☑ **Six marks** will be allocated.

☑ State points or facts which you **recall** from your **knowledge.**

☑ Make sure you **link the points** you make.

☑ Give clear **reasons to support** any points you make.

☑ Include **evidence to support** your point of view or recommended course of action. This could be supporting information from your knowledge or from the scenario.

Worked example

Sean is 70. He has lung cancer and is not responding to treatment. His doctor has told him that he is likely to die within the next three to six months. Sean meets his palliative care nurse and talks about his needs and preferences. When the time comes, he would prefer to die in his own home or in his local hospice. Sean's wish is that he can be with his family when he dies. He is also worried about how his wife, Jenny, will cope with his death.

Explain how Sean's palliative care nurse will support him following this discussion in the period leading up to his death.

6 marks

Sample response extract

The palliative care nurse will talk to Sean and Jenny about what they might experience over the coming months so they have time to reflect and be prepared emotionally and physically. They will explain what help is available and help plan care for them both, including Sean's pain relief. They will ensure that other carers know Sean's preferences and discuss his wishes with local hospice staff. The nurse might help the couple cope with practical planning for his death, for example asking if they have a made a will, so Sean will know that Jenny will have less to worry about.

 Links See page 80 to revise care in hospices and page 100 to revise care for older adults.

As you read a scenario, notice:
- the focus of the scenario, e.g. end-of-life care
- details about the service users, e.g. gender, age, relationships
- the specific needs, e.g. healthcare, social and personal care needs
- the workers providing care and support, their roles and responsibilities and how they help, day to day.

- You must write about Sean's needs.
- You could include Jenny's needs.
- You must write about how the palliative care nurse will support Sean.
- You should not write about what happens after Sean dies.

You can refer to the palliative care nurse as 'he', 'she' or 'they'.

You can use phrases such as 'for example' to link and develop your points.

- Consider access provision for wheelchair users, such as ramps and toilet facilities.
- Think about other physical disabilities, as the question refers not only to wheelchair users but the wider requirements of the Equality Act, for example sight and hearing impairments, arthritis, cerebral palsy.
- State ways in which schools can meet the requirements.
- Link and develop your points, using examples.
- Include evidence to support your answer.

Now try this

Mike and Jean are both wheelchair users. They both work in local schools. Mike is a head of science and Jean is a deputy head. Their schools have facilities that meet the requirements of the Equality Act 2010.

Explain ways in which the schools might meet the requirements of the Equality Act 2010, which apply to people with physical disabilities.

 Links See page 63 to revise the Equality Act 2010.

'Discuss' questions

'Discuss' questions are the final question following the scenario and require you to answer in some detail. Here are some examples based on extracts from scenarios.

Answering 'discuss' questions

✓ **Eight marks** will be allocated.

✓ Your answer should be based on facts which you **recall** from your **knowledge**.

✓ You must **explain** and **link** the points you make.

✓ Give clear **reasons to support** your points.

✓ Write about **different aspects** of the topic and show how they **interrelate**.

✓ Give different **points of view**, both positive and negative.

✓ Include **evidence in support** of your point of view or recommended course of action. This could be supporting information from your own knowledge or from the scenario.

Worked example

Older people who are unable to live in their own homes sometimes move into residential care settings. They are looked after by staff who provide them with personal care, such as help with washing, dressing, toileting and eating. Staff who work in these settings have to think about how to empower the residents, leading to better mental and physical health.

Discuss ways that health and social care workers empower older people who live in residential care settings. **8 marks**

Links See page 81 to revise residential care and page 65 to revise empowerment.

The key term here is **empower**. You should notice key terms and use the introduction to your answer to say what you understand by them.

Your introduction should give meaning and context to the points made, showing that you have read the question accurately.

Sample response extract

Before discussing how health and social care workers empower older residents, it is important to clarify what I mean by empowerment. Empowerment is a key principle in health and social care and it underpins the ways that care is provided. It means giving people (as far as possible) the ability to make their own decisions about the sorts of care and treatment they want and need. Empowerment gives people a say in the ways that they are supported and cared for. It is important for individuals because it enables them to attain their rights, to challenge attempts to deprive them of their rights, to express their beliefs and preferences and to have a say in matters which affect them. It also places people at the heart of service provision.

There are different ways that the term 'empowerment' is used and understood. This extract from a response clarifies what the term means in a health and social care setting, and shows how different aspects of empowerment interrelate. The answer would go on to relate clearly to the question, expanding on each of the points and linking them together.

Now try this

Delusha is a resident in a care home for older people. She needs help with all her daily routines. She is unable to hear clearly and this can make her impatient. She swears at care workers and often refuses to cooperate. Delusha's care workers are experienced in supporting residents with specific needs and who sometimes exhibit challenging behaviour.

Discuss the ways that care workers might support a resident such as Delusha.

Think about what the scenario tells you, to help focus your answer:
• Facts about Delusha
• What the care workers do.
Remember: linking the points you make is an important aspect of your discussion.

Links See page 100 for more about care of older adults with specific needs.

Long-answer questions

Half of the marks on your paper will be given for 6- and 8-mark questions. Here is an extract of a good answer to a 6-mark question, based on an extract from a scenario.

Worked example

Fonzi is 8 years old. He refuses to eat healthy foods and is unwilling to exercise. He often has a note from his parents to excuse him from school sports lessons. He has put on a lot of weight and is now obese. His parents are unconcerned about his weight gain and are both obese themselves. Fonzi fell over recently and damaged his arm. The doctor who treated Fonzi asked him and his parents about their diet and whether they took any exercise.

Explain ways that Fonzi could be supported to lose weight.

6 marks

What to note in this scenario:
- Information about Fonzi's health.
- The support Fonzi gets from his parents.
- The role of healthcare workers, e.g. the doctor.
- How Fonzi's teacher might support him.

What to think about as you read:
- What sort of support might Fonzi need?
- What sort of support might Fonzi's parents need?
- Which health and social care workers might provide support for Fonzi and his family?
- How might the family members' progress (weight loss) be monitored?
- How might the health worker challenge their right to eat what they want?

Sample response extract

Fonzi needs to lose weight quickly if he is to become healthy. Both he and his parents need support. When Fonzi returns to school, he will be measured and given advice about losing weight. The school will arrange for him and his parents to be seen by a school nurse sent by the local authority. Fonzi's parents will receive a letter about his weight with information about how to contact a support worker and outlining services that are available locally. Then they might look online for information. The NHS website has some steps for success, including how to be a good role model and encouraging healthy eating. Finally, Fonzi's GP might become involved and refer Fonzi and his parents to a dietitian.

This extract from an answer sets the context and refers back to the scenario, stating Fonzi's needs as an introduction to how he will be supported.

You need to show knowledge of how child health is monitored and of the role of health workers, in this case by a school nurse sent by the local authority. You need to expand the point, showing what further support is available for Fonzi.

This answer connects and links the points made. It also states what most people do when they want to know something – look online.

This answer shows knowledge of the next stage of support and the healthcare workers involved.

Links See pages 56–61 to revise roles and responsibilities of health and social care workers and page 74 to revise holistic approaches to care.

Coherent answers

When you write answers to 'explain' or 'discuss' questions, you need to show that you can **connect** the points you make. This is how your answers will be **coherent**. In simple terms, your answer has to make sense.

Now try this

Write another paragraph explaining how Fonzi's teacher could support him to lose weight.

State at least two things the teacher might do. Explain how those things will impact on Fonzi and his weight loss. Make sure that you develop and link your points.

Concise answers

Being concise means answering a question without adding information that is not needed. Here are some examples based on extracts from answers and scenarios.

Short-answer questions

'**Identify**' and '**describe**' questions require concise and specific answers. Don't write a lot of points that aren't needed. Instead, write concisely and spend your time on the longer questions. See pages 106 and 107 to revise short-answer questions.

Long-answer questions

'**Explain**' and '**discuss**' questions require longer answers but you should still focus your answer. You could note down a brief plan of key words to help you stay focused as you make, link and develop your points. See pages 108–110 to revise long-answer questions.

Abdul has broken his leg in an accident. He has received treatment in hospital and has returned home.

Explain ways that care workers could support Abdul to improve his health.   6 marks

Sample response extract

Abdul will only improve his health if he gets physiotherapy. The physiotherapist will come to Abdul's house and help him there. The physiotherapist will be trained to help Abdul. The physiotherapist will help Abdul to get better …

Improved response extract

The most effective way to support Abdul to improve his health would be to provide him with regular physiotherapy sessions …

This start to the answer is not concise. It unnecessarily repeats the word 'physiotherapist' several times. It also makes some general statements that are not needed and are not a good use of time.

This start to the answer makes a relevant point clearly and concisely. It is a good example of how to spend your time in the exam in the most useful way.

Now try this

David has returned home after treatment in hospital for a heart complaint. He had difficulty in ordering food that met his needs and preferences. He is vegetarian because he is opposed to taking life to eat meat or fish. When he tried to discuss it, the person delivering meals did not seem to respect his viewpoint.

Describe two ways that David might have experienced discrimination as a hospital in-patient.

Sample response extract

David experienced discrimination when he went to his local hospital. There seemed to be no vegetarian option available even though he tried to order it. Vegetarianism is important to David because he does not want to eat meat, as he disagrees with killing animals for food. David is unhappy about the discrimination and reports it to the hospital.

Rewrite the extract from the answer about David so that it is concise.

Focus on key points:
- that David felt discriminated against in hospital
- the lack of vegetarian food
- that his needs and preferences were not met
- that his viewpoint did not seem respected.

Cell structure and function

The cell is the fundamental unit of all living organisms. Cells are made up of a collection of molecules. The size and shape varies depending on the cell's specialised function. In order for cells to survive in the body they must carry out a variety of functions.

Basic cell structure

Revise what you know about animal cell structure before learning about human cells in more detail.

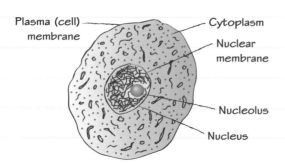

Plasma (cell) membrane — Cytoplasm — Nuclear membrane — Nucleolus — Nucleus

Cell functions

All cells share some basic functions. Others also have specialist functions.

- **Respiration:** cells require and absorb oxygen to produce heat and energy.
- **Growth:** cells grow to maturity by manufacturing proteins. They may then divide or specialise.
- **Excretion:** waste products pass out through the cell membrane.
- **Irritability:** cells can respond to a physical, chemical or thermal stimulus.

Human cell structure in detail

- **Cell membrane:** an outer coating which selectively transports substances into and out of the cell.
- **Nucleus:** the control centre of the cell, regulating its general and specialist functions.
- **Ribosomes:** made of ribonucleic acid (RNA) and protein, they manufacture other proteins.
- **Rough and smooth endoplasmic reticulum:** this manufactures, stores and transports materials within and outside of the cell.
- **Mitochondria:** situated in the cytoplasm, these supply the cell's energy source.
- **Centrioles:** essential for cell division.
- **Lysosomes:** contain enzymes which digest worn out parts of the cell for recycling and elimination of waste products.
- **Golgi apparatus:** modifies and stores manufactured protein and transports it out of the cell.

Mitochondrion   Centrioles   Smooth endoplasmic reticulum   Cell membrane   Nuclear membrane   Ribosomes   Lysosomes   Cytoplasm   Golgi apparatus   Rough endoplasmic reticulum   Nucleus

Make sure that you can draw and label a diagram of a human cell.

Cell division

Human cells **reproduce** by the process of **mitosis,** when structures like chromosomes and centrioles **replicate**. Then the cell **divides** into two identical daughter cells.

Nucleic acids

- **DNA** (deoxyribonucleic acid) carries the cell's **genes** as **chromosomes**. Genes are coded 'instructions' for making proteins and for cell function.
- All three types of **RNA** are involved in the decoding (**transcription**) of DNA to make proteins.

Enzymes

Enzymes are the **protein catalysts** that enable metabolic reactions at low temperatures. Enzymes are involved in all the cell functions of respiration, growth, excretion and irritability.

Now try this

Describe how proteins are involved in all cell functions.

You could cover the role of proteins in growth, the control of cell reactions and the manufacture of other proteins.

Tissue types: connective tissue

Tissues consist of many of the same type of cells, classified according to structure, location, size, shape and function. Connective tissue is one of the four tissue types.

Tissue types

There are **four** main types of tissue, which each then have subtypes:

 Epithelial tissue – thin sheets of epithelial cells make up the coverings and linings of the body and its organs and organ systems (page 114).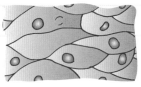

Muscle tissue – contraction of muscle tissue gives movement, and also aids internal processes such as digestion and circulation (page 115).

Connective tissue – has a supportive, structural role in the body, but also includes blood (this page).

Nervous tissue – conducts electrical impulses through the body, enabling the fast transfer of information (page 115).

> You need to know where these different tissue types may be found in the body and how they are adapted to their functions.

The functions of connective tissue

- To provide **structural** support, such as for **bones** and **cartilage** in the skeletal system, and **areolar tissue** which bonds tissues like skin and muscle.
- To **protect** – the skull protects the brain, and the ribs protect the heart and lungs.
- To **transport** substances in the **blood.**
- To **insulate (adipose** tissue contains fatty deposits to help to prevent heat loss).

Main connective tissue types

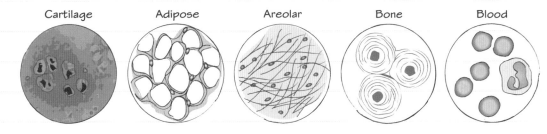

Cartilage   Adipose   Areolar   Bone   Blood

Now try this

Complete a table like this to show the four main tissue types and their functions in the body.

Tissue type	Function
Epithelial	
	transfer of information via electrical impulses
Muscle	
	structure, support and transport in the body

Tissue types: epithelial tissue

Tissues consist of many of the same type of cells, classified according to structure, location, size, shape and function. Epithelial tissue is one of the four tissue types.

Epithelial tissues

Epithelial tissues cover the body and line cavities, hollow organs and tubes. They are also found in glands of the **endocrine system**, where hormones are made that regulate different bodily functions, such as growth, reproduction and sleep.

You need to know about the **four** types of **simple epithelial tissue** and the **two** types of **compound epithelium**.

Functions

The functions of epithelial tissues are to:

- **protect** underlying structures, for example skin protects all internal tissues and organs
- **secrete**, for example **goblet cells** in the lining of the digestive system secrete enzymes and mucous
- **absorb**, for example the lining of the lungs absorbs oxygen from the air.

Simple epithelial tissue

There are **four** types of simple epithelium, each consisting of a single layer of cells.

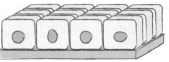

① Simple cuboidal

② Simple squamous

- Cilia
- Cell membrane
- Goblet cell
- Nucleus

> You need to know the differences between the four types of simple epithelium.

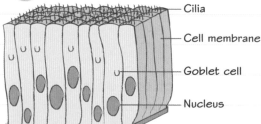

③ Simple columnar

④ Ciliated

Compound epithelium

① **Simple compound epithelium** consists of several layers of cells, the outer layer of which may be worn away.

② In **keratinised compound epithelium** like our skin, the outer layers of cells are dead, flattened and filled with a protein called keratin. This gives the tissue a waterproof outer layer.

> Simple compound epithelial **tissues** are found where the body is subject to wear and tear.

Simple compound epithelial tissue

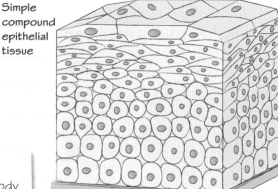

1 Identify the tissue shown in the photomicrograph and suggest where in the body such tissue might be found.

2 Make a sketch of the tissue shown and label it.

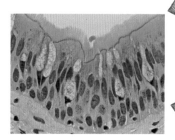

> Think about the structures shown in the photomicrograph and how these relate to the function of the tissue. This will give you a clue about where in the body it could be found.

> Include these labels: cilia, nucleus, goblet cells. Use the relevant figure above to help you find the correct positions for these labels.

Tissue types: muscle and nervous tissue

Tissues consist of many of the same type of cells, classified according to structure, location, size, shape and function. Muscle and nervous tissue are two of the four tissue types.

The three main muscle tissues

1 **Striated** (skeletal or voluntary) tissue is under conscious control, enabling us to move our bones.

2 **Non-striated** (smooth or involuntary) tissue is concerned with many internal body processes and functions, such as peristalsis in the digestive system.

3 **Cardiac** tissue is found only in the heart wall. It is not under conscious control and never tires.

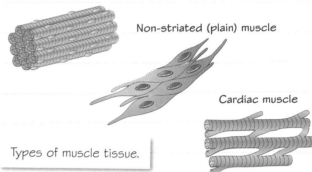

Striated (striped) muscle

Non-striated (plain) muscle

Cardiac muscle

Types of muscle tissue.

Characteristics of muscle tissue which contribute to muscle functioning

- **Contractability**: the ability to shorten and thicken.
- **Irritability**: the ability to respond to stimuli created by nerve impulses.
- **Extensibility**: the ability to stretch.
- **Elasticity**: the ability to return to its original shape following contraction.

The two types of nervous tissue

1 **Neurones** (with properties known as excitability and conductability)

- A neurone is a specialised nerve cell that receives stimuli, converts it to a nerve impulse and transmits this to other neurones, muscles and glands.
- Neurones occur as single cells and in groups in certain areas of the body, such as the spinal cord.
- A neurone consists of a cell body, an axon and many dendrites.

2 **Neuroglia** (glial or non-excitable cells)

- These support and protect the neurones.
- They are smaller and more numerous than neurones, forming over 50% of brain tissue.

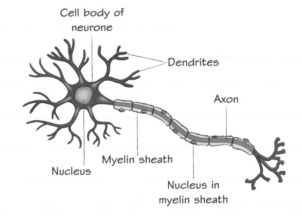

Cell body of neurone

Dendrites

Axon

Myelin sheath

Nucleus

Nucleus in myelin sheath

Neurones receive stimuli at the dendrites. A nerve impulse travels along the axon to the terminals. These form connections with other neurones, muscles or glands.

Now try this

Complete a table like the one below.

Muscle tissue type	Location in body	Function
Striated		
Non-striated		
	heart	

Major body organs

You need to know the locations of the major organs in the human body, and the structure and functions of each. Make sure you can label them.

Brain, skin, heart and lungs

Brain: in the skull. The **nervous centre** that controls all life functions.

Skin: a protective layer on the outer surface of the body.

Heart: situated in the central chest area. Circulates the **blood** to all tissues, which is essential for life.

Two **lungs:** located on either side of the heart. Facilitate the exchange of gases during **respiration**.

Sexual organs

Uterus and **ovaries** (in females): situated in the lower abdomen. Involved in reproduction.

Testes (in males): in the groin. Secrete testosterone and produce sperm.

Digestive organs

Liver: in the upper right of the abdomen. Involved in **digestion** and **excretion** of waste products.

Pancreas: behind the stomach. Secretes vital digestive **enzymes**.

Stomach: around the midline of the body, slightly to the left. Important in **digestion**.

Large intestine: (cecum and colon) where water reabsorption takes place.

Small intestine (duodenum and ileum): where the main food **absorption** takes place.

Kidneys and bladder

Two **kidneys**: on either side of the body, above and slightly behind the large intestine. Secrete urine, which is collected and stored in the **bladder** ready for excretion.

Now try this

Complete the table by adding the name of an organ that is part of each organ system. Can you add more than one example for some systems?

Look at the organs in bold above and work out the organ system for each from the description of its function.

Organ system	Example organ(s)
Nervous system	
Cardiovascular system	
Respiratory system	
Digestive system	
Reproductive system	

Energy metabolism

Humans use the chemical energy stored in food molecules as an energy source for life processes. We also use the simple products of digestion to build the new complex molecules that our bodies require.

Transformation of energy

An important law of physics is **the law of conservation of energy**. According to this law energy can neither be created nor destroyed. It can, however, be tranformed from one form into another. Forms of energy include chemical, heat, sound, electrical and light.

Bodies are good at converting the chemical energy in food into other forms of energy, for example into heat energy to keep warm, kinetic energy to move about, electrical energy to send nerve impulses and sound energy to speak or make noises.

What is metabolism?

The body converts ingested food into the chemicals and energy it needs to grow and function.

- Cells can build up complex molecules from the simple products of digestion.
- In cells, chemical processes release stored energy from the products of digestion.

The rate at which energy is released from cells is known as the **metabolic rate.** Metabolism involves two processes: **catabolism** and **anabolism.**

Basal metabolic rate (BMR)

This is the rate of metabolism when the body is at rest, in a warm environment, and when food has not been consumed for at least 12 hours. In this state, the energy released is just sufficient to meet the essential needs of the vital organs, such as heart, lungs, brain, and kidneys, thereby keeping the body alive.

Catabolism

The chemical breakdown of complex substances, such as carbohydrates, proteins and glucose, is accompanied by the release of energy.

- If the body has plenty of oxygen, **aerobic respiration** takes place. The products are carbon dioxide and water, which are excreted through the lungs.
  In cells, aerobic respiration takes place in the **mitochondria**.
- If there is insufficient oxygen, **anaerobic respiration** occurs. The product is lactic acid. In cells, anaerobic respiration takes place in the **cytoplasm**.

Anabolism

Anabolism is the opposite of catabolism. It is the building up of larger molecules from smaller ones, for example proteins from amino acids. Examples of anabolism include:

- building muscle tissue
- creating new cells
- mineralising bone.

Now try this

1 Compare anabolic and catabolic reactions.
2 Compare aerobic and anaerobic respiration.

Remember, catabolism and anabolism are opposite types of reaction.

They take place under different conditions and have different products.

117

Inheritance and genetic variation

Many characteristics are inherited. A wide range of disorders and disabilities occur as a result of genetic inheritance.

Genetic inheritance

- Children inherit certain **characteristics** from their parents.
- Genetic information, which is passed from parent to child, is contained in **genes**. These are carried by **chromosomes** in the nucleus of cells.
- A gene is a section of **DNA** (deoxyribonucleic acid) which controls the development of specific characteristics. Each chromosome contains many genes.
- In each cell, humans have 46 chromosomes (23 pairs) that carry about 30,000 genes.
- Although humans all look roughly similar they are not identical; the differences in appearance are known as **genetic variation**.
- Variation occurs when a child inherits characteristics from both parents (one set of 23 chromosomes from the mother and a second set of 23 chromosomes from the father).

Sex determination: an example of genetic inheritance

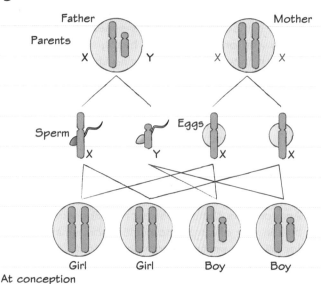

At conception

Females inherit one X chromosome from their mother and one from their father. Males inherit an X chromosome from their mother and a Y chromosome from their father. **Sex-linked conditions** are inherited via the sex chromosomes.

Chromosomal abnormalities

These can be classified into two basic groups:

1 In **numerical** abnormalities, there are either missing chromosomes or additional chromosomes.

2 In **structural** abnormalities, part of a chromosome may be missing, duplicated, inverted (upside down) or translocated (transferred to another chromosome).

Chromosome abnormalities usually occur when there is an error in cell division. The likelihood of a child inheriting a chromosome abnormality increases with maternal age. **Down's syndrome** is caused when a child inherits three copies of chromosome 21 instead of the usual two copies.

Using a Punnett square

To save drawing out complex diagrams, you can use a Punnett square to represent sex determination and other genetic crosses.

This Punnett square shows the sex chromosomes carried by eggs and sperm, and the resulting **genotypes** (genetic make-up) of the potential embryos.

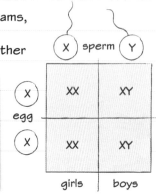

Now try this

1 What is genetic variation?
2 Explain why, when a baby is conceived, there is a 50% chance it is a boy and a 50% chance it is a girl.

Refer to the Punnett square to explain why the chance of having a boy is equal to that of having a girl.

Mendelian principles

The **principles of Mendelian inheritance** describe how some **traits** (appearances) result from the inheritance of a single gene copy (**allele**) from the female and an allele from the male. The probability of inheriting such traits is predictable.

Single gene disorders

Alleles for genes that cause single gene disorders can be either **recessive** or **dominant**. Only one copy of a dominant allele is required for that characteristic to be expressed, whereas two copies of a recessive allele must be present for that characteristic to appear. In **partial dominance**, an individual with one normal allele and one affected allele will exhibit a mild form of the disease. Examples of single gene disorders include:

- phenylketonuria (PKU) (recessive)
- cystic fibrosis (recessive)
- Huntington's disease (dominant)
- sickle cell disease (partially dominant).

 Links Look at page 120 to revise the effects of some conditions.

Key terms

Allele: alternative versions of a gene, giving different traits.

Trait: a genetically determined characteristic.

Dominant allele: if present, the trait is always expressed.

Recessive allele: two copies of this allele must be present for expression of the trait.

Homozygous: inheriting two identical copies of the same allele for a gene, one from the female and one from the male. These may be two dominant alleles or two recessive alleles.

Heterozygous: inheriting two different alleles for a gene, one recessive and one dominant.

Genotype: genetic makeup.

Phenotype: resulting appearance from the genetic makeup.

Dominant gene disorders

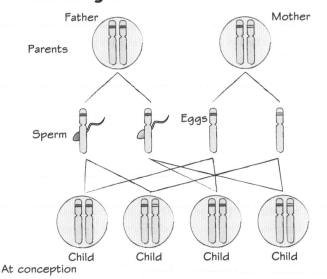

Parents — Father / Mother

Sperm / Eggs

Child Child Child Child
At conception

There is a 1 in 2 (50%) chance that a child of these parents will inherit the dominant gene disorder. There is a 50% chance that the child will inherit normal genes from both parents and be unaffected.

Multi-factorial conditions

Most human diseases are not caused by inheriting a single gene. Some disorders are caused by a combination of many genes and environmental factors such as lifestyle choices.

Representing genes with letters

To avoid drawing complex diagrams, you can represent single gene inheritance with letters. Capital letters are used for dominant genes and lower case letters for recessive genes. Rr would be a **heterozygous** individual. You can use **Punnett square** diagrams (page 118) to work out the potential allele combinations from a genetic cross and the probabilities of the resulting **phenotypes** and **genotypes**.

Now try this

Draw a diagram like the one above, or use a Punnett square, to represent the inheritance of a recessive single gene disorder. Start with two parents who each have a dominant normal gene and a recessive gene for the disorder. Give the probability of these parents having a normal child, an affected child and a child who is a carrier.

People who have a dominant normal gene and a recessive gene for a disorder are called **carriers**. They can pass on the genetic disorder but are unaffected themselves.

Genetic and chromosome disorders, and testing

Here are some causes and effects of genetic and chromosome disorders, and methods for diagnostic testing.

Diagnostic methods

Both tests for genetic disorders carry a small risk of miscarriage during pregnancy.

1 **Amniocentesis**. A small sample of amniotic fluid is removed from the womb, using a thin needle, under ultrasound control. The fluid contains foetal cells that can be tested for genetic disorders. The test is usually carried out between 15 and 18 weeks of pregnancy.

2 **Chorionic villus sampling**. A small sample of cells is removed from the placenta, containing foetal cells that can be tested for various genetic conditions. The test is usually carried out between 11 and 14 weeks of pregnancy.

Down's syndrome

Cause: when three copies of **chromosome 21** are present (one extra copy). It is associated with older maternal age (over 35 years), but also occurs in the children of younger women. Approximately 1 in 1000 births are affected.

Individuals with Down's syndrome commonly have the following features:

- short stature
- a flat, round face
- a large tongue
- a learning disability.

Some heart conditions are more common in children with Down's syndrome. Generally, life expectancy is good, with many people living until 50 or 60 years of age.

Huntington's disease

Cause: a dominant genetic condition which damages **nerve cells** in the brain.

Symptoms: affects movement, cognition, balance, awareness, judgement and mood.

Treatment: genetic testing confirms the diagnosis. There is no cure, although medication is used to relieve some of the symptoms. The prognosis is usually 10 to 25 years from diagnosis with progressive neurological degeneration during that time.

Phenylketonuria (PKU)

Cause: a recessive genetic condition that is present from birth.

Symptoms: the body is unable to break down the amino acid **phenylalanine**, which builds up to cause **brain damage**, leading to epilepsy, learning difficulties and behavioural problems.

Treatment: Babies are routinely screened with a heel-prick blood test during their first week of life. The condition is treated with a low-protein diet and amino acid supplements.

Sickle cell disease (SSD)

Cause: a partially dominant inherited **blood disorder** caused by gene mutation. It is much more common in people of African, Caribbean, Middle Eastern and Asian origin.

Symptoms: red blood cells develop abnormally. Rather than being flexible and disc shaped, they become rigid and crescent shaped; haemoglobin is defective. Blood vessels may become blocked by abnormally shaped red blood cells, resulting in tissue and organ damage, and severe pain (sickle cell crisis). **Sickle cell trait** (SST) is a mild version caused by inheriting a single faulty gene and one normal gene. It is thought to confer some protection against malaria.

Treatment: centres on the prevention of crisis episodes and pain relief.

Cystic fibrosis

Cause: a recessive genetic condition resulting from a mutation in the gene CFTR. If two affected genes are inherited, the lungs and digestive system become clogged with thick, sticky mucous. Individuals with a normal dominant gene and a recessive affected gene are carriers, but not affected.

Symptoms: persistent cough, respiratory infections, poor appetite and weight loss.

Treatment: physiotherapy, antibiotics and bronchodilators are used to alleviate symptoms. In severe cases a lung transplant may be considered.

Now try this

Choose **one** of the conditions caused by a mutation in a single gene and draw a diagram to show how it may be inherited.

Links Look at pages 118 and 119 to revise diagrams of genetic inheritance.

Homeostasis: temperature and blood pressure

Homeostasis means regulation of the body's internal environment. You need to know some examples of homeostatic mechanisms.

Maintaining balance

Homeostasis maintains the body's internal environment within normal limits despite external changes. This control is brought about by systems that detect and respond to internal changes. Usually these systems are **negative feedback mechanisms**.

Positive feedback, or amplifier mechanisms, also control certain factors, including blood clotting, but are much less common.

Controlled factors

- ✓ Core body temperature.
- ✓ Blood glucose levels.
- ✓ Water and electrolyte concentrations.
- ✓ pH of body fluids.
- ✓ Blood pressure.
- ✓ Blood and tissue oxygen and carbon dioxide levels.

Blood pressure

Negative feedback mechanisms reverse deviations from the physiological norms. If an abnormal state is detected, such as a fall in blood pressure, there is a response to the stimulus. The body takes action to correct the imbalance (e.g. raise the blood pressure).

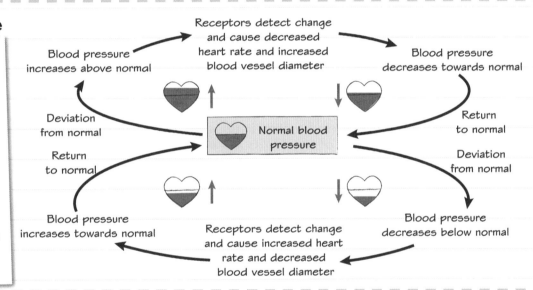

Body temperature

This is regulated by negative feedback. The body balances the amount of heat produced and lost to the environment to achieve a normal core temperature (36.0–37.5°C).

Body temperature is regulated by the **hypothalamus** in the brain:

- **Cool blood:** hypothalamus sends nerve impulses via the **autonomic nervous system** to constrict the skin arterioles to prevent heat loss, and to contract striated muscles (shivering) to produce heat. Hypothermia sets in when the body temperature falls below 35°C.
- **Hot blood:** hypothalamus sends nerve impulses to dilate the skin arterioles, enabling loss of heat, and stimulates sweat glands to increase perspiration.

Some of these **physiological signs** (reactions of the body) are symptoms of a **fever**, as the body attempts to control its temperature.

Body heat

Heat is produced in the body by:

- contractions of striated muscles
- metabolic reactions in the liver
- peristalsis and chemical reactions in the digestive system.

Heat loss occurs:

- through the skin
- in exhaled breath, urine and faeces.

Now try this

Produce a simple diagram indicating how negative feedback mechanisms control body temperature.

 Refer to the diagram above. Start by putting 'normal body temperature' in the box in the middle. Now complete the diagram with information about control of body temperature.

121

Homeostasis: glucose and fluids

Homeostasis is vital to life and health. Poor homeostasis can be life threatening.

Blood glucose level

Glucose in the blood is controlled mainly by the opposing actions of two hormones, insulin and glucagon, which are made in the **pancreas**.

- **Insulin**, secreted by the islets of Langerhans in the pancreas, **reduces** the blood glucose level. Secretion of insulin is stimulated by an increase in blood glucose level, for example after eating a meal.
- **Glucagon increases** the blood glucose level. It is secreted in response to low blood glucose and exercise. The **liver** is the site of action of glucagon.

The normal ranges of blood glucose levels are 3.5–5.5 mmol/litre (millimoles per litre) before meals, and less than 8 mmol/litre two hours after meals.

 Links Look at page 116 to revise the locations of the pancreas and liver.

Fluid balance

Approximately 60% of an adult's weight is fluid. To maintain homeostasis, the intake of fluid must balance the output. The intake of fluid is primarily from ingestion of food and drink, but some fluid is produced by the process of metabolism. Fluid loss occurs through urination, defecation, perspiration and exhalation. Excessive fluid loss (dehydration) can also occur as a result of haemorrhage, vomiting and diarrhoea.

Hormones produced by the renal system (adrenal glands and kidneys) and other organs signal to the body to seek out, conserve or expel fluids and electrolytes.

Blood pressure falls Kidneys release renin Angiotensin is produced in the blood This stimulates release of aldosterone from the kidneys Kidneys act to conserve fluid Blood pressure rises again

An example of fluid balance regulation.

Homeostatic failure

If a regulatory mechanism fails to return a physiological measurement to within the normal limits, the resulting abnormal state can quickly become life threatening and urgent medical intervention is needed. For example, in **diabetes mellitus** regulation of blood glucose level is disrupted, resulting in an unusually high blood glucose level, **hyperglycaemia**, or an unusually low blood glucose level, **hypoglycaemia**.

Life-threatening conditions
Extremes of body temperature
Pyrexia (fever) (temperature above 37.5°C)
Hypothermia (temperature below 35°C)
Abnormal blood glucose levels
Hyperglycaemia (regularly above 8 mmol/litre)
Hypoglycaemia (below 3.5 mmol/litre)

Now try this

1 Suggest how injecting insulin can help diabetics prevent hyperglycaemia.
2 Suggest how someone with diabetes might counteract the effects of a hypoglycaemic episode.

Consider what you know about people with normal control of blood glucose levels.

The heart structure and function

The heart is the pump of the cardiovascular system. It delivers a constant flow of blood to tissues all around the body.

Measurements

You need to know about **three** different measurements associated with the heart.

1 **Heart rate**: in a healthy adult, the heart averages 60–80 **beats per minute**. This can be monitored by feeling the **pulse** (the contractions in an accessible artery where it runs parallel to a bone) in the wrist or neck, for example.

2 **Stroke volume**: the amount of blood that is pumped by the heart in one contraction. It is the volume of blood in the ventricles before they contract.

3 **Blood pressure (BP)**: the force exerted by blood on vessel walls:

   • **Systolic BP** is the pressure produced in the arterial system when the left ventricle contracts and pushes blood into the aorta.

   • **Diastolic BP** is the pressure in the arteries when the heart is resting (cardiac diastole).

Structure

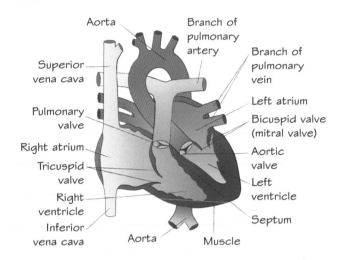

When labelling a diagram of the heart, by convention, left and right are reversed. Imagine you are looking at someone else's heart from the front and labelling **their** left and right atria and ventricles.

The cardiac cycle

The cardiac cycle is the sequence of events in the heart.

 As the atria and ventricles relax (**diastole**), they fill with blood from the vena cava and pulmonary vein.

② The **atria contract** (**systole**), squeezing more blood into the ventricles.

③ Next the **ventricles contract**, squeezing blood into the pulmonary artery and aorta.

The heartbeat

The heartbeat is transmitted through the heart by nervous impulses. Arrival of the impulse at each of the four sites causes a wave of contraction of the **cardiac muscle**.

Regulation

The **sympathetic nervous system** speeds up the heart rate, for example during exercise or stress, and the **parasympathetic system** slows it down, for example during rest or sleep. The hormone adrenaline also causes the heart rate to increase during the 'fright, flight or fight' response.

Now try this

Name the type of muscle found in the human heart.

 Recall that there are three types of muscle. Look at page 115 to revise muscle types.

The cardiovascular system

The cardiovascular system consists of the heart, the blood vessels and the blood.

Double circulation

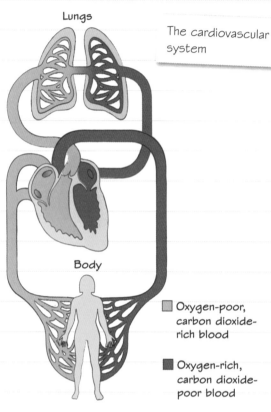

Lungs

The cardiovascular system

Body

☐ Oxygen-poor, carbon dioxide-rich blood

■ Oxygen-rich, carbon dioxide-poor blood

① **Pulmonary circulation**
The right side of the heart pumps blood to the lungs, where gas exchange takes place. Oxygen (O_2) diffuses into the blood and carbon dioxide (CO_2) diffuses out of the blood and into the air sacs for exhalation.

② **Systemic circulation**
The left side of the heart pumps blood into the body where cells take up oxygen and nutrients. Tissue wastes are passed into the blood for excretion.

Blood vessels

Starting at the heart:
- The **aorta** is the largest blood vessel, leaving the left ventricle of the heart to supply oxygenated blood to the rest of the body.
- Many major **arteries** branch off the aorta to supply different areas of the body with oxygen. Arteries have thick, muscular and elastic walls.
- The arteries lead to smaller blood vessels called **arterioles**, which deliver blood to the capillaries in body organs and tissues.

In the body tissues and organs:
- **Capillaries** supply the cells and tissues with nutrients from the blood. Their walls are only one cell thick, to maximise the rate of diffusion into and out of the blood.
- Capillaries unite arterioles and **venules** in the cells and tissues.

Returning to the heart:
- Venules feed into **veins** which carry deoxygenated blood and waste back towards the heart. The pressure in veins is lower than in arteries, so their walls are thinner and less muscular.
- Veins have **valves** at intervals to prevent the backflow of blood.
- Major veins feed into the inferior **vena cava** and superior vena cava, returning deoxygenated blood to the right atrium of the heart.

Now try this

Complete this table by naming the diagrams of the blood vessels and by stating briefly how structure relates to function in each case.

Blood vessel	Cross section	How structure relates to function
	Thicker smooth muscle layer — Fibrous layer of connective tissue — Endothelium — Lumen	
	Thicker smooth muscle layer — Fibrous layer of connective tissue — Endothelium — Lumen	
	Endothelium — Lumen	

Refer to the descriptions of the different types of blood vessels above to work out which diagram shows an artery, a capillary and a vein.

Blood structure and function

Blood is composed of different cell types suspended in a fluid called **plasma**. The cells have different functions.

Components of blood

 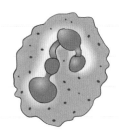

1 **Red blood cells** have no nucleus, contain **haemoglobin** and have a flat shape, which gives them a high surface-area-to-volume ratio for the efficient **carriage of oxygen**.

2 **White blood cells** fight infection, for example by:
- engulfing pathogens (a process called **phagocytosis**)
- releasing destructive enzymes
- producing antibodies.

3 **Platelets** These cell fragments help the blood to clot at the site of injury.

The four main functions of blood

 Transport

 Regulation

 Defence

 Clotting

Examples of body functions regulated by the blood are body temperature and pH balance.

 Links Look at pages 121 and 122 to revise the role of blood in homeostasis.

Transport

As well as the cells mentioned above, blood transports:
- dissolved gases such as oxygen and carbon dioxide
- nutrients like glucose and amino acids
- salts
- waste products of cell metabolism
- white blood cells to the site of infection
- enzymes, antibodies and hormones
- plasma proteins, which have roles in blood clotting.

Now try this

Describe how blood is adapted to carry out its four main functions

Consider which parts of the blood carry out each of the four functions. Don't forget that plasma (the matrix) is part of the blood and has important functions.

Cardiovascular disorders

Many disorders are associated with the **cardiovascular system**. Some affect the **heart** structure and function, some affect a particular type of blood vessel, while others affect the **blood** composition and function.

Sudden and chronic disorders

There are **two** types of disorders: **acute** (sudden), such as a heart attack, and **chronic** (long term), such as angina. Disorders can vary in severity.

- **Life-threatening disorders** include blood clots and leukaemia, a cancer in which high numbers of abnormal white blood cells are made at the expense of normal blood cells.
- **Relatively mild disorders**, such as anaemia, may be controlled by medication.

Some conditions are treated by surgery, for example heart valve replacement.

Stroke

A stroke, also known as a **cerebrovascular accident (CVA)**, is a life-threatening condition that occurs when the blood supply to the brain is interrupted. There are **two** main causes:

- **haemorragic**: when a blood vessel in the brain bursts
- **ischaemic**: when a blood clot blocks the blood supply to the brain.

Transient ischaemic attacks (TIAs) occur when there is a temporary interruption to the blood supply. It is a risk factor for a stroke in the future.

Coronary heart disease (CHD/ atherosclerosis)

Coronary arteries are narrowed by a gradual build-up of fatty matter in the vessel walls, forming a deposit called a **plaque** or **atheroma**.

Arteries eventually become so narrow that oxygen-rich blood cannot pass through, causing a condition called **angina**.

Small parts of the atheroma can break off and cause a complete blockage.

If this occurs in a coronary artery, it results in a **heart attack**.

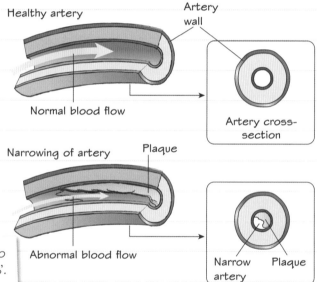

Healthy artery — Artery wall — Artery cross-section — Normal blood flow — Narrowing of artery — Plaque — Abnormal blood flow — Narrow artery — Plaque

> CHD is commonly referred to as 'narrowing of the arteries'.

Hypertension

Hypertension is also known as **high blood pressure**.

- A blood pressure reading higher than 140/90 mm Hg is an indication of hypertension.
- This increases the risks of heart attack, stroke, heart failure and kidney disease.
- The patient often has no symptoms.
- Blood pressure may be controlled by lifestyle changes and/or medication.

Anaemia

Anaemia is due to a **lack of iron** in the body.

- This results in fewer **red blood cells**, affecting the amount of oxygen supplied to tissues and organs.
- People with anaemia may be tired, pale and short of breath.
- If anaemia is not treated, people may become more susceptible to illness and infection. Extreme anaemia may result in heart and lung problems.
- Medication (iron) is the most common form of treatment. A diet that is rich in iron (green vegetables, meat, wholegrains and pulses) may also help.

Now try this

Identify **three** acute disorders and **three** chronic disorders affecting the cardiovascular system.

> List all the different conditions that are mentioned on this page. Decide whether each is acute (sudden) or chronic (long term).

Respiratory system structure

The respiratory system structure allows oxygen in the air to enter the body, and to be taken up by cells and tissues. The respiratory system also eliminates carbon dioxide from the body.

Structure of the respiratory system

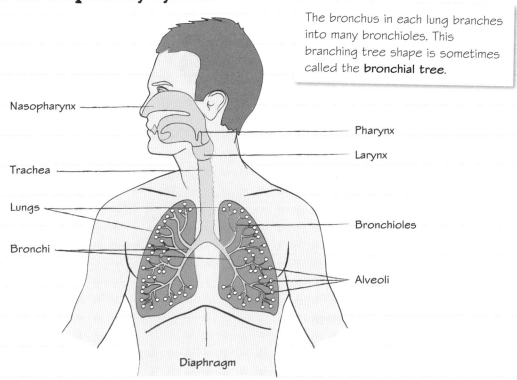

The bronchus in each lung branches into many bronchioles. This branching tree shape is sometimes called the **bronchial tree**.

Labels: Nasopharynx, Pharynx, Larynx, Trachea, Lungs, Bronchi, Bronchioles, Alveoli, Diaphragm

Upper airways

In the air passages of the **nose**:

- The tiny hairs (**cilia**) of **ciliated epithelial tissue** begin to filter atmospheric air.
- **Goblet cells** in the ciliated epithelial tissue secrete mucous to trap dust and bacteria, and to moisten the air.
- Cilia sweep the mucous, dust and bacteria away from the airways, preventing their entry into the body.
- Blood capillaries warm the air.

The air is warmed further as it passes through the **nasopharynx**, **pharynx** and **larynx**.

Air then passes into the **trachea** – a large, strong tube which is held open by rings of hyaline **cartilage**.

Lungs

- The **trachea** divides into two – the right and left **bronchi**, which enter the right and left **lungs**.
- Each **bronchus** then divides into smaller **bronchioles**.
- Bronchioles then subdivide into **alveoli** (small air sacs). Each warms and moistens inhaled air, bringing it close to gas exchange surfaces during inspiration, and transporting waste gases out during expiration.
- The **alveoli** are thin-walled and covered with tiny capillaries. This enables the exchange of oxygen into the blood and carbon dioxide out of the blood, to be exhaled. In an adult each lung contains millions of tiny alveoli.

 Links Look at page 114 to revise ciliated epithelial tissue.

 Now try this

Describe how the tissue in the nose is adapted to its function.

Refer to the characteristics of ciliated epithelial tissue that prevent the entry of foreign bodies into the respiratory system, and that warm and moisten air.

Respiratory system function

The respiratory system allows oxygen in the air to enter the body and it also eliminates carbon dioxide.

Ventilation

Ventilation (**breathing**) is the movement of air in and out of the lungs, not to be confused with **respiration** (gas exchange). The average adult ventilation rate is 12–15 breaths per minute.

Breathing rate and depth are regulated by the **autonomic nervous system** (see page 139), specifically by two parts of the brain called the **medulla oblongata** and the **pons**. These structures receive information about the levels of oxygen and carbon dioxide in the blood, and respond by sending nerve impulses to the respiratory muscles.

Muscles

Two types of muscles are involved in ventilation.

 The **diaphragm** is a dome-shaped muscle below the thoracic cavity.

 The **intercostal muscles** occupy the spaces between the 12 pairs of ribs.

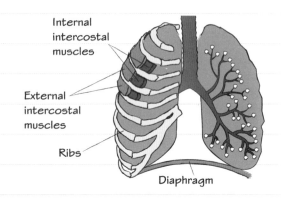

Inspiration and expiration

- During **inspiration**, the diaphragm and the intercostal muscles **contract** simultaneously increasing the volume of the thoracic cavity, and lowering the pressure in the air passages and alveoli, causing air to be drawn into the lungs.

- **Relaxation** of these muscles causes a decrease in thoracic volume, pressure to rise, and **expiration**.

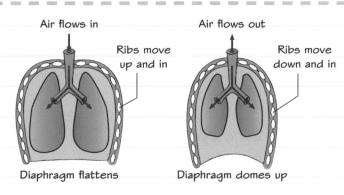

Air flows in — Ribs move up and in — Diaphragm flattens

Air flows out — Ribs move down and in — Diaphragm domes up

Gaseous exchange and diffusion

Gas exchange at the respiratory membrane is a continuous process, independent of the respiratory cycle, with oxygen and carbon dioxide exchanging across the walls of the alveoli at the same time.

Diffusion is the movement of particles from an area of high concentration to an area of low concentration. In the lungs the difference in concentration of gases in the alveoli and gases dissolved in capillary blood leads to diffusion.

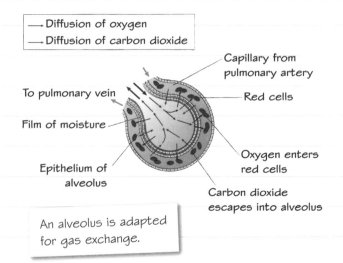

— Diffusion of oxygen
— Diffusion of carbon dioxide

To pulmonary vein
Film of moisture
Epithelium of alveolus
Capillary from pulmonary artery
Red cells
Oxygen enters red cells
Carbon dioxide escapes into alveolus

An alveolus is adapted for gas exchange.

Now try this

Describe how the structure of alveoli makes them suited to the function of gas exchange.

The diagram of an alveolus above tells you everything you need to know.

Respiratory disorders

Respiratory diseases have similar signs and symptoms, although they have different causes.

Asthma

Cause
A common **inflammatory** disorder of the airways when the bronchi are oversensitive. When triggered, the bronchi swell, narrow and produce excess mucous.

Symptoms
Breathlessness, coughing, **wheezing** and a 'tight' feeling in the chest. Various things can trigger an attack, including **allergens** (for example pet hair and pollen), pollution, cold air, exercise and emotional stress.

Treatment
There is no cure for asthma, but in most cases it can be controlled with medication.

Chronic obstructive pulmonary disease (COPD)

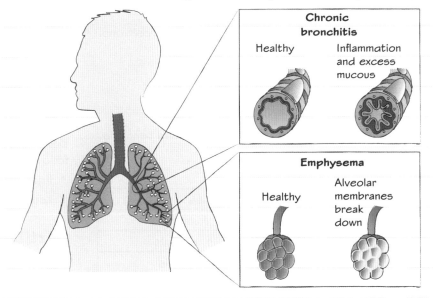

Chronic bronchitis — Healthy / Inflammation and excess mucous

Emphysema — Healthy / Alveolar membranes break down

Cause COPD is the name given to a collection of respiratory disorders, including chronic **bronchitis** and **emphysema**. The main cause of COPD is **smoking**.

Symptoms **Cough**, excess mucous production and breathlessness, especially on exertion.

Treatment Medication can relieve some symptoms.

Pneumonia

Pneumonia   Healthy

Inflammation causes fluid and blood cells to leak into the alveoli

Thicker alveolar walls

Cause Inflammation and fluid occur in the alveoli of one or both lungs, usually due to an **infection**.

Symptoms Include a **high body temperature**, breathlessness and a cough with thick mucous.

Treatment Patients are often treated in hospital with antibiotics and oxygen therapy.

Lung cancer

Cause
Smoking causes around 90% of lung cancers, and also causes cancers in many other parts of the body, including mouth, throat, lips, larynx and oesophagus.

Symptoms
Only develop in the later stages of the disease and include a persistent **cough**, coughing up blood, breathlessness, tiredness, weight loss and **pain** when breathing and coughing.

Treatment
Lung cancer may be treated with surgery, chemotherapy and radiotherapy.

Smoking can also cause pneumonia, emphysema, COPD and bronchitis, and can worsen conditions such as asthma.

Now try this

A peak-flow meter is a simple mechanical device that measures the maximum volume of air a person can expire and an oximeter is an electronic finger-tip device that measures the amount of oxygen in the blood. Suggest why a GP might use these tests in the initial diagnosis of respiratory disorders.

The skeletal system

The human skeleton is made up of the axial skeleton and the appendicular skeleton.

Functions of the skeletal system

- ✓ Protects vital organs and spinal cord.
- ✓ Gives support and shape in different positions.
- ✓ Source of blood cell production.
- ✓ Storage of minerals.
- ✓ Provides attachment sites for skeletal muscles (to enable movement).
- ✓ Incorporates cartilage, ligaments and tendons.

Types of bones

Type	Examples
Long bone	femur, humerus
Short bone	tarsals, carpals
Flat bone	cranium, pelvis
Irregular bone	vertebrae
Sesamoid bone	knee cap

Bones

A function of bones is to create blood cells. This happens in **two** ways:

- **Red blood cells** are made in **cancellous bone**.
- **White blood cells** are made in the **bone marrow**.

Ligaments and tendons

Bones join to other bones and to muscles in the following ways:

- ligaments join bone to bone
- tendons join muscles to bone.

Cartilage

Cartilage protects the ends of bones where they may rub against each other.

Structure of a long bone

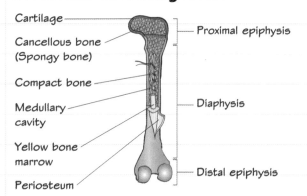

Cartilage
Cancellous bone (Spongy bone)
Compact bone
Medullary cavity
Yellow bone marrow
Periosteum
Proximal epiphysis
Diaphysis
Distal epiphysis

Note that the epiphysis and diaphysis are separated by epiphysial plates.

Proximal and distal

Two terms in the diagram are used regularly in health and social care:

 Proximal means nearest to the point of attachment.

 Distal means furthest away from the point of attachment.

The human skeleton

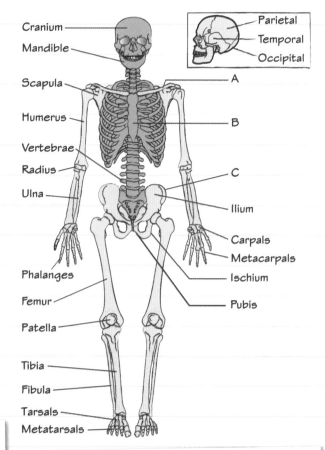

Cranium
Mandible
Scapula
Humerus
Vertebrae
Radius
Ulna
Phalanges
Femur
Patella
Tibia
Fibula
Tarsals
Metatarsals

Parietal
Temporal
Occipital
A
B
C
Ilium
Carpals
Metacarpals
Ischium
Pubis

There are 33 vertebrae in the **vertebral column** (spine). Twelve pairs of ribs join to the 12 thoracic vertebrae. The femur is the longest and strongest bone in the body – if it is fractured the resulting blood loss can kill.

Now try this

You can choose from **sternum, pelvis** and **clavicle**.

Look at the diagram of the human skeleton above. State the names of bones A, B and C.

Joints and movements

Joints occur where two or more bones meet. They enable the body to move. They can be classified as **fibrous**, **cartilaginous**, or **synovial**.

Joints

Type	Characteristics	Diagram	Example
Fibrous	• Very little movement • Bones separated by fibrous tissue or cartilage		Skull Pelvis
Cartilaginous	• Slight movement • Bones separated by disc of cartilage	Cartilage	Vertebral column
Synovial	• Free movement • Ends of bones covered in cartilage and separated by a cavity that is filled with fluid	Bone Synovial membrane Cartilage Capsule Joint cavity containing synovial fluid	There are six types of synovial joints: 1 pivot (e.g. proximal radioulnar joint) 2 hinge (e.g. elbow, knee) 3 condyloid (e.g. wrist) 4 saddle (e.g. thumb) 5 ball and socket (e.g. shoulder, hip) 6 plane/gliding (e.g. patellofemoral and acrimioclavicular joints).

Terms used to describe movements at joints

Movement	Description	Example
Abduction	movement away from midline of body	raising leg at hip joint
Adduction	movement towards midline of body	lowering arm at shoulder
Extension	straightening limbs at a joint	straightening elbow
Flexion	bending limbs at a joint	bending knee
Circumduction	a circular movement around a fixed point	turning head at neck
Gliding	movement in more than one direction	twisting wrist

Now try this

Describe the types of movements that are possible at the shoulder and at the knee.

Shoulder and hip joints are both ball-and-socket joints, with a similar range of movements, and elbow and knee joints are both hinge joints.

Skeletal disorders

Disorders of the skeletal system result from one of four causes. You need to know about these causes and some examples of types of conditions.

Skeletal disorders

Disorders of the skeletal system be the result of:

1. **accidents**, for example **fractures** (complete or incomplete breaks in bones)

2. **dietary deficiencies**, for example childhood rickets where there is defective **calcification** (hardening) of bones due to a lack of dietary calcium or a lack of vitamin D

3. **illness or disease**, for example osteoporosis (when bone loses density and becomes brittle)

4. the **ageing process**, for example **osteoarthritis**, a degenerative condition in which cartilage is worn away.

Osteoarthritis

Cause

Wear and tear in joints means that cartilage becomes damaged.

Symptoms

Stiff, swollen and painful joints.

Treatment

Four key things can help to minimise the symptoms of osteoarthritis:

- Regular exercise to reduce stiffness.
- Maintaining a healthy weight to reduce strain on hip and knee joints.
- Wearing joint supports.
- Pain relief medication.

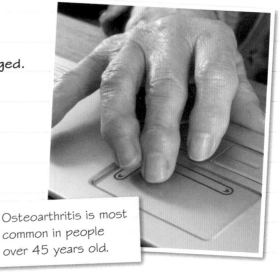

Osteoarthritis is most common in people over 45 years old.

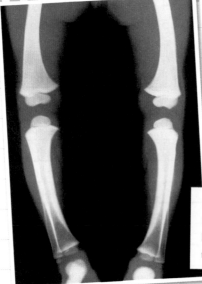

Increase in rickets

Recently, rickets in children has increased in the UK. This is associated with deficiency in calcium and vitamin D, which is formed in the body on exposure to sunlight.

Suggested explanations include that children do not play outdoors as much as they did in the past and that a change in the ethnic mix of the population, to include more people with darker skin, means that vitamin D deficiency is more common.

Bowed legs are a sign of rickets – leg bones are not strong enough to bear the body's weight, leading to malformation of the long bones.

Now try this

Draw a diagram of a synovial joint and indicate the part of the joint damaged in osteoarthritis.

 Refer back to page 131 if you need help with the diagram.

The muscular system and disorders

You need to know about the structure, function and main disorders of the muscular system. The striated muscles of the skeleton have three main functions: movement, maintaining posture and heat production.

Striated muscles

Skeletal or striated muscles are under **voluntary control** and enable movement of bones and joints.

 Look at page 115 to revise the characteristics of muscle tissue.

Contractions

Type	What the muscle does	Example
Concentric	contracts and shortens	climbing stairs
Eccentric	contracts but lengthens due to the load	carrying a load
Isometric	contracts but remains the same length due to the load	in tug-of-war

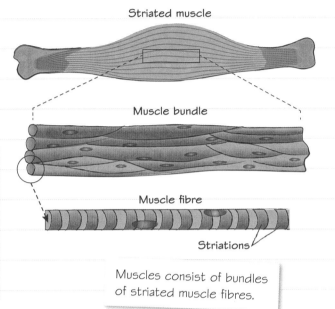

Striated muscle

Muscle bundle

Muscle fibre

Striations

Muscles consist of bundles of striated muscle fibres.

Muscle types

1. **Agonists** (prime movers) are the main activating muscles.

2. **Antagonists** work as a pair with and in opposition to agonists. One relaxes as the other contracts to create movement.

3. **Synergists** work to assist agonist or antagonist muscles.

4. **Fixators** are muscles which stabilise bones, enabling agonists to work effectively.

Disorders of the muscular system

Muscular dystrophy is an inherited progressive condition. Changes occur in the muscle fibres, affecting muscle function. It often begins by affecting one group of muscles but becomes more widespread. Eventually the heart and respiratory muscles are affected, causing death. **Duchenne muscular dystrophy** is the most common type. There is no cure but symptoms can sometimes be relieved by medication and physiotherapy.

Muscle attachments

- The attachment of the muscle closest to the centre of the body is known as the **origin**.
- The attachment furthest from the centre of the body is known as the **insertion**.

There are **three** types of attachment:

1. **Tendons** are strong, fibrous bands which link **muscles to bones** and transmit the contractile force of the muscle to the bone, creating movement. The tendons are quite **inflexible** and do not contract or stretch.

2. **Ligaments** are strong, fibrous **elastic** structures which stabilise joints by joining **bone to bone**. Ligaments are pliable enough to allow movement of a joint but prevent overstretching.

3. **Fasciae** consist of fibrous connective tissue. A fascia separates different muscles, protecting them while allowing them to move alongside one another, e.g. facial muscles can move whereas the skull does not.

Now try this

1. Muscle fibres and their attachments can become damaged. Suggest how this might happen.

2. What signs and symptoms would you expect where there is damage to muscles and their attachments?

Major muscles

Muscles work in groups to coordinate body movements. You need to know the names and locations in the body of the major muscles.

Major muscles

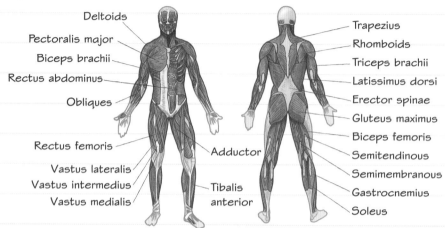

Deltoids
Pectoralis major
Biceps brachii
Rectus abdominus
Obliques
Rectus femoris
Vastus lateralis
Vastus intermedius
Vastus medialis
Adductor
Tibalis anterior
Trapezius
Rhomboids
Triceps brachii
Latissimus dorsi
Erector spinae
Gluteus maximus
Biceps femoris
Semitendinous
Semimembranous
Gastrocnemius
Soleus

Examples and actions

Muscle	Action
Erector spinae	Extension, lateral flexion and rotation of the vertebral column
Rectus abdominus	Flexion of the vertebral column (to allow a sitting-up action)
Internal and external obliques	Flexion and rotation of the vertebral column (to allow side bending)
Trapezius	Enables movement of the scapula and shoulder joint, and pulls head backwards
Latissimus dorsi	Extension, adduction and medial rotation of the humerus
Gluteus maximus	Extension, abduction and lateral rotation of the femur
Biceps brachii	Flexion and supination of the forearm
Triceps brachii	Extension of the forearm and adduction of the arm
Deltoids	Flexion, abduction and lateral rotation of the arm
Pectoralis major	Flexion, adduction and medial rotation of the arm
Adductors	Flexion of the hip joint. adduction and lateral rotation of the femur
Tibialis anterior	Dorsiflexion and inversion of the foot
Gastrocnemius	Plantar flexion of the foot and flexion of the knee joint
Soleus	Plantar flexion of the foot
Semimembranosus, semitendinosus and biceps femoris: collectively known as the hamstrings	Flexion of the knee and extension of the hip
Rectus femoris, vastus lateralis, vastus medialis and vastus intermedius: collectively known as the quadriceps	Extension of the knee joint and flexion of the hip joint

 Links Look at page 131 to revise some of the terms that describe movements.

Now try this

Consider which muscles you use when standing up from a sitting position.

Try standing up. Are you using muscles in your legs, stomach and/or back?

The digestive system

The alimentary canal is a long tube through which food passes (mouth to anus) in order to be digested (broken down) into useful molecules. It is made up of the oesophagus, stomach, duodenum, ileum and colon.

The digestive system

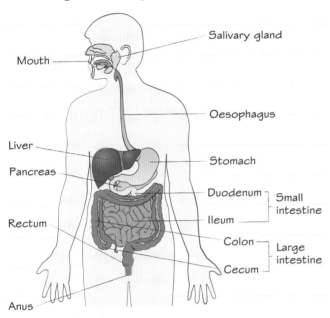

Salivary gland
Mouth
Oesophagus
Liver
Pancreas
Stomach
Duodenum ⎤ Small
Ileum ⎦ intestine
Rectum
Colon ⎤ Large
Cecum ⎦ intestine
Anus

> You need to know about the structure and function of these parts of the digestive system.

Ingestion

1 Food is **ingested** (taken in) through the **mouth**, where it is chewed up (masticated) and formed into a ball (bolus) by the tongue. to enable swallowing.

Peristalsis

2 The food is pushed into the **oesophagus** and is conveyed by **peristalsis** (alternate antagonistic contractions of the longitudinal and circular muscles of the wall of the alimentary canal) to the **stomach**.

Digestion

3 Food enters the stomach through the cardiac sphincter (a muscle which opens and closes the stomach bag). In the stomach, the food is churned up mechanically and is chemically broken down by gastric juices to a liquid (**chyme**). Food is in the stomach for about five hours, while protein digestion begins.

4 Chyme passes through the pyloric sphincter muscle into the **duodenum** (the first part of the **small intestine**). Peristalsis continues the mechanical breakdown of food, while gastric juices assist with chemical digestion.

Absorption

5 **Absorption** of digested food is in the next part of the small intestine (and the **ileum**).

6 Once nutrients from digested food have diffused into the bloodstream, they are transported to cells to metabolise.

Egestion

7 Undigested food passes into the **large intestine**, where absorption of water takes place and faeces are formed and stored. Mucous lubricates the passage of faeces to the **rectum**.

8 Faeces are stored in the rectum before expulsion (**egestion**) via the **anus**, which is controlled by two sphincter muscles that remain closed except during defecation.

Now try this

Complete the table to revise the functions of different sections of the alimentary canal.

Part of the alimentary canal	Function
	Breaks food up into smaller pieces
	Food passes from the mouth to the stomach
Stomach	
	Mechanical breakdown of food and chemical digestion
	Absorption of the products of digestion
Large intestine	
Rectum	
	Defecation

Enzymes and products of digestion

You need to know about the main digestive enzymes, their sites of secretion and the products of the reactions they catalyse.

Digestive enzymes

Enzymes assist with the chemical digestion of food to enable effective absorption in the small intestine.

Salivary amylase

There are three pairs of **salivary glands** in the mouth (sublingual, submandibular and parotid). These glands secrete salivary **amylase** in response to the sight and smell of food. This starts breaking carbohydrates into simple sugars.

Intestinal juice

This is released by glands in the duodenum and completes the breakdown of nutrients.

Pancreatic juice

This is produced by the **pancreas** and secreted into the duodenum. It contains three main enzymes:

* **trypsin** (a **protease**) which is involved in breaking proteins into peptides and amino acids
* **pancreatic amylase** for the further breakdown of starches
* **pancreatic lipase** which breaks down lipids into fatty acids and glycerol.

Bile

The **liver** produces an alkaline liquid called **bile**, which is stored in the gall bladder before entering the duodenum. Bile neutralises chyme and breaks up fatty droplets.

Products of digestion

Food group	Type of enzyme	Products of reaction	What happens to the products
Proteins	Protease	Peptides and amino acids	**Peptides** and **amino acids** pass through the capillaries of the small intestine into the bloodstream and are carried to the **liver** where they are made suitable for use in body tissues. They are stored in the liver until required; any excess is **deaminated** and excreted as urea by the **kidneys**. Their main function is to produce proteins to repair damaged cells and produce new cells. They are also needed to produce enzymes.
Carbohydrates	Amylase	Simple sugars	**Glucose**, a sugar and a product of carbohydrate digestion, enters the bloodstream to be carried to the **liver** where it is regulated and stored for use in the body tissues. Any excess which the liver cannot store is converted to fat. Glucose provides energy for cell functions.
Fats	Lipase	Fatty acid and glycerol	**Fatty acids** and **glycerol** (the products of fat digestion) pass into the **lacteals** and are transported through the **lymphatic system** before reaching the bloodstream. These provide energy in the body.

Vitamins and **minerals** enter the blood capillaries and are transported to tissues to assist with cell metabolism and many body functions, including blood clotting and immune responses.

Now try this

Complete the table, showing enzyme types, the food groups they digest and products of digestion.

Enzyme type	Substrate	Products of digestion
protease		peptides and amino acids
	starch	
		fatty acids and glycerol

Absorption of digestive products

Following the chemical breakdown of food molecules, absorption of nutrients occurs in the small intestine. The final function of the alimentary canal is the expulsion of waste.

Absorption

- The majority of nutrients are absorbed in the **ileum**.
- The epithelium of the ileum is folded into structures called **villi**. These hugely increase the surface area of the small intestine to improve the efficiency of absorption.
- **Microvilli** on the epithelial cells of the small intestine also enable absorption to take place.
- Villi have a good capillary **blood supply** to carry absorbed nutrients to larger blood vessels. Villi also contain lymph vessels known as **lacteals**. These two characteristics enable effective diffusion of nutrients from digested food out of the small intestine.

A single villus of the small intestine

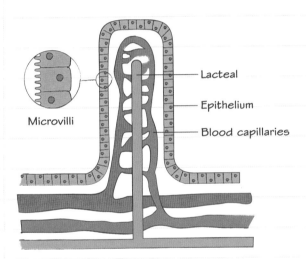

Microvilli

Lacteal

Epithelium

Blood capillaries

This is where the products of digestion diffuse into the blood in the capillaries and into the lymph fluid in the lacteals. The epethelial cells are covered in microscopic protrusions called **microvilli**.

Section through the wall of the small intestine

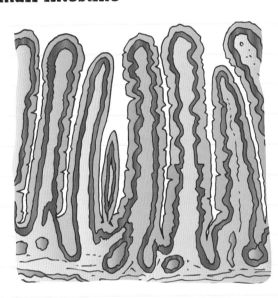

You can see how villi increase the surface area available for the absorption of nutrients.

Micro-organisms in the gut

Beneficial micro-organisms help to keep the alimentary canal healthy by:

- assisting with the absorption of undigested carbohydrates
- suppressing harmful microbial growth
- stimulating an immune response to harmful bacteria
- helping to prevent inflammatory bowel disease.

Waste

After absorption of nutrients by the body, any undigested food is passed into the large intestine where water is reabsorbed and faeces are produced. The faeces are stored in the rectum before expulsion via the anus.

Now try this

Track the digestive process taken by a protein-rich food from ingestion through to egestion.

 Use information above and on pages 135 and 136 to help you.

Digestive disorders

All parts of the digestive system can be affected by diseases, both acute and chronic.

Gastric ulcers

Ulcers are open sores in the lining of the digestive system, most commonly in the stomach and the first few centimetres of the duodenum. Common causes are infections and long-term or high-dose use of anti-inflammatory drugs. They are more frequent in males. The most common symptom is a burning pain in the centre of the abdomen. Usually, ulcers are treated with medication to reduce stomach acid. Possible complications include haemorrhage, perforation and gastric obstruction, any of which may be fatal.

Hepatitis

This is an inflammation of the liver, usually as a result of a viral infection, but can be alcohol-related. Symptoms include muscle and joint pain, pyrexia (fever), nausea and vomiting, headaches and jaundice, but many people are unaware they have the disease.

- **Hepatitis A.** Usually a short-term illness; preventative vaccinations are available.
- **Hepatitis B.** Often short term, but can be chronic; vaccinations are available.
- **Hepatitis C.** The most common viral type in the UK; passed on in body fluids, particularly blood; treated by antiviral medications; no vaccine is yet available.
- **Alcoholic hepatitis** can lead to **cirrhosis** (irreversible scarring) and liver failure.

Jaundice

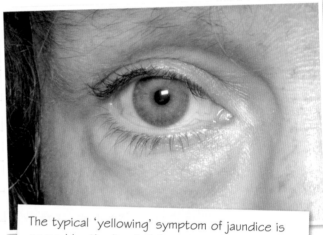

The typical 'yellowing' symptom of jaundice is caused by the liver's failure to break down all the components of ageing red blood cells.

Coeliac disease

This is a common digestive disorder caused by an adverse reaction to gluten, a protein found in wheat and other cereals. It affects around 1 in 100 people in the UK. Symptoms include diarrhoea, flatulence, abdominal pain, weight loss and tiredness. There is no cure, but symptoms can usually be controlled by a gluten-free diet. Long-term complications are rare, but can include osteoporosis, iron-deficiency anaemia, and vitamin B- and folate-deficiency anaemia.

How coeliac disease affects villi

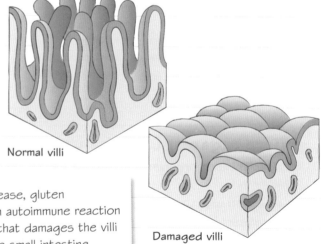

Normal villi

Damaged villi

In coelic disease, gluten stimulates an autoimmune reaction in the body that damages the villi which line the small intestine.

Now try this

Consider how damage to the villi might result from coeliac disease.

Describe the structure and function of the villi in the small intestine.

 Links Look at page 137 to revise the structure and function of villi.

The nervous system

The nervous system **senses** information about internal and external factors, **analyses** information received and instigates an appropriate **response**. It is divided into two parts: the CNS and the PNS.

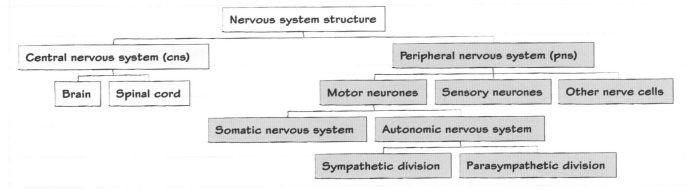

CNS and PNS

Different parts of the nervous system work together.

The **CNS** (**brain** and **spinal cord**) is the control centre. It coordinates the body's voluntary and involuntary activities.

The **PNS** (**sensory** and **motor neurones**, and other nerve cells) is subdivided into

- the **somatic nervous system**
- the **autonomic nervous system**.

Autonomic nervous system

The autonomic nervous system controls **automatic** body actions (e.g. **breathing** and **heartbeat**) by conducting nerve impulses to and from the CNS. It is divided into **two** parts:

1 **Sympathetic nervous system**: prepares the body for dealing with emergencies by increasing the heart and breathing rates, dilating blood vessels, stimulating sweat glands and decreasing gastrointestinal activities.

2 **Parasympathetic nervous system**: balances the actions of the sympathetic nervous system by creating conditions for rest and sleep.

Neurones

The functional units of the nervous system are **neurones**. They receive and respond to stimuli and initiate actions by transmitting electrical impulses.

There are **three** types of neurones:

1 **Sensory (afferent) neurones**: transmit stimuli from **sensory organs** and **receptors** to the brain and spinal cord. Sensations include heat, pain, taste and smell.

2 **Motor (efferent) neurones**: carry messages from the CNS to muscles, organs and glands to stimulate activities.

3 **Association (mixed) neurones**: link sensory and motor neurones and help to keep messages and responses functioning effectively.

Transmission

Junctions between neurones are called **synapses**. Chemicals called **neurotransmitters** transmit an electrical impulse from one neurone to the next, across a synapse.

Properties

Neurones have **two** major properties:

1 **Excitability**: the ability to respond to a stimulus by converting it to a nerve impulse.

2 **Conductibility**: the ability to transmit impulses to muscles, glands, and other neurones.

Responses

Sensory neurones respond to **mechanical** stimuli (touch and pressure), **thermal** stimuli (heat and cold) and **chemical** stimuli (external sources or internally released by the body).

🔗 **Links** Look at page 115 to revise the structure of a neurone.

Now try this

Suggest why the sympathetic nervous system is sometimes referred to as 'fight or flight', and the parasympathtic nervous system as 'rest and digest'.

Think about what structures the sympathetic and parasympathetic nervous systems regulate and what responses they might bring about in these two situations.

Disorders of the nervous system

There are many disorders which affect the nervous system. Some specifically affect the brain or spinal cord, and others affect nerves, or even just one specific nerve.

Parkinson's disease

This is a progressive degeneration of the brain due to loss of nerve cells which, in turn, leads to a lack of **dopamine** (a chemical messenger that helps to transmit signals in the brain).

In the UK, 1 in 500 people have this condition. The disease occurs more frequently in males. There are three main symptoms:

- tremor
- slow movements
- stiff, inflexible muscles.

Patients may also complain of depression, insomnia and memory problems. There is no cure, but symptoms can be relieved with medication, physiotherapy and, occasionally, surgery.

Other common conditions

Condition	Further information
Epilepsy	causes seizures
Motor neurone disease	degeneration of motor neurones and muscle wasting
Brain tumour	cancerous growth in the brain
Sciatica	leg pain from compression of a nerve from the spinal cord
Meningitis	bacterial or viral inflammation of the membranes in the brain and spinal cord
Cerebral palsy	coordination problems following early brain damage

Multiple sclerosis (MS)

MS is a progressive condition affecting the brain and spinal cord, causing problems with movement, balance, sensation and vision. Diagnosis is most frequent in people aged 20 to 30 years. The most common form is relapsing–remitting MS, in which symptoms are intermittent, although gradually progressive. Symptoms include:

- fatigue
- difficulty walking
- numbness and muscle stiffness
- blurred vision, balance and coordination problems
- cognition difficulties
- urinary incontinence.

Dementia

This is a very common condition affecting approximately one in three people over the age of 65 years. It is more common in women. It is a complex disorder, with over 100 different types of dementia currently being recognised. Signs and symptoms can be many and varied, but often include:

- memory loss
- delayed thoughts
- lack of understanding
- using incorrect or inappropriate language
- altered emotional responses
- lack of decisiveness
- impaired judgements
- depression.

Multiple sclerosis is a neurological condition that affects the nerves and is caused when the immune system is not working properly. There is no cure but symptoms may be relieved or lessened with medication.

Now try this

Name **five** common disorders which affect the nervous system and suggest which parts of the nervous system are most affected in each case.

The endocrine system

You need to know about the structure and function of the endocrine system – the hypothalamus, pituitary gland, ovaries, adrenal glands, testes, thyroid gland and pancreas.

Structure of the endocrine system

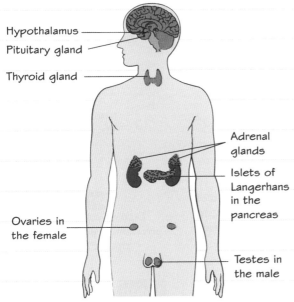

Hypothalamus
Pituitary gland
Thyroid gland
Adrenal glands
Islets of Langerhans in the pancreas
Ovaries in the female
Testes in the male

Functions

There are three functions of the endocrine system:

1 **Regulation** of body activities (e.g. growth)

2 Control of the **reproductive** process

3 **Homeostasis**

 Endocrine glands secrete hormones (chemical messengers) which diffuse into the bloodstream.

The endocrine glands

1 **Hypothalamus:** this region of the brain controls the **pituitary gland** by producing **releasing** and **inhibiting hormones** that regulate our moods, thirst, sleep, hunger, etc.

2 **Pituitary gland:** secretes hormones that are important in the **regulation of growth**, control of the **sex organs** and **osmoregulation**, including:

- **growth hormone** controls the growth of bone, muscle and soft tissue
- **follicle stimulating hormone (FSH)** stimulates the release of ova or sperm
- **luteinising hormone (LH)** causes ovulation and the formation of the corpus luteum in the ovary and secretion of testosterone from the testes
- **oxytocin** causes contractions of the uterus during childbirth
- **antidiuretic hormone (ADH)** causes water reabsorption in the kidneys.

3 **Thyroid:** secretes:

- **calcitonin** to regulate blood and tissue calcium levels
- **thyroxine** to control growth, development and metabolic rate.

4 **Adrenal glands** secrete:

- **adrenaline:** enables the body to react to stress ('**fight or flight**' response) by increasing heart and breathing rates, and redistributing blood to the muscles.
- **aldosterone:** acts in the kidneys to control sodium, potassium and water balance, stabilising blood volume and **blood pressure.**

5 **Pancreas:** cells called **islets of Langerhans** secrete two hormones:

- **glucagon** increases blood glucose levels
- **insulin** reduces blood glucose levels.

6 **Ovaries:** secrete:

- **oestrogen:** involved in development of secondary sex characteristics and regulation of the reproductive system
- **progesterone:** secreted after ovulation and linked to potential pregnancy.

7 **Testes:** secrete **testosterone**, which is involved in the development of male secondary sex characteristics (see page 5) at puberty.

Now try this

List **three** specific functions of the endocrine system and give an example of a hormone that is involved in each function.

Endocrine disorders

You need to know about disorders of the pancreas and thyroid gland.

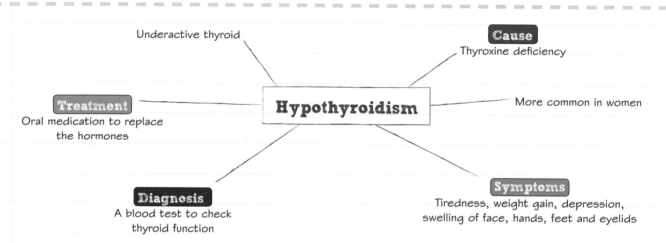

Prediabetes: slightly raised blood glucose levels mean diabetes is more likely to develop

Common: 1 in 16 adults in the UK

Increasing in prevalence

Cause
Absence of, or resistance to, insulin

Type 1: sudden onset, can be life threatening

Diabetes mellitus

Type 2: gradual onset, strong link to obesity

Diagnosis
Testing urine for glucose and, if positive, specialised blood testing. Type 1 is usually diagnosed in childhood. Type 2 often begins in middle age, although many younger people are being diagnosed with Type 2 because of links with obesity levels.

Acute complications: hypoglycemia (low blood glucose levels) and ketoacidosis (high levels of ketone blood acids).

Treatment
Type 1: insulin injections; Type 2: diet, exercise, and possibly medication; for some with advanced Type 2 diabetes, insulin injections also.

Symptoms
Excessive thirst, increased urination, tiredness, weight loss, thrush, blurred vision

Underactive thyroid

Cause
Thyroxine deficiency

Treatment
Oral medication to replace the hormones

Hypothyroidism

More common in women

Diagnosis
A blood test to check thyroid function

Symptoms
Tiredness, weight gain, depression, swelling of face, hands, feet and eyelids

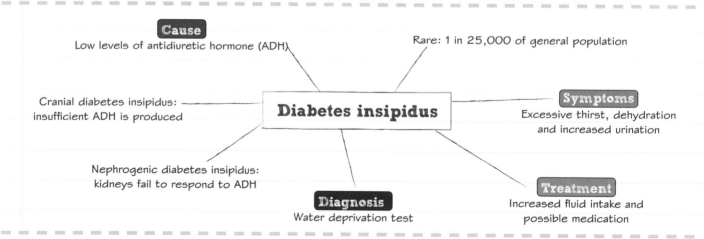

Cause
Low levels of antidiuretic hormone (ADH)

Rare: 1 in 25,000 of general population

Cranial diabetes insipidus: insufficient ADH is produced

Diabetes insipidus

Symptoms
Excessive thirst, dehydration and increased urination

Nephrogenic diabetes insipidus: kidneys fail to respond to ADH

Diagnosis
Water deprivation test

Treatment
Increased fluid intake and possible medication

Now try this

If a medical term begins with 'hypo', what does this tell you? Give some examples of conditions that begin with 'hypo'.

Lymphatic and immune systems

The main functions of the lymphatic and immune systems are tissue drainage, preventing and fighting infection, and transport of fats.

Lymph

This is the colourless, watery fluid formed from **tissue fluid** and found within lymphatic vessels. It contains cells called **lymphocytes.** These white blood cells are responsible for immunity. They are produced and matured within **lymphatic organs**, which include **lymph nodes**, the thymus gland, spleen and tonsils (see page 144).

Lymphocytes

These white blood cells are part of the **immune system**. Two immune responses are produced by different types of lymphocytes:

 B-lymphocytes produce **antibodies** to supress and destroy antigens.

 T-lymphocytes recognise infected and abnormal cells and destroy them.

Lymphocytes can respond quickly to repeat infections, giving us **immunity**.

Lymphatic vessels

The lymphatic vessels network carries lymph and assists the blood in returning **tissue fluid** from the tissues back to the blood system and heart, also helping to maintain blood volume and blood pressure.

Lymph vessels start with **lymph capillaries,** which are tubes, closed at one end, originating in the spaces between tissues. The lymph capillaries join up to form larger lymph vessels, which contain one-way **valves** to prevent backflow of fluid. As the lymph vessels join together they become larger, eventually forming two large ducts: the **thoracic duct** and the **right lymphatic duct**, which enter into the **subclavian veins**, enabling fluid to be returned to the heart.

Lymphatic system

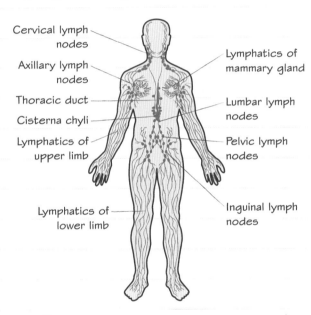

Cervical lymph nodes
Axillary lymph nodes
Thoracic duct
Cisterna chyli
Lymphatics of upper limb
Lymphatics of lower limb
Lymphatics of mammary gland
Lumbar lymph nodes
Pelvic lymph nodes
Inguinal lymph nodes

The majority of body tissues have lymphatic vessels, exceptions being the central nervous system (CNS), bones, the corneas of the eyes and superficial skin.

Lymph nodes

Found at intervals along lymphatic vessels, lymph nodes are oval-shaped structures covered with connective tissue. They filter and trap cell debris or micro-organisms which may cause infection, so that the lymph entering the blood does not contain any impurities. Lymph nodes appear in clusters at joints, and are particularly effective when joint movement occurs

Superficial nodes are common in the neck, axillae (armpits) and groin. Most of the **deep lymph nodes** are found alongside blood vessels in the thoracic, abdominal and pelvic cavities.

Now try this

Name the structures in the lymphatic system that filter the lymph fluid. Explain why their function is important in maintaining health.

Lymphatic organs and disorders

In addition to the lymph nodes, the three major organs of the lymphatic and immune systems are the spleen, the thymus gland and the tonsils.

Location of lymphatic organs in the human body

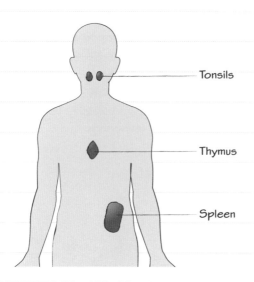

Tonsils

Thymus

Spleen

 The spleen

This is the largest organ of the lymphatic system, lying in the left hypochondriac region of the abdomen. It has four main functions:

- **Phagocytosis**: the spleen filters the blood, destroying and recycling parts of red blood cells and other cells, and the broken down products are transported to the liver.
- **Storage of blood**: the spleen contains up to 350 ml of blood. In emergencies, such as haemorrhage, it can rapidly return most of this to the circulatory system.
- **Immune response**: the spleen contains T-and B-lymphocytes. The proliferation of lymphocytes during serious infections can cause the spleen to become enlarged.
- **Erythropoiesis**: the spleen and liver are involved in foetal blood cell production, and in emergencies the spleen can also produce blood cells in adults.

 Thymus gland

Behind the sternum and extending towards the neck, this gland consists of two lobes, enclosed within a fibrous capsule. Some lymphocytes originating in stem cells of the red bone marrow enter the thymus, where they develop into activated T-lymphocytes. Actions of the thymus gland enable each T-lymphocyte to react to one specific antigen.

 Tonsils

Composed of lymphatic tissue and located on either side of the pharynx, the palatine tonsils provide defence against micro-organisms entering the mouth and nose.

The tonsils contain both B- and T-lymphocytes.

Hodgkin's disease (lymphoma)

Cause A malignant cancer involving progressive enlargement of lymph nodes in the body. B-lymphocytes multiply abnormally and collect in parts of the lymphatic system, particularly in the lymph nodes.

Symptoms Painless swellings in the neck, armpit or groin area.

Diagnosis Requires a biopsy.

Treatment Although this is an aggressive cancer, it is treated effectively with chemotherapy and radiotherapy.

Leukaemia

Cause A rare family of tissue cancers that lead to overproduction of lymphocytes (white blood cells).

Symptoms Pale skin, tiredness, breathlessness and unexplained bleeding.

Diagnosis A blood test.

Treatment Chemotherapy and radiotherapy; bone marrow and stem cell treatments. Remission occurs when no leukaemic cells can be found in the blood or bone marrow.

Now try this

Which is the largest of the lymphatic organs and what are its four functions?

The renal system and disorders

The renal system's primary function is to control the composition, volume and pressure of blood (homeostasis).

Structure and function

The two **kidneys** are bean-shaped organs. They lie on the posterior wall of the abdomen, partly protected by the lower rib cage. The right kidney is slightly lower than the left, due to the space taken up by the liver. Each kidney has over a million **nephrons** (filtration units) and numerous collecting ducts to transport **urine**.

The functions of the kidneys are:

* **filtration** of **waste** products and **toxins** from the blood
* **formation** of **urine**
* **regulation** of **water** and **salt** balance in the body
* **regulation** of **blood pressure** and blood **volume**
* **maintenance** of the normal **pH balance** in the blood.

The two **ureters** carry urine from the kidneys to the bladder, a pear-shaped sac in the pelvic cavity which stores urine until it is expelled via the **urethra**. In a female, the urethra is about 4 cm long, but in males it is 18–20 cm.

The renal system

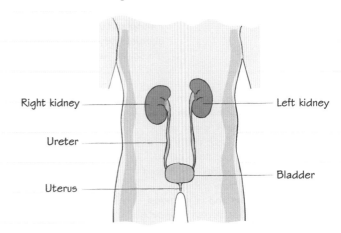

Right kidney
Left kidney
Ureter
Bladder
Uterus

The renal system maintains the correct fluid balance in the body.

Urination

For **micturition** (urination) to take place, the **urethral sphincter muscle** relaxes and muscular contractions occur in the bladder wall, forcing the urine out through the urethra.

Urinary tract infections (UTIs)

These are common, especially in females.

Symptoms:

* pain or a burning sensation when urinating (dysuria)
* frequent urination
* lower abdominal pain
* cloudy or dark, strong-smelling urine.

Treatment: Most UTIs do not require treatment, but a short course of antibiotics may be prescribed. Long-term complications are rare, but may include kidney damage.

Good personal hygiene can help prevent UTIs, and some evidence suggests that drinking cranberry juice regularly can also help.

Renal failure

Occurs when the kidneys' ability to carry out their normal functions are impaired.

Acute renal failure has rapid onset (less than two days).

* **Symptoms:** fatigue, oedema (swelling due to fluid retention in tissues), kidney pain, hand tremor, decreased appetite and changes in urination habits.
* **Treatment:** diuretic drugs, intravenous fluids and electrolytes, and possible short-term dialysis.

Chronic renal failure is asymptomatic (symptomless) in the early stages.

* **Symptoms:** tiredness, oedema, nausea, blood in the urine and confusion, developing as the disease progresses.
* **Treatment:** diagnosis is usually by blood or urine testing. There is no cure, but it can sometimes be controlled by medication. Dialysis or kidney transplant may be considered.

Now try this

Suggest why oedema may be a symptom of kidney failure.

Revise what you know about normal kidney function. What could happen to blood and tissue fluid if the kidneys stop working properly?

The female reproductive system

The main functions of the female reproductive system are the production of sex hormones and eggs, and protection and support of an embryo and foetus if fertilisation takes place.

Structure and functions of the female reproductive organs

Fallopian tubes are 5–10 cm long, extending from each ovary to the side of the uterus. They carry the egg (ovum) from the ovary to the uterus, using a peristaltic (muscular wave) action. Fertilisation of the ovum takes place in the fallopian tube.

The **ovaries** have two main functions: producing **eggs** (ova) and secreting **oestrogen** and **progesterone**. Each ovary contains masses of cells called ovarian follicles, within which egg cells develop. From puberty, one ovum ripens and is released each month. Oestrogen supports the development of sexual characteristics and progesterone prepares the uterus lining for implantation of a fertilised egg.

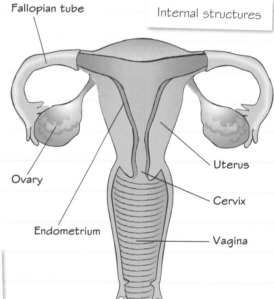

Internal structures

The **uterus** is a muscular organ behind the urinary bladder. After puberty, during regular monthly cycles, the uterus is prepared to receive a fertilised egg. If a fertilised ovum is not implanted, the uterine lining is shed and a new cycle begins. If the ovum is fertilised, an embryo develops and becomes a foetus, protected and supported by the uterus.

You need to understand how the internal and external diagrams relate to one another.

The **cervix** is the neck of the uterus, which protrudes through the anterior wall of the vagina. Sperm enter the uterus here.

The **vagina** is a **lubricated** fibromuscular tube which connects the internal organs of the female reproductive system with the external genitalia.

External structures

The **vulva** is the collective name for the external opening of the vagina and the other outer genitalia, including the labia and clitoris.

The female external genitalia are the entry point for the penis, they receive sperm during intercourse, and provide a passage for menstruation and childbirth.

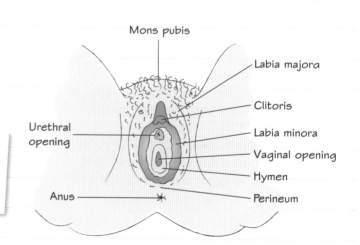

Now try this

What is the function of the uterus, if fertilisation of an egg occurs in a fallopian tube?

The male reproductive system

The main functions of the male reproductive system are production, maturation, storage and delivery of sperm.

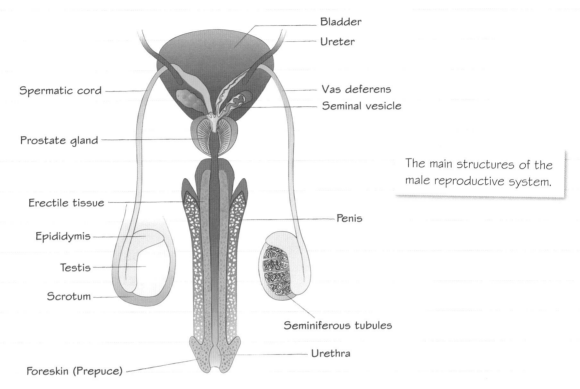

Bladder
Ureter
Spermatic cord
Vas deferens
Seminal vesicle
Prostate gland
Erectile tissue
Penis
Epididymis
Testis
Scrotum
Seminiferous tubules
Urethra
Foreskin (Prepuce)

The main structures of the male reproductive system.

Structure and functions

- **Penis**: an external organ comprised of erectile tissue, with a rich blood supply. When stimulated by sexual activity, the penis becomes erect and **ejaculates semen** (around 10% of which is sperm). The semen is carried via the urethra, which passes through the prostate gland, and extends to the end of the penis. This can **deposit semen into a woman's vagina**.
- **Scrotum**: a sac which lies behind the penis and is divided into two compartments, each containing one **testis**. Being outside the body, the scrotum **maintains the testes at lower than body temperature**.
- **Testes**: glands with two main functions: the **production of male sex hormones** (collectively known as **androgens,** the most important of which is testosterone) and the **formation of sperm cells**.
- **Epididymis**: this tube joins the testis to the vas deferens. It **transports** and **stores** sperm cells produced in the testes.
- **Vas deferens**: a muscular tube leading from the epididymis to the seminal vesicles. Its function is to **transport mature sperm** to the urethra.
- **Seminal vesicles**: sac-like pouches which join the vas deferens to form an ejaculatory duct. The seminal vesicles **produce the fructose in semen**, which provides sperm with a source of energy. The vesicles also **contract and expel semen** during ejaculation.
- **Prostate gland**: located in front of the rectum, and behind the symphysis pubis, completely surrounding the urethra as it leaves the bladder. During ejaculation the prostate gland **secretes a thin milky fluid**, which assists with **sperm mobility** and **thickens the semen**, making the retention of sperm in the woman's vagina more likely.

Now try this

1 What is the collective term for the male sex hormones?
2 Where are they produced?

Reproductive system disorders

Both males and females may experience disorders of their reproductive systems.

Infertility

Some disorders of the reproductive system may make it difficult for a couple to conceive.

> ### Reproductive health
> Many people think their reproductive health is a private matter and are reluctant to seek medical help if they have a problem.
>
> ### Sexually transmitted infections
> A number of sexually transmitted infections (STIs) can affect both females and males.

Hydrocele

Condition
Fluid collects in the scrotum, around one or both testes, causing swelling.

Symptoms
The condition is not painful or harmful, but is often uncomfortable and can cause embarrassment.

Treatment
Hydroceles often resolve without treatment but, if not, the fluid may be aspirated (drawn off) or surgery may be required.

Polycystic ovary syndrome

Condition
Common features are the development of cysts in the ovaries, irregular or no ovulation and high levels of male hormones in the body.

Symptoms
Include irregular or no periods, unexplained weight gain, excessive hair growth on face and body, skin problems and difficulty getting pregnant.

Treatment
There is no cure, but symptoms can be treated with medication and, in more severe cases, surgery.

Benign prostatic hyperplasia (BPH/hypertrophy)

Condition
A non-cancerous enlargement of the prostate gland, common in older men. The enlarged prostate gland can partly block the urethra, causing problems with urination.

Symptoms
Difficulty starting urination, weak flow of urine, dribbling after urination, pain when urinating increased, frequency, urgency, and inability to empty the bladder fully.

Treatment
Medication or surgery, depending on the severity of the condition.

Endometriosis

Condition
Endometrial tissue grows outside the uterus, often in the ovaries and fallopian tubes.

Symptoms
The tissue responds to sex hormones secreted during the menstrual cycle, causing bleeding into the lower abdomen and cysts in the ovaries.

Treatment
Untreated, it can lead to pelvic inflammation and adhesions, and infertility. There is no cure, but treatments include pain relief, hormone therapy and surgery.

Prostate cancer

Condition
The most common male cancer in the UK (especially in men over 50 years old).

Symptoms
Often do not occur for some time. They include difficulty starting urination, weak flow of urine, dribbling after urination, pain when urinating, increased frequency and urgency, inability to fully empty the bladder.

Treatment
Diagnosis involves physical examination, blood tests and biopsy. If the cancer has not spread elsewhere, treatment options include surgery, radiotherapy and hormone therapy.

Now try this

Why should a man seek medical advice sooner rather than later, if he is experiencing poor urinary flow, as well as increased frequency and urgency?

Think about the similarity in symptoms between different prostate problems and the treatability of prostate cancer if identified before it has spread.

Gametes, fertilisation, conception and growth

Fertilisation

Conception occurs when a male sperm **fertilises** a female egg, forming an **embryo,** which implants into the wall of the uterus. After conception, the embryo grows to form a foetus, and growth continues after birth throughout childhood.

Fertile window

An egg survives in a fertilisable form for as little as eight hours after ovulation. Sperm is able to fertilise the egg for about 24 hours. So, the period for conception, or **fertile window**, is relatively short in the monthly cycle. If the ovum is not fertilised, decreasing oestrogen and progesterone levels lead to menstruation and the beginning of a new cycle.

Two types of cell division: mitosis and meiosis

Meiosis is a series of two divisions, giving four cells with half the usual number of chromosomes. Meiosis is vital for **gamete** formation.

Mitosis is cell division that results in the production of two identical cells. Mitosis is important in **growth**.

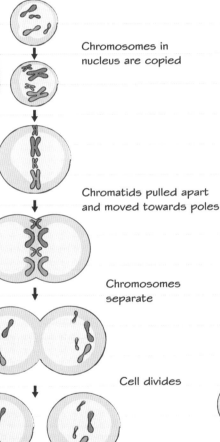

Chromosomes in nucleus are copied

Chromatids pulled apart and moved towards poles

Chromosomes separate

Cell divides

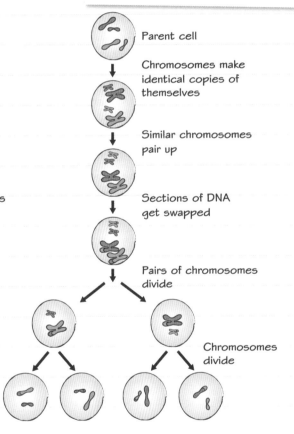

Parent cell

Chromosomes make identical copies of themselves

Similar chromosomes pair up

Sections of DNA get swapped

Pairs of chromosomes divide

Chromosomes divide

DNA replicates so that chromosomes are copied. When the cell divides, each daughter cell receives a copy of every chromosome.

DNA replicates so that chromosomes are copied. Similar chromosomes pair up and may exchange sections of DNA before they separate into daughter cells. A second cell division gives a total of four gametes, each with half the normal number of chromosomes.

Now try this

Suggest why couples are advised to try to conceive for a year before seeking medical help.

Think about the fertile window and why this can influence the time it takes a woman to become pregnant.

Gamete production

Meiosis leads to the production of gametes (reproductive cells). In humans, gametes have only 23 chromosomes, instead of the usual 46. When the male gamete (sperm cell) and the female gamete (egg) unite, 23+23 chromosomes make 46 and the embryo has genetic information from both parents.

Had a look ☐   Nearly there ☐   Nailed it! ☐

Foetal growth through the trimesters

Pregnancy has three trimesters. You need to know which foetal developments take place during each trimester.

The developments that take place during pregnancy

First trimester		Month	Week
This stage is crucial to development. • As the fertilised egg grows, the **amniotic sac** develops, helping to protect the embryo throughout pregnancy. • The **placenta** develops. This organ transfers nutrients from the mother to the baby, and transfers waste from the baby. • The baby's body structure and **organ systems** develop. • **Miscarriages** and birth defects most commonly occur during this time. • Many women experience **symptoms** including nausea, fatigue, breast tenderness and frequent urination.		One	1–4
		Two	5–8
		Three	9–13

Second trimester		Month	Week
This is a period of rapid development. The baby's head is the largest part of the body. • The **body will grow** to be in proportion. • The baby's **gender** becomes apparent and **facial features** also develop rapidly. • The baby has developed and functioning **organs, nerves and muscles**. • **Skeletal bones** are also developing.		Four	14–17
		Five	18–21
		Six	22–26

Babies born before 26 weeks may survive but are at risk of developing health problems.

Third trimester		Month	Week
During this stage the baby **gains weight**. • Most **internal systems** are well developed. • The **lungs** mature towards the end of the pregnancy. • The **skeleton** is fully developed, although bones continue to harden. • Towards the end of this stage, the baby's head **descends into the mother's pelvis** ready for the birth.		Seven	27–30
		Eight	31–35
		Nine	36–40

Babies born before 37 weeks' gestation are described as 'premature'.

Birth

Newly delivered **neonates** (newborns) are covered in mucous, maternal blood and body fluids. Immediate assessment of the baby involves attributing an **Apgar Score** which assesses the vital signs and determines if resuscitation or medical treatments are required.

Birth may take place in different ways:
• Birth in vertex position: head-first presentation through the vagina
• Breech birth: legs/buttocks first through the vagina
• Caesarian birth: delivery through surgical incision in the mother's abdomen and uterus, usually in response to complications.

Now try this

Suggest why babies who are born in the second trimester may develop health problems.

The developments that normally occur in the third trimester must happen after the birth of a premature baby.

Prenatal development and teratogens

Many factors affect foetal development. Some effects are positive and some are negative.

Positive effects

👍 Diet

Good nutrition is important during pregnancy. **Folic acid, calcium, protein and iron** are vital for foetal development. Folic acid and iron supplements may be prescribed. Many women prefer to eat organic produce, which is grown without chemicals. No matter how they are produced, washing vegetables and fruits before eating is important.

👍 Prenatal care

Monitoring as part of prenatal (**antenatal**) **care** can help to detect problems early, so that action can be taken to ensure the foetus remains healthy. Health professionals assess foetal development and may intervene if necessary. They can offer advice on how to maintain a healthy pregnancy and on preparations for the birth.

👍 Good health

As well as balanced nutrition, maintenance of good health includes reducing stress and taking exercise. **Moderate** exercise is usually recommended in pregnancy as it improves the mother's **emotional state** and can increase **oxygen flow** to the foetus. Activities such as walking, swimming and yoga are particularly good for pregnant women.

Negative effects

👎 Alcohol

Drinking alcohol during pregnancy can cause **foetal alcohol syndrome**, which is characterised by a small head and an abnormal facial appearance. Maternal alcohol consumption also increases the risk of autism, Down's syndrome, cerebral palsy, heart, lung and kidney defects, slowed growth and learning disabilities.

👎 Smoking

Smoking **tobacco** (and other substances) during pregnancy can cause a baby to have **low birth weight**, learning difficulties and respiratory problems. There is evidence that babies born to smokers are more susceptible to **sudden infant death syndrome** (cot death).

👎 Drugs

Taking illegal drugs during pregnancy can cause birth defects, is linked to low birth weight, and may result in withdrawal symptoms in the baby after the birth.

Medicines should only be taken in pregnancy if prescribed by a health professional – even over-the-counter medicines and herbal remedies are potentially harmful.

Teratogens

These are agents that cause birth defects. Examples include:

- ✓ some **viruses**, for example rubella and HIV
- ✓ some **drugs**, for example thalidomide that was widely prescribed in the 1950s for morning sickness, until it was found to cause limb defects
- ✓ **cigarette smoke** and **alcohol**
- ✓ some **chemicals**, such as mercury
- ✓ **radiation**, such as x-rays.

Now try this

Explain why it is important for women to attend antenatal appointments, even if they feel well.

Health professionals may advise pregnant women on any of the positive and negative factors outlined on this page.

Congenital disorders

Congenital disorders are medical conditions or disabilities that are present at birth, such as spina bifida, cerebral palsy and the effects of rubella. Some congenital disorders can be life threatening in infancy. Others, although present from birth, are not diagnosed until later in life.

Causes

Causes can be:

- **genetic** problems, such as lack of oxygen or brain injury during labour and birth
- **teratogens**, which can affect the normal development of an embryo and foetus. For example, rubella virus is a teratogen that can cause congenital rubella syndrome.

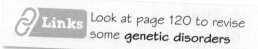 **Links** Look at page 120 to revise some **genetic disorders**

Congenital rubella syndrome

Condition A mother who catches the rubella virus during pregnancy can pass it on to her unborn child. The risks of congenital effects are greater if she contracts the disease during the first trimester of pregnancy.

Symptoms Deafness, visual problems, heart conditions and blood disorders, and damage to the central nervous system (CNS), including an abnormally small head.

Treatment Treatments vary according to the symptoms.

 Links Look at page 150 to revise developments during the first trimester.

Cerebral palsy

Condition A general term covering many neurological conditions affecting movement, balance and coordination. It can be a result of infections during pregnancy or problems at birth. There are also genetic causes.

Symptoms People with this condition are often unable to walk without support, and may have spasms and uncoordinated limb movements. The degree of disability can vary.

Treatment There is no cure but the effects can often be reduced by physiotherapy, occupational therapy, medication and sometimes surgery.

Spina bifida

Condition Spina bifida is a **neural defect** (malformation of the spine and spinal cord). There are several types.

Symptoms In the first month after conception, the embryo grows a neural tube, which will eventually develop into the spine. In a foetus with spina bifida, the spinal column does not develop normally and, in some cases, the spinal cord is also affected. Spina bifida may range from incomplete development of some vertebrae to a gap in the vertebrae that allows the spinal membrane to protrude, to a larger gap that allows part of the spinal cord to protrude into a sac on the back.

Treatment Often surgery is performed to repair the defect, but it can result in loss of sensation, paralysis and incontinence.

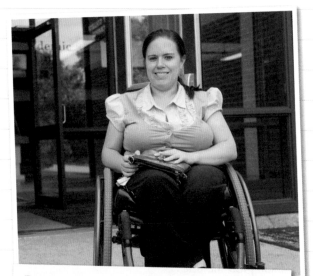

People with some congenital disorders may need support with mobility and other needs.

Now try this

Name the teratogen in congenital rubella syndrome.

Clinical trials

Clinical trials are used to evaluate the benefits of a specific treatment, or to find out whether there are side effects.

Testing

Clinical trials involve human participants and aim to evaluate specific medical interventions. Clinical trials can be used to:

- test vaccines or new medicines
- evaluate procedures, such as blood tests and scans
- evaluate nutritional changes, physical therapies or psychological interventions.

Clinical trials help to establish if:

- treatments are safe
- side effects are likely to occur
- new treatments are more beneficial than the existing ones.

Double-blind trials

Clinical trials need to be fair and provide **accurate, unbiased** results.

- In some clinical trials the researchers know who is receiving the treatment but the patients do not – this is known as a **single-blind trial**. Patients' beliefs cannot influence the result.
- In a **double-blind trial**, neither the researchers nor the patients know who is receiving the treatment and who is getting an alternative (**placebo**). This is believed to be one of the most reliable styles of clinical trial because nobody can influence the results, which improves the reliability of the study.

Reliability

If patients don't know whether they are receiving a treatment or a placebo, their beliefs cannot influence the results of the trial. If researchers also do not now which group of patients is undergoing treatment and which is the **control group**, they cannot influence the results, thereby improving the reliability of the study.

Placebo

A placebo is a 'dummy' treatment with no known medicinal properties. In some clinical trials, some patients receive the drug being tested and others receive a placebo. However, there is evidence of the '**placebo effect**', where placebos are beneficial to patients. It seems that, if you believe a treatment will improve your health, symptoms may improve.

Control groups

Participants in a clinical trial are usually randomly allocated to either the group that is given the treatment being tested or the group that is given either a placebo or a previously established treatment. For a **valid** test, conditions within the two groups must be as similar as possible. For example, participants in each group should be of similar ages, with similar symptoms and the groups should have a similar gender mix.

Sample size

For trials to be reliable and valid, the sample must be large enough to be certain that the results could not be by chance. Many researchers test the **statistical significance** of their trial results. A clinical trial on just 20 patients would not be considered reliable, but a trial on 1000 patients would.

Risks and ethics

Risks in testing new medicines and treatments include possible side effects. People who take part in trials may forgo conventional treatment in the hope of receiving a new treatment, but may only have a placebo. They must understand the risks and give their **informed consent**.

Agencies

Agencies involved in monitoring and regulation of testing, making sure that testing is ethical, include:

☑ National Institute for Health Research, UK Clinical Research Collaboration, Association of Medical Research Charities, Medical Research Council, Cancer Research UK

☑ NHS Trusts, health departments of UK universities, Medicines and Healthcare Products Regulatory Agency.

Now try this

Discuss **three** ways of making clinical trials fair and reliable.

 You could cover three of these: blinding of trials, randomisation of samples, sample sizes, use of controls and placebos.

Epidemiological studies and data analysis

Epidemiology is the study of disease patterns, causes and effects in populations. Data analysis is the process of evaluating data in order to form a conclusion.

Public health

Epidemiology looks at **health and illness** in a particular population over a specified period of time. It helps **identify disease risk factors** and assists in targeting **preventative healthcare.**

Statistics

Statistics is a mathematical science that allows health professionals and scientists to test data to see whether they support a valid conclusion.

Incidence and prevalence

- **Incidence** is the **rate** at which new cases of a disease occur in a population, indicating the **risk** of contracting a condition.
- **Prevalence** is the number of affected individuals in a population at one time, so it indicates how **widespread** a condition is.

Morbidity and mortality

- **Morbidity** is the **prevalence** or **incidence** of a **disease** in a population
- **Mortality** is the rate of death in a population, usually given per 1000 people or as a percentage.

Effective data analysis

- Data should be **monitored** throughout a study to allow for modifications in the sampling or methodology.
- Data and subsequent analysis should be **presented** in a simple and clear form. A series of simple tables or graphs is preferable to one complicated table or graph.
- Any **limitations** in the data should be clearly stated.
- A **negative result** (one that does not prove the hypothesis) is as important as a positive one.

Data use

Data analysis skills are used by health professionals to evaluate the **efficacy of medical procedures** and the **health effects of lifestyle choices**.

✓ The Office for National Statistics (ONS) compiles, analyses and disseminates census and health statistics.

✓ Bodies such as the World Health Organization (WHO) study disease occurrences and leading causes of deaths linked to specific groups and demographic populations.

✓ Reputable sources of health statistics are vital for reliable and valid research.

Now try this

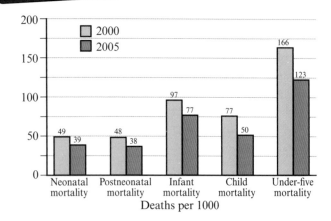

Death rates per 1000 for children at different developmental stages in 2000 and 2005. (Source: adapted from the *Ethiopian Demographic and Health Survey, 2005*).

Consider which groups show the largest mortality rates and which show the smallest rates. Consider the differences in the data between the two years. What is the overall trend?

The bar chart shows child mortality. Summarise this epidemiological data.

Data analysis skills: statistics, bar charts and histograms

Data analysis skills are used to evaluate the efficacy of medical procedures and the effects of lifestyle choices. You need to be able to analyse data presented in bar charts and histograms, and it is also helpful to understand simple statistical language.

Statistical terms

Term	Meaning
Statistics	A mathematical science that allows health professionals and other scientists to test their data to see whether it supports a valid conclusion.
Mean	**Average** of the data, calculated by adding up all scores and dividing the total by the number of scores
Median	Value at the **midpoint** when scores are ordered lowest to highest.
Mode	The **most common** score in the data
Range	The **difference** between the highest and lowest scores
Standard deviation	How widely the results are **distributed** and how widely the data is spread from the mean

Ways of presenting data

Good data presentation makes data analysis much easier. The type of data determines the most appropriate presentation.

Bar charts

These are suitable for presenting data in **discrete** (separate) groups. Note the gaps between the bars. These tell you that the data is discrete. Bar charts enable comparisons to be made between groups.

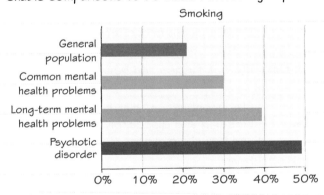

This bar chart shows the percentage of people with different mental health problems who choose to smoke.

Histogram

A histogram groups **continuous data** (various values within a range) into **classes**. There are no gaps between the bars, which tells you that the data is continuous. When analysing a histogram, consider whether the classes that have been used are appropriate.

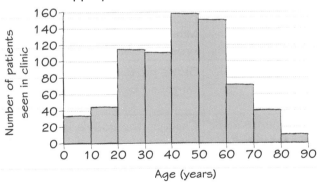

This histogram shows the number of patients seen in a clinic by age group.

Now try this

1. Would a **bar chart** or a **histogram** be the most appropriate presentation of the data below?
   Causes of COPD: Smoking 80%, Work-related fumes, dust and chemicals 15%, Air pollution 5%

2. From this data, what is the most common cause of COPD?

3. Referring to the **bar chart** above, is there a link between the severity of someone's mental illness and the likelihood that they will smoke?

4. Referring to the **histogram**, suggest why fewer patients aged 80 to 90 were seen than any other age group. Does the histogram suggest that people in this age group are the healthiest?

Links Look at page 129 to revise COPD.

Data analysis skills: graphs and tables

Data analysis skills are used to evaluate the efficacy of medical procedures and the effects of lifestyle choices. You need to be able to analyse data that is presented in graphs and tables.

Line graphs

These display **continuous data** (various values within a range). They are very useful for showing **trends**.

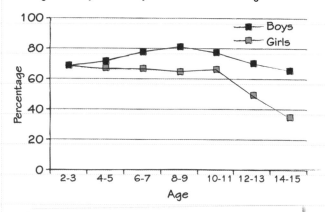

This line graph shows the percentage of girls and boys in different age groups who do the recommended amount of physical activity.

Scatter graphs

This type of graph is used to plot lots of separate data points to test whether there is a relationship (**correlation**).

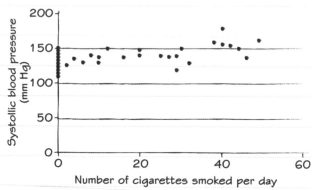

This scatter graph shows blood pressure against the number of cigarettes smoked per day.

Tables

Tables are used to show data that fall under separate headings. Tabulation aids data analysis as it shows clearly which data are associated with which headings.

This table shows the possible side effects of different types of treatment for prostate cancer.

Managing side effects		
Treatment	**What it does**	**Possible side effects**
Surgery	Removes the cancerous tissue and the prostate	Urinary incontinence, erectile dysfunction (ED) and infertility
Hormone therapy	Minimises presence of androgens which fuel prostate cancer growth	ED, hot flushes and bone loss
Radiation	Slows prostate cancer cell growth by targeting cells externally or by injection	ED, incontinence, diarrhoea, rectal bleeding and discomfort during urination and bowel movement
Immunotherapy	Changes the body's immune system to kill cancer cells	Fever
Bone-related treatments	Inhibits bone loss and fractures and relieves pain from prostate cancer in the bone	Tiredness, diarrhoea, nausea and weakness
Chemotherapy	Targets cancer cells that grow quickly including cancer cells metastasised to the bone	Hair loss, fragile bones and nervous system disorders such as confusion, depression, headaches and nausea

Now try this

1. Describe the **trend** shown by the **line graph** above.
2. Referring to the **scatter graph**, do you think there is a **correlation** between the number of cigarettes smoked and blood pressure?
3. Referring to the table, name the three prostate cancer treatments that cause erectile dysfunction.

Data analysis skills: pictorial presentation

Data analysis skills are used to evaluate the efficacy of medical procedures and the effects of lifestyle choices. You need to know how to analyse pie charts, sociograms and pictograms.

Pie charts

Pie charts show data as a proportion (**sector**) of a whole circle.

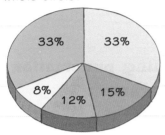

This pie chart shows the proportions of different food types in a healthy diet.

Recommended daily amounts

☐ 33% - Bread, rice, potatoes, pasta and other starchy foods

☐ 33% - Fruit and vegetables

☐ 15% - Milk and dairy foods

☐ 12% - Meat, fish, eggs, beans and other non-dairy sources of protein

☐ 8% - Foods and drinks high in fat and/or sugar

Sociogram

This is a way of recording interpersonal relationships. The direction of the arrows can be used to show who initiated contact.

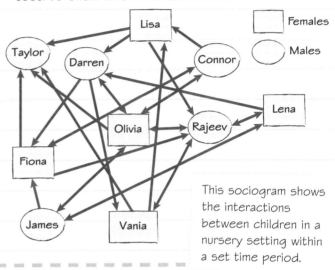

☐ Females
○ Males

This sociogram shows the interactions between children in a nursery setting within a set time period.

Pictogram

Pictograms use pictures to represent data in order to create interest. This type of data presentation is often used in health education posters and leaflets, as a way to engage the reader.

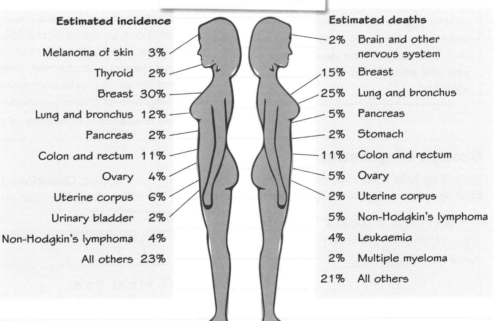

ONCOLOGY Epidemiology
Female cancer statistics

Estimated incidence

Melanoma of skin	3%
Thyroid	2%
Breast	30%
Lung and bronchus	12%
Pancreas	2%
Colon and rectum	11%
Ovary	4%
Uterine corpus	6%
Urinary bladder	2%
Non-Hodgkin's lymphoma	4%
All others	23%

Estimated deaths

2%	Brain and other nervous system
15%	Breast
25%	Lung and bronchus
5%	Pancreas
2%	Stomach
11%	Colon and rectum
5%	Ovary
2%	Uterine corpus
5%	Non-Hodgkin's lymphoma
4%	Leukaemia
2%	Multiple myeloma
21%	All others

Now try this

1. Referring to the **pie chart** above, which food types should make up the greatest **proportion** of a healthy diet?

2. Referring to the **sociogram**, are there any children who did not initiate contact with others?

3. Analyse the **pictogram**. (a) Identify the most common female cancer. (b) Which female cancer is the biggest killer?

Your Unit 3 exam

You will have 1 hour and 30 minutes to complete the Unit 3 exam paper. You need to answer each part of **every question.**

Types of question

- Define
- State
- Which
- In which

- To which
- Identify
- Complete
- Outline

- Describe
- Explain
- Compare and contrast
- Provide a key

- What
- Deduce
- By how many
- To what extent

How to answer each question type is explained on pages 159–167.

Number of marks

The paper is worth 90 marks in total. The marks are shown at the end of each part of each question and range from 1 to 8 marks. The number of marks indicates the amount of time you should spend on each question. The amount of writing space available will give you an idea of how much detail is needed.

Spelling, punctuation and grammar

Make sure that your answers are clear, using accurate spelling, punctuation and grammar.

Read the question

Always read the **whole question** and **accompanying information** before starting to answer it. Some questions may relate to conditions or illnesses you are less familiar with. The information provided with the question may give you sufficient background to enable you to answer the related questions correctly. Make sure that you **answer the question you are asked**, not one you wish for!

Focus of questions

In the exam, groups of questions are focused on:

- **the structure and organisation of the human body,** e.g. questions on some of the following: how cells work, characteristics of tissues, the structure and function of body organs, energy in the body, human genetics. Make sure you can **label diagrams** of the heart, lungs, brain, stomach, liver, pancreas, duodenum, ileum, colon, kidneys, bladder, ovaries, testes, uterus, skin.
- **the structure, function and disorders of body systems,** e.g. questions on some of the following: homeostatic mechanisms, cardiovascular, respiratory, skeletal, muscular, digestive, nervous, endocrine, immune and lymphatic, renal, male and female reproductive systems. Make sure you can **label diagrams** of these systems.
- **medical research** – how data is collected and used.

Groups of questions

You will be told what each group of questions is about. For example, **Questions 1–3 are about the heart.** Each question may start with a diagram or piece of information. Each question may then be broken into parts.

State names or locations of specific structures
Complete a table
Outline why certain features are important
Describe physiological processes, e.g. cell division
Define terminology
Deduce probability
Examples of what you might be asked to do
Describe the structure of specific cells, tissues or organs
Compare and contrast procedures or treatments
Complete a diagram to identify how a system would react in a given situation
Explain why certain symptoms occur in a disorder or particular disease
Explain the functions of specific organs or systems

Now try this

A number of problems can occur during delivery of a child, which may lead to a caesarean birth. Define the term *caesarean birth*.

Provide a short factual statement giving the meaning (e.g. to define breech birth, you might answer: 'Legs/buttocks first through vagina'. Give an accurate definition. You would receive no marks if you answered 'upside down'.)

'State' and 'Which' questions

'**State**' and '**Which**' questions require you to quickly recall facts or features relating to anatomy and physiology or to specify one or more items from a list. These are generally short-answer questions and your answers should be brief. One mark is awarded for each answer.

Worked example

The diagram shows the renal system of a human.

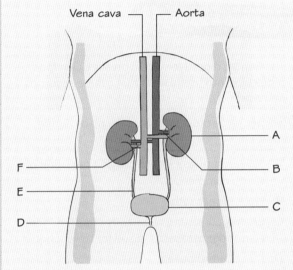

(a) State the letters that label the kidney and urethra. `2 marks`

Sample response extract

Kidney   A ....

Urethra   D ....

(b) State the name of structures B, C and E. `3 marks`

Sample response extract

B   Renal artery ....

C   Bladder ....

E   Ureter ....

(c) These are some different disorders.

> **A** Urinary tract infection
> **B** Diabetes mellitus
> **C** Dementia
> **D** Spina bifida

Which is a disorder of the renal system? `1 mark`

Sample response extract

A ....

Revise diagrams

Questions that give you diagrams and ask you '**state**' or '**which**' questions can be quick to complete. Make sure that you include diagrams in your revision, and practise your labelling skills for each system. Short-answer questions may be worth 1 to 3 marks, so you should not spend too long on them. If you do not know the answer, move on and come back to tackle all parts of the question at the end. Give an answer even if you are not sure.

You may be given a diagram showing structures labelled with letters.

You may be given names of structures and asked to **state** the corresponding letters.

You may be given letters and asked to **state** the corresponding names of structures.

You may be asked **which** item or statement from a list is an example of a particular location, structure, characteristic, function, disorder or situation. You must select the correct item from the list. No detail is required.

Now try this

Which letter points to the renal vein?

You may be asked **which** letter on a diagram points to a structure.

Links Look at page 145 to revise the human renal system.

'Identify' and 'Complete' questions

'**Identify**' questions require you to recall your knowledge. '**Complete**' questions require you to provide brief answers. One mark is awarded for each part of the answer.

Worked example

> Blood glucose level is regulated by a negative feedback system.

Identify how the system responds after a meal by completing the diagram.   **4 marks**

'**Identify**' questions require you to indicate the main features or function of something, showing your recall and understanding of facts. In this example, you need to identify how a system would respond by completing a diagram.

Sample response extract

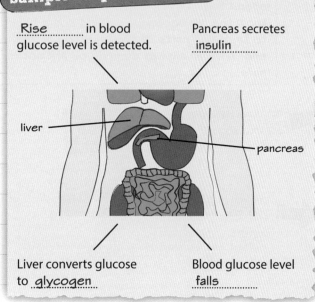

<u>Rise</u> in blood glucose level is detected.

Pancreas secretes <u>insulin</u>

liver

pancreas

Liver converts glucose to <u>glycogen</u>

Blood glucose level <u>falls</u>

Complete questions require you to provide facts to complete a table or fill in gaps on a diagram or in sentences.

In this example, you need to recall your knowledge of the process of digestion to complete the table.

🔗 **Links** Look at page 122 to revise regulation of blood sugar level.

Worked example

> The human digestive system breaks down food molecules into useful units that can be absorbed into the body.

Here are some processes that take place during digestion.

A Salivary amylase is secreted and digestion of starch commences.

B Water is reabsorbed.

C Chyme, consisting of partially digested food, acid and proteases, is mixed for several hours.

D Faeces are expelled.

E Faeces are stored.

F Small molecules are absorbed into the bloodstream.

Complete the table with the relevant letter to show where each stage of digestion occurs.   **6 marks**

Sample response extract

Location in alimentary canal	Process
Mouth	A
Stomach	C
Small intestine	F
Large intestine	B
Rectum	E
Anus	D

Now try this

Identify how the negative feedback system that controls blood sugar level responds to a fall in glucose by completing this diagram.

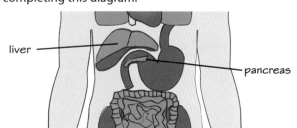

liver

pancreas

| Fall in blood glucose level is detected |

| Liver secretes .... |

| .... is converted to .... |

| Blood glucose level .... |

'Outline' and 'In which'/ 'To which' questions

'**Outline**' questions ask you to provide a summary, overview or brief description of a topic, and are worth up to 3 marks. '**In which**'/'**To which**' questions ask you to specify a particular item and are worth 1 mark.

Worked example

The diagram shows a red blood cell, platelets and white blood cell.

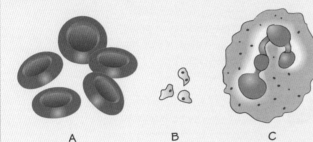

A   B   C

(a) **To which** body system do the cells in the diagram belong?   1 mark

   A Digestive
   B Respiratory
   C Cardiovascular
   D Skeletal

> '**To which**' and '**In which**' questions usually require a one or two-word answer.

Sample response extract

C ....

(b) **In which** part of an adult are red blood cells produced?   1 mark

> This question asks you to outline how the function of a red blood cell relates to the fact that it has no nucleus. Be guided on how much to write by the space available and marks allocated.

Sample response extract

Bone marrow ....

(c) **Outline** why the cell labelled A has no nucleus.   3 marks

Sample response extract

The main function of the erythrocyte or red blood cell is to transport oxygen. Without a nucleus, there is more room for haemoglobin, the chemical that combines with and carries oxygen. The lack of a nucleus allows the cell to have a flattened shape, which increases its surface-area-to-volume ratio and, therefore, the efficiency with which oxygen can diffuse in and out.

> You need to provide a brief **descriptive** outline, summarising the key points. Use separate sentences to outline each of the main points you wish to cover in your answer.

White blood cells fight infection in three main ways, which you should briefly describe. Platelets have one function.

 Links   Look at page 124 to revise functions of the blood.

Now try this

1 Outline the main functions of the cells labelled B in the diagram above.

2 Outline the main functions of the cells labelled C in the diagram above.

'Describe' questions

'Describe' questions require you to **recall knowledge** and **provide a clear account**, in your own words, of, for example, a structure, function, system or disorder. These questions are worth up to 4 marks.

Worked example

One function of striated muscle is the generation of heat.

Describe what happens during shivering when a person's body temperature falls.   4 marks

You are being asked how the body regulates its temperature when it is cold. The amount of space and the number of marks are a guide as to how long your answer should be.

Sample response extract

Muscle action generates heat. If the body temperature falls, the striated muscles are stimulated to contract in the action of shivering. This generates heat, which raises the body temperature.

This clear description of shivering and its effect demonstrates a good understanding of this homeostatic body function.

 Links Look at page 121 to revise homeostasis in relation to body temperature.

Worked example

The stages of foetal development fall into three trimesters.

Describe how a foetus develops during the second trimester of pregnancy.   4 marks

You must read the question carefully and only describe information that answers the question – additional, but irrelevant, information will not be rewarded.

Sample response extract

Foetal development during the second trimester of pregnancy is very rapid, with changes taking place almost daily. The body continues to grow, and the baby's gender will become apparent. Facial features also develop rapidly. The baby will develop functioning organs, nerves and muscles, and skeletal bones also develop.

This answer is correctly limited to developments in the second trimester.

 **Links** Look at page 150 to revise foetal development.

Now try this

Coronary heart disease is a disorder of the cardiovascular system.

Describe the changes in the body of a person who has coronary heart disease.

You need to describe changes within the coronary arteries and the effects of these on the person.

 Links Look at page 126 to revise coronary heart disease.

'Explain' questions

'Explain' questions require you to answer in detail to demonstrate understanding. You need to **give clear reasons** to support an opinion, view or argument and link your points. Read the questions carefully, as you may need to provide explanations for more than one feature or aspect of a process or condition. 'Explain' questions are usually worth between 2 and 4 marks.

Worked example

Respiratory disorders affect the airways and lungs.

Explain how smoking leads to the development of respiratory disorders.   4 marks

You are being asked to explain changes that happen in a person's respiratory system if they smoke regularly.

Sample response extract

Cigarette smoking damages the cilia in the airways, therefore reducing the person's ability to filter the air they are breathing in, and making it more difficult for them to clear secretions from their airways. The tar produced by smoking also damages the cells in the lungs. Such damage or irritation leads to diseases such as lung cancer, COPD and bronchitis, and aggravates conditions such as asthma.

Words such as '**therefore**' lead onto reasons and explanations.

This is a strong answer because it clearly explains the adverse effects of smoking on the respiratory system.

 Links Look at page 129 to revise respiratory disorders.

Worked example

Negative feedback mechanisms help to maintain stable conditions within the body.

Explain how negative feedback mechanisms help to maintain homeostasis in the body.   4 marks

This question asks you to demonstrate an understanding of homeostasis, and how negative feedback mechanisms help to achieve it.

Sample response extract

Negative feedback mechanisms help to keep aspects such as blood pressure and body temperature stable by reversing changes in the body's physiological 'norms'. If a fall in blood pressure or temperature is detected, the body is stimulated to react and attempts to correct the imbalance. When the 'norms' are restored, homeostasis (a constant state) is achieved.

This answer uses specific physiological processes as examples to illustrate the explanation.

 Links Look at pages 121 and 122 to revise homeostasis.

Now try this

The liver has many functions, including a role in digestion.

Explain the functions of the liver in relation to digestion.

For example, the liver plays a role in sugar, fat and protein metabolism. You should explain at least two of these aspects.

 Links Look at pages 122 and 136 to revise some of the liver's functions.

163

'Compare and contrast' questions

'Compare and contrast' questions require you to identify the main factors or features of two or more structures, functions or disorders. You need to explain the **similarities (comparing)** and **differences (contrasting)** as well as the **advantages** and **disadvantages**. The questions are usually awarded between 2 and 6 marks.

Worked example

> Metabolism involves both catabolic and anabolic processes.
>
> **Compare and contrast** the metabolic processes of catabolism and anabolism.
> **6 marks**

If you are asked a 'compare and contrast' question, there will always be some similarities and some differences. You need to cover both!

Sample response extract

> These two metabolic processes are almost the opposite of each other, although they are both involved in providing energy for the body's cells. Catabolism involves the breakdown of complex substances to form simpler ones, whereas anabolism builds up larger complex molecules from smaller ones. Anabolism uses the molecules which are broken down during catabolism to build stronger body structures.

This extract correctly makes links between the two processes, not just describing each one separately.

This extract clearly covers the main similarity (being involved in providing energy), and also describes the significant differences (breaking down and building up molecules).

 Links Look at page 117 to revise metabolism.

Worked example

> Diabetes is a disorder of sugar metabolism.
>
> Compare and contrast Type 1 and Type 2 diabetes mellitus.
> **6 marks**

To answer this question, you need to show knowledge of the similarities and differences between Type 1 and Type 2 diabetes.

Sample response extract

> There are a number of differences between Type 1 diabetes and Type 2 diabetes. Firstly, in Type 1 the pancreas does not produce insulin, and there is sudden onset of the illness, whereas in Type 2 diabetes either not enough insulin is produced, or the body is resistant to the insulin, and onset is gradual. Type 1 diabetes is usually diagnosed in childhood, whereas Type 2 most often begins in middle age, although many younger people are now being diagnosed with Type 2. This is likely to be due to increasing obesity levels as there are definite links between obesity and Type 2 diabetes, but no links with Type 1. The main similarity between these two types of diabetes is that the symptoms are the same, as are the possible complications.

The answer covers a lot of the differences. However, it is a lengthy answer, and only briefly mentions similarities.

 Links Look at page 142 to revise diabetes.

Now try this

Compare and contrast Type 1 and Type 2 diabetes mellitus.

Make sure that your answer is concise and balanced with both differences and similarities.

'Provide a key' and 'What' questions

These are data analysis questions based on **graphs and diagrams**. You may be asked to **provide a key** for some data, perhaps identifying the lines on a graph. In '**what**' questions, you may be asked to identify a fact from data on a graph. Usually, you get 1 mark for each correct part of the answer.

Worked example

Three disorders of the respiratory system are cystic fibrosis, chronic obstructive pulmonary disease (COPD) and pneumonia.

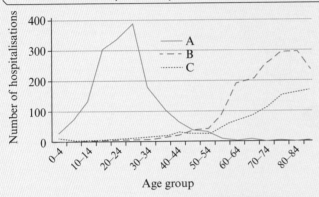

Age group

'Provide a key' questions require you to link an item, such as a line on a graph, to another, such as a label in a key.

(a) **Provide a key** for the graph by matching a letter to the correct disease. The first one has been done for you. **3 marks**

Sample response extract

Pneumonia: _C_____

Cystic fibrosis: _A_____

COPD: _B_____

Cystic fibrosis is an inherited disease. People with the disease have a shorter than average life expectancy, and it is likely to affect children from birth, with most hospitalisations in early adulthood.

(b) In **what** age range does the number of hospitalisations for pneumonia rise above 100? **1 mark**

Sample response extract

_70 to 74_____

This refers to the point on line C where the number of hospitalisations rises above 100.

Now try this

Diabetes is a disorder that affects sugar metabolism.

Post-glucose blood sugars in a typical diabetic person and a non-diabetic person

(a) Provide a key for lines on the graph: Diabetic and Non-diabetic.

(b) What is the maximum blood glucose level in mg/100 ml in a person with diabetes after glucose is given?

You need to decide which of the lines is likely to represent the blood glucose level in a non-diabetic person and which represents the level in a diabetic person, after glucose is taken. You can read this value from the graph.

'Deduce' questions

These are data analysis questions based on **graphs and diagrams**. For 'deduce' questions you will be asked to reach a conclusion about some data by reasoning. These questions are usually worth a maximum of 8 marks.

Worked example

Studies of a family with a genetically inherited condition, cystic fibrosis, revealed a family tree as shown below. A and B were carriers of the faulty allele but did not have the disorder themselves.

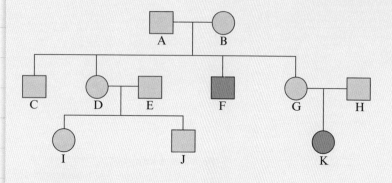

⬤ Women with cystic fibrosis

◯ Women without cystic fibrosis

◼ Men with cystic fibrosis

◻ Men without cystic fibrosis

This type of question can carry up to 8 marks. This is reflected in the amount of space provided for the answer.

Deduce the probability of an individual with F's genotype being born to parents A and B. You must include a suitable genetic diagram in your answer.   `8 marks`

f = cyctic fibrosis allele
F = normal allele

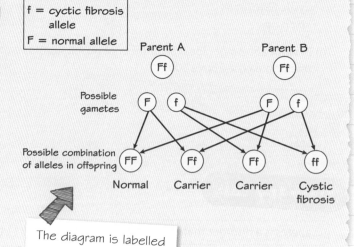

Sample response extract

F's genotype is ff because cystic fibrosis is a recessive condition and he is affected by the disease. Both parents A and B must be Ff, with one normal allele and one cystic fibrosis allele, because they are carriers for the recessive condition. Parents A and B can have children of genotypes FF, Ff and ff in the ratio of 1:2:1, as shown by the genetic diagram, so F has a probability of 25% of having a genotype of ff.

The diagram is labelled accurately and clearly.

Now try this

Referring to the family tree in the question above, deduce the probability of A and B having a child with the same genotype as themselves (a carrier). You must include a suitable genetic diagram in your answer.

First you must recall the genotype of a carrier of cystic fibrosis. Then you should work out the probability of a carrier being born to parents who are both carriers.

'By how many' and 'To what extent' questions

These are data analysis questions based on **tables** of data, graphs or diagrams. They are usually worth between 1 and 3 marks. **'By how many'** questions require you to calculate a quantity in relation to another. **'To what extent'** questions require you to give reasons or evidence to support an opinion, view or argument, explaining how you came to your conclusion.

Worked example

The Office for National Statistics (ONS) presented data on the doctor-diagnosed prevalence of diabetes by weight status and gender for adults aged 18 years and over between 2010 and 2012, in England. The results are shown in the table.

Table 1: Doctor-diagnosed diabetes prevalence by weight status and gender for adults aged 18 years and over, 2010–12, England

	Underweight	Healthy weight	Overweight	Obese (incl severely obese)
Female	1.9 %	1.9 %	4.3 %	10.7 %
Male	0.0 %	3.3%	6.0%	14.6%
TOTAL	1.3 %	2.4%	5.2 %	12.4 %

(a) **By how many** times has the likelihood of getting diabetes increased for adults who are male and obese, compared with adults who are male and of a healthy weight? `2 marks`

Sample response extract

$$\frac{14.6}{3.3} = 4.4$$

4.4 times as many obese men are diagnosed with diabetes as men of healthy weight.

Workings show how you arrive at your answer.

You need to demonstrate a clear understanding of the data presented.

(b) **To what extent** do the data presented in the table demonstrate a link between obesity and diabetes? `3 marks`

Sample response extract

The figures in the table suggest that being obese or severely obese significantly increases the risk of developing diabetes. Being a healthy weight (or being underweight) carries less than a 2.5% chance of developing diabetes. The likelihood of developing diabetes in those who are overweight increases to 5.2%, and for obese individuals the risk rises to over 12%. These figures demonstrate a clear link between obesity and diabetes. This link is also strongly supported by numerous research studies and medical opinion.

This extract shows understanding of the data. A stronger answer could comment on the differences between statistics for females and males.

The question asks about the data given – this part of the answer is not proven by the data.

Now try this

Write a paragraph identifying to what extent the likelihood of having diabetes varies between males and females, based on the data given above.

Purpose of research

The purpose of research is to find out information or gain knowledge. The aim of a particular piece of research is usually to answer a specific question.

Research in health and social care

There are four key purposes of research in health and social care.

1. To improve outcomes for people using services.

2. To inform policy and practice.

3. To extend knowledge and understanding.

4. To identify weaknesses or gaps in provision.

Research leading to improvement

Research in health and social care helps to shape society. It explores different issues and leads to better practice and policy, for example changes in treatment of health conditions, and changes in practice in providing care and support.

What is research?

Research is a systematic or orderly procedure that explores issues to establish facts or reach new conclusions.

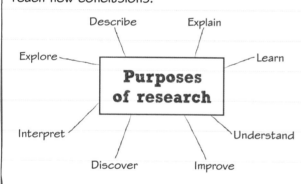

Describe   Explain

Explore ——   —— Learn

Purposes of research

Interpret   Understand

Discover   Improve

Benefits of research

Research helps to form policy that leads to improved outcomes for people who use services, such as older people.

What is the starting point?

Questions that lead to research

Here are three examples of types of questions that lead to important research projects.

1. **What** is the cost of care at the end of life?

2. **Why** do some cancer patients use services and others do not?

3. **How** can pressure on hospitals be reduced in winter?

Research studies usually start by asking a question.

Now try this

Make up a question of your own that could start a research study, using 'What', 'Why' or 'How'. Show how your question relates to the purposes of research in health and social care.

 Your question should relate to one or more of the purposes of research listed above on this page.

Issues in health and social care

Issues of concern in health and social care include the effectiveness of treatments of health conditions, how far lifestyle factors contribute to health and social care needs, and the changing health, social care and welfare needs in society.

Reviews and research

Research leads to improvements in care provision, policy and practice. Sometimes reviews are a reaction to a particular event, such as the death of a child. Such reviews can be forms of research.

Types of issues

The main three types of issues for research in the health and social care sector are:

1 health conditions

2 lifestyle factors

3 social care and welfare needs.

When planning research, you can look at what is 'topical' (current) by following the news or organisations in your field.

Researching the main issues

The effectiveness of different types of treatment

Health trends among certain age groups (for example, children or older people)

Health conditions

Health trends in particular areas of the country (or in types of areas, such as cities or rural areas)

The success of strategies for avoiding certain health conditions

Ideas for research into the main issues

The prevalence of particular lifestyle choices in certain age groups

How far certain lifestyle factors contribute to health and social care needs

Lifestyle factors

The success of strategies to mitigate the effects of these factors

The effect of lifestyle factors on the demand for services

Services provided to individuals with specific needs and the effect of these services on individuals' wellbeing

Social care and welfare needs

The effectiveness of practices in providing care and support to individuals with specific needs

The success of these practices in promoting individuals' independence and wellbeing

Examples of recent reviews and research

✓ 'Exploring the cost of care at the end of life'

✓ 'Evaluating Age UK's Integrated Care Programme'

✓ 'Reducing winter pressure on hospitals'

✓ 'Cancer patients' use of health and social care'

✓ 'National evaluation of integrated care pilots'

Now try this

The ageing population is a major current challenge facing the health and social care sector. Suggest a related research topic for each of the three types of issues identified on this page.

Find out how research in these areas has influenced policy or practice. Watch the news, read a newspaper or search the internet for current ideas.

Planning research

You need to know how a piece of research is planned, and understand the research methodologies, ethical issues and planning and research skills involved. This will help prepare you to carry out your own review of secondary sources in order to evaluate research in the field.

The research process

Key stages of the research process include:

1 Research planning, rationale and objectives (pages 170–171)

2 Use of research methodology (pages 172–175)

3 Selecting target group and sample (page 176)

4 Considering ethical issues (pages 177–182)

5 Conducting research and selecting, analysing and interpreting sources (pages 183–192) and evaluating and applying research (pages 193–203)

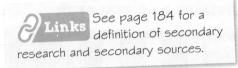 **Links** See page 184 for a definition of secondary research and secondary sources.

Achievable objectives

Research objectives should be SMART:

- **S**pecific
- **M**easurable
- **A**chievable
- **R**ealistic
- **T**ime-related.

Project proposal outline

Here is an example of a proposal outline that shows the structure and steps of a study.

Name of project proposal:	Name:
Date:	Title:
Rationale, achievable objectives, measures for success: (How will you know it's achieved its objectives? Will it be completed on time? Will the outcomes be reliable?)	
Research question/hypothesis:	
Design: (What form will the research take? What methods will it use? Who is the target group/sample? What skills are required?)	
What are the **ethical issues**, including considerations for consent and for preventing harm?	
When and how will the research be conducted and analysis and interpretation of the data take place? How will the research be monitored and modified if need be?	
When and how will the evaluation of research take place, and conclusions be drawn and presented? What are the implications for future research, practice and provision?	

Timescales and monitoring

Researchers often use a calendar or chart to plan timescales and produce a visual project plan. They break down the stages to create a timeline and use a ticklist to monitor progress and check quality. They reflect on progress by asking:

- Am I adhering to my timeline?
- Am I achieving what I set out to do?
- What barriers have I encountered?
- How can I overcome them?

If something isn't working, it can be changed so it is back on track.

Select research methods

Research methods need to show reliability and validity of results. Triangulation uses different research methods to investigate the same question from different angles and increases the validity of results. For example:

Observations: tracker observations to see behaviours of elderly people.

Structured interviews: with the elderly to find out about their views.

Questionnaires: to staff asking them for their views on supporting elderly people.

Now try this

1 What does triangulation mean?
2 What is the benefit of triangulation?
3 State **three** things to consider when setting and monitoring realistic timescales.

Rationale for research

When planning a piece of research, it is important to identify the **topic** and **rationale** (the reason for doing the research).

Choosing a research topic

Choose a topic that will:

- draw on a personal interest
- sustain your interest for the whole project
- be relevant to your work
- be achievable
- be ethical.

Breadth of topic

Start with a broad topic area and then narrow down your focus. Here is an example.

Topic: Health

Issue: Discrimination in healthcare

Narrow issue: Should obese people pay for healthcare related to their condition?

Case study

 Topic

For 5 years, Gill has been working with an organisation, carrying out key research into children in social care. Some of the children have experienced multiple foster carers. The organisation is aware that this affects the children's behaviour, and Gill wants to explore the impact on their confidence and self-esteem. She has focused on her field (children in care) and broad topic (the impact on children of having multiple foster carers).

3 **Research title**

Gill has to decide on a working title for her research which gives an idea of what the study is about. Her research title could be:

'Exploring the impact of being placed with multiple foster parents on children's psychological wellbeing'.

2 **Rationale**

The organisation's rationale (or reason) for the research is the view that frequent changes of foster parents are detrimental to children's wellbeing.

Gill may be able to gather evidence to support this **hypothesis**. This could lead to a change in the way children in care are managed.

Hypothesis

This is an idea or possible explanation for something, based on limited evidence, which is used as a starting point for an investigation.

4 **Research questions**

Gill has decided to investigate these specific research questions:

1 What is the impact on children's psychological wellbeing when experiencing frequent changes in foster carers?

2 Does the impact differ with the children's gender and age?

Now try this

Choose one of the issues below. Define a broad topic for research, narrow it to a more detailed issue, and suggest a rationale for researching the issue, and a working title.

(a) Health conditions   (b) Lifestyle factors   (c) Social care and welfare needs

You may find it helpful to follow the steps shown in the 'Breadth of topic' box above, and then the same process as Gill in the case study above.

Quantitative methods

When planning and conducting quantitative research, your methods will produce data that can be analysed statistically (e.g. number of hours spent exercising). Data are measurable and can help generate a hypothesis (e.g. those who don't exercise may be at higher risk of a stroke).

Controlled conditions

Quantitative research looks **objectively** at attitudes, opinions, responses and other aspects of behaviour to learn about the way people behave in their everyday lives. Quantitative research is usually used to explore an issue under controlled laboratory situations. The ability to **control** (limit) the variables is high, and there are ample opportunities to observe.

Some experimental studies are conducted on animals in laboratories, for example, Harry Harlow's experiment with monkeys on 'the Nature of Love' in the 1950s.

Producing quantitative data

Numerical data for **quantitative analysis** can be produced using six key methods:

1. experiments
2. observations
3. interviews
4. checklists
5. questionnaires
6. surveys.

Experiments

Quantitative research looks at the effects of one thing on another (cause and effect) using **experiments**. For example, to find out if pepper makes a person sneeze, you could give one group pepper to sniff and another group salt and watch the reactions of both groups. The **hypothesis** would be: 'If you give a participant pepper to sniff, they will sneeze.'

Using closed questions

Quantitative studies use 'closed questions' that require only a yes or no answer. For example, it is possible to establish:

- how many people are in a category (e.g. number of people with diabetes)
- frequency (e.g. number of diabetic episodes)
- specialist information (e.g. blood sugar levels).

Analysing quantitative data

Quantitative experiments are usually analysed numerically and by making **statistical inferences**. Conclusions can be drawn based on what the data indicates. An example is data compiled from local authorities and GP surgeries, to identify trends and whether methods of care and support, or treatment for health conditions, are successful.

Presenting quantitative data

Some key ways of presenting quantitative data are using a histogram, bar chart, a line graph, a pie chart, or charts that show the mean, the mode and the median.

 Links Look at pages 194–196 to revise interpretation of quantitative data.

Now try this

1. What are quantitative methods usually used to explore?
2. Give **one** example of a hypothesis.
3. Give **two** examples of a method that could produce numerical data.

You need to be able to choose and evaluate appropriate research methods, and identify and evaluate methods in research carried out by others.

Qualitative methods

When planning and conducting qualitative research, your methods will produce data that is descriptive and cannot easily be measured statistically (e.g. emotions shown by facial expression). Research takes place through words about what the person thinks or how they feel (e.g. explaining fears about treatment).

Listening to people

Qualitative methods look **subjectively** at human behaviour and interpret what people say about their feelings and experiences.

Qualitative researchers believe the best way to understand things is to listen to what people say and to observe what they do, instead of quantitative research methods such as controlled laboratory situations.

Qualitative research may be used alongside quantitative research, for example, by finding the number of people choosing a particular health product (quantitative) and exploring the reasons for their choice (qualitative).

Exploratory research

Qualitative research is sometimes called **exploratory** because it explores reasons and motivations for people saying and doing things.

Producing qualitative data

In qualitative research you try to develop understanding of what people are saying or doing by analysing their words and actions. The researcher may ask participants to provide explanations of their feelings, opinions and experiences. Alternatively, they may observe behaviour and interpret what those behaviours may suggest. Data can be gained through a range of methods including:

 interviews

 case studies

 questionnaires

 observations.

Using open questions

Qualitative research methods, such as interviews, usually contain 'open questions' that require an answer with a description or explanation, for example:

'What happened when treatment was proposed for your illness?'

Methods in qualitative research

There are many different methods you can use in qualitative research. Here are three key methods.

Case study: an up-close, in-depth examination of a subject

Diary: participants keep a diary that is analysed by researchers, usually over a long period of time

Key methods of qualitative research

Focus group: a group of people are asked about their opinions, attitudes and beliefs about something

Links Look at pages 197–199 to revise interpretation of qualitative data

Look at pages 197–199 to revise interpretation of qualitative data

Now try this

1 What are qualitative methods usually used to explore?
2 Give **two** examples of a method you could use in qualitative research.

You need to be able to choose and evaluate appropriate research methods, and identify and evaluate methods in research carried out by others.

Advantages and disadvantages

When planning, conducting, reporting and evaluating research, you need to know the advantages and disadvantages of the main research methods. This can help you to identify, select and use methods suitable for different research purposes and evaluate their reliability.

1 Observations

Observations can produce both **qualitative** and **quantitative** data:

👍 Observer can see what is happening.

👍 Not expensive to carry out.

👍 Data can be more reliable.

👎 Participants may be uncomfortable.

👎 People may behave differently when being watched.

👎 Time consuming.

2 Experiments

Experimentation usually produces **quantitative** data:

👍 Good for discovering cause and effect.

👍 Allows control over variables.

👍 Can be replicated.

👎 Not typical of real-life situations.

👎 Behaviour of participants may be limited.

👎 Participants may guess the purpose of research and subconsciously influence the data.

3 Interviews

Interviews can be used to gather both **qualitative** and **quantitative** data:

👍 Direct feedback from participants.

👍 Topics can be explored in depth.

👍 Opportunities to explain and clarify.

👎 Time consuming and costly.

👎 Researchers need to be well prepared.

👎 Researchers' own opinions may influence the way participants respond to questions, and this may bias results.

4 Questionnaires and surveys

Can be used to gather both **qualitative** or **quantitative** data:

👍 Can gain large amounts of information.

👍 Can be carried out quickly.

👍 Cheap and not time consuming.

👎 Doesn't always give insight into feelings, motivations or behaviours.

👎 Participants may not tell the truth.

👎 Questions may be misinterpreted.

Using qualitative and quantitative methods

Using qualitative and quantitative methods together is known as mixed methods design.

👍 In-depth information

👍 Increases reliability

👍 Increases validity

👎 Time consuming

👎 Difficult to manage

👎 Can be difficult to analyse

Q1 What colour jelly bean do you like best?

Red ☐ Green ☐ Orange ☐

Q2 What is it about this colour that you like best?

_____

This research is identifying the most popular colour of jelly bean among children, using a mixed method design. It can find out **how many** children prefer red jelly beans but also **why** they prefer red jelly beans. Question 1 is a **closed question**. Question 2 is an **open question**.

Now try this

1 Describe a research method you could use to use to find out whether a person uses alternative therapies.

2 Give one advantage and one disadvantage of using this method.

 State your method and explain briefly how you could carry out the research.

Research questions

When planning and conducting research, you need to think carefully about the types of questions to ask in order to achieve the reliable results that you need.

Research questions

Here are some examples of research questions for qualitative studies:

1 What do patients think of cuts in funding?
2 What are the effects of integrating male and female wards?

Here is an example of a question with a **sub-question:**

Question:

What are the effects of parenthood on single mothers?

Sub-question:

Are there differences in perceptions associated with the age of the mother?

Researchers think carefully about the questions used in research. They may use closed or open questions, or a mixture, with a focus on achieving reliable results.

Closed and open questions

Closed and open questions can be used in interviews, questionnaires and surveys.

Here's an example of a **closed question**.

'How many cigarettes do you smoke a day?'

Here's an example of an **open question**.

'Tell me, what happened when you tried to give up smoking?'

Scaled questions

Some questions ask respondents to select their answer from a scale, for example from strongly disagree to strongly agree, or to rate their response according to a number scale, perhaps from 1 to 10. These scales are sometimes referred to as **Likert** scales.

These questions allow a wider variety of responses than closed questions but answers still can be analysed systematically. Here is an example.

I am satisfied with the standard of care I have received today:

Agree strongly ☐   Agree ☐   Neither agree nor disagree ☐   Disagree ☐   Disagree strongly ☐

Now try this

Which of these questions are open and which are closed?

1 Is Macmillan Cancer Support a charity?
2 Have you ever visited someone in hospital?
3 How do you think the latest social care reforms will affect service users?
4 Why do you think it is better for older people to live in their own homes?
5 How many minutes of exercise do you do on average each day?
6 At what age did you stop smoking?

Remember the criteria for deciding if a question is open or closed:

- Open questions allow participants to respond in their own words.
- Closed questions require a yes/no answer, a numerical answer or selecting an answer from limited choices.

175

Target groups and samples

The **target group** or **target population** is the subset of the whole population that is relevant to your research. When planning, conducting, reporting and evaluating research you need to be able to identify the target population for a particular research project.

Sampling methods

A sample is a subset of the target group of your research. The challenge is to ensure that the sample is **representative** of the target group. Researchers use data from the sample to make **predictions** about the whole target population. Below are **four** different types of sampling you need to know about.

Advantages of sampling

✓ It is **cheaper** to gather data from a sample than from the whole target population.

✓ It is **quicker** to collect data from a sample.

✓ It is **easier** to analyse data from a sample and calculate statistics.

If you want to research attitudes to managed care amongst the elderly, your target population might be adults in the UK aged 65 or over. Your sample should be selected to represent the target population as accurately as possible.

① Random sample

Every member of the target group has an equal chance of being chosen.

Picking names out of a hat would produce a random sample.

② Systematic sampling (*k*-in-1 sample)

Every kth member of the target group is selected for the sample.

Choosing every fifth member of the target population produces a k-in-1 sample.

③ Stratified random sample

The target group is divided into subsets (called **strata**). A proportional number of members of each stratum is randomly selected for the sample.

There are twice as many boys as girls, so twice as many boys are included in the sample.

④ Cluster sample

The target group is divided into subsets. One or more entire subset is selected for the sample.

The target group has been divided into boys and girls. All the girls have been selected for this cluster sample.

Now try this

A primary school wants to research the diets of its pupils.

1 Identify the target population for this research.

2 Describe two different sampling methods the school could use for this research.

 Describe the sampling methods as specifically as possible.

Ethical principles

When planning, conducting, reporting and evaluating research, researchers must be ethical by showing respect for the participants and treating them according to some basic principles.

Being ethical

Being ethical means that you conduct yourself according to certain standards and treat people properly.

A **code of conduct** may be used to spell out the standards of behaviour that are required.

The Nuremberg Code

This is a set of ethical principles that guides research on human subjects. It was devised in 1947 following the Nuremberg Trials after the end of the Second World War. These included trials of Nazi doctors who had carried out terrible experiments on Jewish prisoners.

Some ethical principles

Ethics are guidelines. Here are some ethical principles that could guide any aspect of human behaviour, from how we conduct ourselves in our personal lives, to behaviour in business and research:

- ✓ Promote the truth.
- ✓ Avoid error.
- ✓ Cooperate and collaborate.
- ✓ Maintain confidentiality.
- ✓ Be accountable.
- ✓ Be trustworthy.
- ✓ Be professional.
- ✓ Respect the dignity of participants.
- ✓ Be socially responsible.
- ✓ Respect human rights.

Ethical conduct with children

All research should be carried out to a strict code of conduct and not harm consenting participants. For subjects under 18, both parent and child are required to give their consent, which may be withdrawn at any time.

Ethics in research

Here are examples of organisations that conduct research projects and use a set of principles for ethical conduct:

- Health Research Authority (has taken over the role of the National Social Care Research Ethics Committee)
- British Psychological Society (BPS)
- Medical Research Council (MRC)
- The National Research Ethics Advisors Panel (NREAP)
- National Institute for Health Research
- Human Fertilisation and Embryology Authority
- Human Tissue Authority.

Universities and other centres of research usually have an ethics committee to oversee research projects.

Researchers, harm and consent

Researchers have a **duty** not to cause **harm** to their subjects through their research. Harm could be **physical**, **emotional** or **material** (to property). To avoid causing harm, researchers should behave ethically, following appropriate codes of conduct, and must gain **informed consent** from participants.

Participants must understand what is going to happen during the research and formally agree to take part. The principle of consent is central to the Nuremberg Code. **Mental capacity** is required in order to give informed consent.

Links Look at page 180 to revise informed consent.

Now try this

1 Name **three** ethical principles.
2 What is the main purpose of an ethical code of conduct?

Safeguarding ethics

When planning, conducting, reporting and evaluating research, researchers must ensure that no harm is caused to participants or wider society. Correct conduct in research has implications for the whole of society.

Risk assessment

Researchers have a duty to minimise people's exposure to risk when they take part in research. Risk assessment is used to identify and mitigate sources of possible harm.

Risk assessment cycle

Identify potential risk → Assess risk to participant → Identify ways to control risk → Evaluate controls → (back to Identify potential risk)

Data protection

Researchers must follow the law (Data Protection Act 1998) and their organisation's **data protection policy and procedures** when they keep data and documents about participants or use photographs. This helps to ensure appropriate use of data and participant **confidentiality**.

- Personal data should be stored in a locked cabinet or on a password-protected computer.
- When you report data you should not use actual names or refer to traceable locations.
- Data can only be used for the purpose for which it was collected and for which the data provider gave their consent.

Links Look at page 181 to revise the Data Protection Act 1998.

Conflicts of interest

Conflicts of interest in research should be avoided by:

- **peer review:** scrutiny of research findings by another expert in the field prior to publication
- **participant review:** people who took part in the research have the opportunity to comment and may request that their data is excluded
- **mentoring** by an expert, allowing researchers to discuss their work with another professional
- maintaining a **professional distance** to ensure objectivity
- protecting people who **disclose** ethical concerns through **whistleblowing procedures**.

Impact of unethical conduct through misuse of results

Andrew Wakefield was the author of a *Lancet* paper that linked autism with the MMR (measles, mumps, rubella) vaccine. Following a two-year investigation, Wakefield was found guilty of conflict of interest, selective reporting of data and unethical dealings with children. The paper led to a fall in the take up of the MMR vaccine and an increase in the incidence of these preventable diseases, which can have dangerous side effects. Complications of measles include blindness and miscarriage; mumps can lead to male infertility and meningitis, and rubella can cause foetal defects.

Now try this

1. Identify **one** key procedure researchers should follow under the Data Protection Act 1998 to ensure participant confidentiality.

2. State **two** ways of avoiding conflicts of interest in research.

Confidentiality

When planning and conducting research, researchers must ensure that participants know that their information remains **confidential**. Researchers have a **professional duty** to make sure that confidentiality is **safeguarded**.

Why is confidentiality important?

Successful research relies on participants volunteering truthful **personal information** about their health, feelings, beliefs, attitudes and actions. They are more likely to be honest when they **trust** the researcher not to divulge their information.

What is professionalism?

Professionalism means having the qualities, skills, competence and behaviours expected of individuals belonging to your profession. **Safeguarding confidentiality** is an aspect of professionalism in research.

Confidentiality for all participants

Researchers have a duty to protect the confidentiality of participants, whatever their role. Depending on the focus of your research, caregivers and other professionals may be participants.

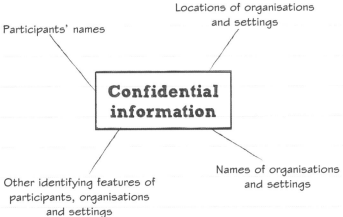

Participants' names

Locations of organisations and settings

Confidential information

Other identifying features of participants, organisations and settings

Names of organisations and settings

Gatekeepers

Researchers sometimes need to gain **gatekeeper approval** for research. The gatekeeper is the person responsible for allowing research to take place in their setting. Issues of confidentiality would focus on the gatekeeper's identity and the name and location of the setting.

If you wanted to observe daily routines in a large care home, for example, you would need to gain gatekeeper approval.

How is confidentiality protected?

Confidentiality is protected through:

- the law, e.g. the Data Protection Act 1998
- organisational data protection policies and procedures which implement the 1998 Act
- a professional approach
- professional codes of conduct
- ethical research codes, such as the Nuremberg Code
- regulatory bodies
- anonymising data.

Anonymity

Research data that has been **anonymised** cannot be traced back to the original providers of the data, although pieces of data from each individual are linked together for analysis.

When referring to individuals, researchers can use initials or reference numbers instead of names.

Now try this

What information should always remain confidential in research studies involving:

1 individual people?

2 observations of large groups of people?

Be aware of the different information that should be protected in different types of research study.

Informed consent

When planning and conducting research, you must always obtain a participant's consent before proceeding with the research. Informed consent is an important principle of the Nuremberg Code and is central to professional conduct in research. **Understanding** and **agreement** together make up informed consent.

1 Understanding

It is important that participants are fully aware of what they are being asked to do and can assess whether they wish to take any risks that may be associated with the research. The participant must have the opportunity to ask questions about the project and to have their concerns addressed. To be **informed**, the participant must understand:

- the aims of the research
- potential benefits to policy, practice and provision procedure
- what will happen during the project
- any potential risks in taking part
- how their data will be treated
- what will happen to the results at the end.

2 Agreement

In giving their consent, the participant agrees to take part in the study that the researcher has described. If the project changes in any way, further informed consent is required.

Obtaining informed consent

Remember that participants may include caregivers and other professionals, as well as those in receipt of care. All participants must give informed consent.

Vulnerable groups and safeguarding them

Special safeguards should be in place when researching vulnerable groups such as:

- children aged under 16
- elderly people
- those lacking mental capacity
- individuals in a dependent or unequal relationship
- people with learning or communication difficulties
- patients in care
- people in custody or on probation
- people engaged in illegal activities, such as drug taking.

Vulnerable people should be protected and be accompanied by a responsible adult when being interviewed or observed to make sure they are treated properly, their human rights are protected and the information they give is recorded without bias.

Capacity

To give informed consent, a participant must have a certain level of mental capacity in order to understand the project and agree to take part. Vulnerable people must give their consent to take part if they can, but a **responsible person** must also give their informed consent.

Now try this

1 What does 'informed consent' mean?
2 Why is it important to gain informed consent from all participants?
3 Why should you take account of the participant's level of understanding when asking for consent?

Legislation

When planning, conducting, reporting and evaluating research, researchers have to adhere to several different legislative frameworks. You need to know about legislation which is current during delivery of the research and applicable to England, Wales or Northern Ireland, including the Data Protection Act 1998 and the Human Rights Act 1998.

The Data Protection Act 1998

The DPA 1998 is an Act of Parliament covering the UK. It sets out the law on how to **collect, store and process the personal data** of individuals living in the UK, including those who have taken part in research.

Principles of the DPA 1998

Personal information must be:

1. used fairly and lawfully
2. used for specified and limited purposes
3. adequate, relevant and not excessive
4. accurate and up to date
5. kept for no longer than necessary
6. processed under the terms of the Act
7. kept securely
8. not transferred to a country outside the European Union (EU).

How to store data

- Computers and other electronic devices should be password protected.
- Physical documents should be stored in a locked filing cabinet.

Researchers need specific consent to take and store **photographs** and **video** footage of research participants.

Timescale

The DPA 1998 does not define for how long data can be stored. When deciding what is an acceptable timescale, researchers should consider how they might use data:

- ✓ for further research into the subject
- ✓ to write an article or book at a later date.

Researchers need consent to store and reuse participants' data.

The Human Rights Act 1998

Researchers should adhere to aspects of the Human Rights Act 1998 when conducting research.

You do not need to have an in-depth knowledge of the Act, but it is important to know how the Articles of the Act relate to researching children, young people and adults.

Important Articles

Three Articles within the Act relate directly to the rights of research participants:

- **Article 3:** No person should be subjected to torture or inhuman degrading treatment.
- **Article 8:** All individuals have the right to respect of their private and family life, home and correspondence.
- **Article 9:** All individuals have the right to freedom of thought, conscience and religion.

These Articles cover safeguarding the rights of participants, minimising risks, and ensuring informed consent, privacy and confidentiality.

Now try this

1. Give **two** principles of the Data Protection Act 1998.
2. Identify **one** Article from the Human Rights Act 1998 that relates to research participants.

Safeguarding of confidentiality is the common theme in these Acts. Other rights are protected too.

Non-judgemental practice

When planning, conducting, reporting and evaluating research, researchers must remain non-judgemental so that the research is unbiased.

Are you judgemental?

- Do you have strong opinions about things or are you able to keep an open mind?
- Are you good at separating facts from opinions?

Being **non-judgemental** and **objective** are important skills in research.

Objectivity and subjectivity

Objectivity	Subjectivity
fact	opinion
what actually happened	an attitude or judgement
can be proved true or false	cannot be proved true or false

Whether delivering care or conducting research in health and social care, rejecting **stereotypes**, **prejudice** and **discrimination** is important.

Rejecting bias

Bias is usually unintentional, so it can be difficult to reduce. Bias decreases the validity of results and even leads to outright errors.

Taking a non-judgemental approach is vital to good research. It means you don't pre-empt the outcomes of your research and you keep an open mind about the possible results. To be non-judgemental, you must be aware of, and reject, stereotypes, prejudice and discrimination:

- A **stereotype** is a set idea about a group of people that does not reflect their individuality.
- **Prejudice** is an unjustified attitude based on an individual's membership of a particular group. Prejudice is often connected to stereotyping.
- **Discrimination** is the unfair treatment of a person due to prejudice.

Researcher bias

If you are biased, it means you have already made up your mind about something. If you approach research with a bias (an expectation of a particular outcome), you may influence your findings.

For example, you can change how people respond to you by the questions that you ask and by the way you ask them.

Consider these two questions:

- 'How do you feel about cuts in healthcare provision?' (open question)
- 'Do you think cuts in healthcare provision are terrible?' (leading question)

In addition, you may interpret results to give you the answer you expect.

Sample bias

This is bias in the way the sample is selected. If you only contact people who have complained about a service to ask about their satisfaction levels, you will not get an accurate picture of how the service is performing.

Bias in data collection

If you are unaware of the potential for bias, you might only log data that support your hypothesis as these will be more obvious to you.

Now try this

1 Why is it important to take a non-judgemental approach to your research?
2 What is bias and how can it arise?

Primary and secondary research

When planning, carrying out, reporting and evaluating research, you need to be aware of the two types of research, and their selection for suitability and reliability: **primary** and **secondary**.

Primary research

Primary research (**field research**) involves gathering information (data) that has not been collected before. **Primary research methods** include:

- observations
- interviews and focus groups
- case studies
- questionnaires and surveys
- scientific experiments.

Secondary research

Secondary research (desk-based research) involves gathering and analysing existing data. Sources for secondary research include:

- journal articles
- original research
- case studies
- books
- newspapers and other media
- internet.

Advantages and disadvantages

Primary research usually answers a specific question or is used to test a hypothesis in an **original** way.

👍 It is the only way to answer a new question.

👍 You own the research.

👍 Interactive.

👍 You can compare and contrast with other studies.

👍 You can control exactly what information you want to collect.

👍 You can control the reliability of the data.

👍 More varied work.

👍 Current.

👎 Expensive and time consuming.

👎 You need to build knowledge and experience to best conduct primary research.

👎 You need to be careful not to let your own opinion or expectation affect conclusions.

Advantages and disadvantages

Secondary research, such as a literature search, is useful to find out more about a topic in preparation for primary research. It can also bring together the findings of several different pieces of primary research, which provide better proof of a theory together.

👍 A good way to research topic background.

👍 Quick and inexpensive.

👍 Can combine evidence from many sources.

👍 Useful as back-up data when testing a theory using primary research.

👍 May have the benefit of drawing from a range of primary sources.

👎 Sources not always reliable.

👎 Findings may have been biased or unethically gathered.

👎 Sample size may be too small or target group may influence the findings.

👎 The information you are looking for may not exist.

👎 Less current, as it was conducted in the past.

👎 Danger of picking only those sources that support your idea.

Now try this

1 What is the difference between primary and secondary research?

2 Give **two** examples of primary research methods and two of secondary research methods.

Primary and secondary research are complementary strategies and serve different purposes.

183

Literature review

When undertaking research, and in your assessment task for this unit, you need the skills to conduct a literature review of an issue and to know about different types of sources.

What is a literature review?

A literature review (or **literature search**) involves:

- reading and reviewing a wide range of literature on a particular issue, to gain a deeper understanding and find out what has been researched before to inform your own research question
- developing understanding of a topic from primary and secondary sources
- evaluating how reliable a source is. You need to understand where the researchers gathered their information.

Conducting a literature review is an important aspect of research as it will give you an in-depth understanding of the research that has been conducted around the topic, and provides insight into areas that may need to be researched further.

Sources

Primary sources are original documents or eyewitness accounts. Examples are original accounts, letters, diaries, memoirs, official records, photographs, experiments and reports written soon after the event.

Secondary sources are secondhand accounts based on a review of one or more primary sources. They may offer different perspectives, analysis and conclusions, based on examination of multiple primary sources.

Telling the difference

How do researchers **distinguish** between primary and secondary sources? To establish whether a source is primary, ask these questions:

- How does the author know the information?
- Were they present at the event they are recording?
- Does the information come from personal experience?

For example, **Piaget talking about his work** is a **primary source**.

Alternatively, to establish whether a source is secondary, you can ask:

- Is the author reporting on historical events or on material written by others?
- Are conclusions based on many pieces of evidence?

For example, **an author discussing Piaget's work** is a **secondary source**.

Secondary sources v secondary research

Don't confuse secondary sources with secondary research.

☑ A literature review is an example of **secondary research** – it may examine both primary and secondary research. It uses mostly secondary sources.

☑ A **secondary source** is an interpretation of a primary source.

Your set task

In your set task for this unit you will be provided with a research article and asked to research **at least two secondary sources** related to the issue. In the context of your set task, this means you will undertake a literature review for research that relates to the issue in the article you are given. References to secondary sources in this context mean literature that **you** find to use in your set task.

🔗 **Links** The advantages and disadvantages of primary and secondary sources are the same as those of primary and secondary research, which you can revise on page 183.

Now try this

1 What is the difference between secondary research and secondary sources?

2 What is the purpose of a literature review?

3 Give **one** example of a primary source and **one** example of a secondary source of information.

Notes and records of sources

It is important to make **notes**, **record** and **organise** the information that you find out during your **literature review**. This is when you research sources related to your issue and find out about research in related areas. Good organisational skills will allow you to work more efficiently and improve your time management.

Organising your notes

When you carry out your literature searches, you need to make sure you organise your notes so you can find information again. You will need to refer to this information later, as you work with and write up your final report.

There are many ways that you can organise your research, for example:

- computerised records
- a diary
- sticky notes
- index cards.

Effective systems

Computerised records, such as spreadsheets, are easy to keep, update and search.

- Record your information systematically, being careful to complete every field in a spreadsheet.
- Remember to back up important data.
- An index card system is an effective way of recording information on key findings of relevant literature.
- A disadvantage of an index card system can be the need to remember the name and content of each study when searching for it.

What to record

You need to record key features of literature you find. A good way of doing this is to make notes using specific headings:

- title
- author
- source and publisher (e.g. journal, government site)
- date of publication
- page number(s) (books, journals)
- date a webpage was accessed
- URL of webpage
- key points, e.g. what the research was about, methods (for example observations and interviews), key findings
- connections with other sources of information.

Research cycle

The focus of your research may change as you find out more information during your literature review, so it is important to **monitor** and **modify** as you go along.

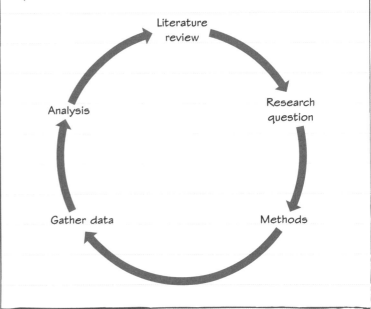

Literature review → Research question → Methods → Gather data → Analysis → Literature review

---

Now try this

Research one piece of literature of your choosing on the advantages and disadvantages of starting nursery at the age of three. Note and organise a record of your research using a spreadsheet or index card system.

 Refer to the list of headings above to record information on your source.

Reading techniques

Different aspects of your research require different reading techniques for different purposes. You might read in four different ways.

 Skim reading

Skim reading means you:
- run your eyes over the text
- read the material rapidly
- take in basic information
- get the gist of what it's about.

People sometimes skim a newspaper for general news or a travel brochure to make an initial assessment about a certain type of holiday.

 Scan reading

Scan reading is similar to skimming in that you do not read the whole piece in depth. However, you do concentrate on certain parts of the document. You:
- read the title
- read the introduction or abstract
- look at pictures and charts
- look at references.

People might scan a bus timetable or a conference guide to find a particular section that they then read in more detail.

 Intensive reading

You use intensive reading if you need an in-depth knowledge of a subject, for example John Bowlby's work on attachment.

This is the form of concentrated reading you should use to prepare for exams.

 Extensive reading

This means reading widely, often for pleasure. It could be the same as intensive reading if you are enjoying your research! Benefits of reading for pleasure include:

👍 increased reading speed

👍 improved comprehension skills

👍 extended vocabulary

👍 better language skills (writing, speaking and listening).

Matching your technique to purpose

When completing your assessment tasks:

✓ you are likely to start by skimming or scanning literature, so you can find key information relating to your topic

✓ you then adopt a more intensive reading style to identify key points within articles and understand the literature more deeply

✓ if there are concepts or ideas that interest or confuse you, you might do some extensive reading to get a richer understanding of theories and previous research.

Highlighting and annotating

Some people find it helpful to use a highlighter pen to pick out important information when skimming, scanning or reading in more depth.

An alternative is to underline important information or you might wish to jot brief notes in the margin.

Make sure you're not writing on a document that will be used by someone else, e.g. a library book.

Now try this

What is the difference between skimming and scanning? When would you use these techniques?

Academic reading and analysis

When conducting and evaluating research, and in your assessment for this unit, you need to undertake academic reading and examine the content of secondary materials. The four key features below can be found in most pieces of current research. You can usually get a good idea of the key aspects of research from an initial skim read, especially of the opening and conclusion. You can then analyse each part in more detail.

 ## Introductions and abstracts

An abstract may be included. It is a summary of the research piece. This is often followed by an introduction. Most openings of a piece of research introduce:

- **what** the study explored
- **how** it explored it
- the **participants**
- the **key findings**
- **recommendations** for future research
- its impact on **policy/practice/provision (the 3P's)**.

 ## Research methodology

This section might also be called **research design** or **study design**. It tells you about:

- **design methods** used, e.g. qualitative, quantitative or mixed methods
- **definitions** of key terms
- **data collection methods** used, e.g. focus groups, questionnaires, interviews, case reports
- **data analysis** used, i.e. the way the data has been analysed so that judgements can be made, e.g. counting the number of people who like the colour green; participants' feelings over a new government incentive.

 ## Results

A section on **results** could include:

- **key research findings** that are presented without being interpreted. Findings are based on methodologies used to gather information. Presentation may include tables and diagrams
- **discussion**, e.g. what the findings illustrate, relationship to other research, implications for practice, limitations and strengths.

 ## Conclusions

Most **conclusions** will give you:

- a **summary** of the study
- the **overall** and **key findings**
- **recommendations** for future research
- **strengths** and **limitations** of the research
- impact on **policy/practice/provision**.

 ## Reference list / bibliography

A reference list / bibliography is provided at the end of the article, which includes sources referred to in the research or read as part of the research.

 See pages 188–189 for information on referencing conventions and techniques.

See pages 188–189 for information on referencing conventions and techniques.

Now try this

Undertake a quick internet search for current research articles on a topic of your choice. Look at the structure of the articles. Choose one and find:

(a) the abstract / introduction

(b) the research methodologies

(c) the results

(d) the conclusion

(e) the references / bibliography.

Referencing conventions

You have to understand and be able to use referencing conventions and techniques. You will be expected to compile bibliographies and reference lists and present them correctly, using academically accepted conventions.

References and bibliographies

These list the **literature** that the writer has read and **cited** (mentioned) in their work.

- A **reference** section lists all the sources that have been cited in a text.
- A **bibliography** takes the same format as a reference section but lists everything you read about the topic, not only the sources you have mentioned in your written work.

Correct referencing is important.

✓ You should always acknowledge the source of any information.

✓ Good referencing increases the validity of your work as it shows that other researchers have published supporting information.

✓ The reader should be able to access any source material that you used – good referencing will help them find your sources easily.

✓ If you know how to read reference lists, you will always be able to find more references for a topic of interest.

Following conventions

Be aware when reading texts that some authors may use the terms 'references' and 'bibliography' differently. The definitions given on this page are conventionally accepted ways of using the two terms.

Referencing systems

There are several referencing systems. The most widely used is known as the Harvard system, which is followed in this guide (see page 189). In your assessment you will need to list your references on the first page of your taskbook using an academic reference system. You must use the referencing system consistently and correctly.

Notation system: footnotes

When reading texts you need to understand the notation system, which is a small superscript number inserted next to the relevant text, like this[1].

[1]Authors give the reference as a **footnote** at the bottom of the page, preceded by the matching number. Footnotes are often given in smaller text.

Notation system: endnotes

Endnotes[2], are referenced in a list at the end of the section of text.

[2]An endnote looks very much like a footnote.

Whether footnotes or endnotes are used, there will also be a **full reference list** at the end of the work.

Avoiding plagiarism

Plagiarism is quoting other people's work without giving them credit. You can fail some courses for plagiarism. To avoid it, you must cite and reference correctly.

✓ You can use quote marks to show that you have used someone else's words, and you must include the reference:
Galotti (2011, p. 400) states that the analytic system is "more deliberate and explicit..."

✓ You can paraphrase (use your own words) and provide a reference:
Galotti compares the analytic and the experiential systems (2011, p. 400).

Now try this

1 Why is it important to cite references correctly, whether in text or in reference lists?
2 What is the difference between a reference section and a bibliography?

Referencing techniques

You will need to understand and use a conventional referencing system for articles and books. A widely used referencing system is known as the Harvard system.

Referencing journal articles

Here is an example of a reference for a journal article:

> Ball, L. (2012) Midwifery education: making sense of the current challenges. *British Journal of Midwifery*, 20(7), pp.516–520.

The information appears in this order:

1 author, last name first, and initial

2 date

3 title of article

4 *journal title*

5 volume (and issue number)

6 page numbers.

Note how the journal name appears in *italics*. In handwritten references, underline the name. The use of punctuation, such as full stops, commas and brackets is also important.

Referencing a book

Here is an example of a reference for a book:

> Sacks, O. (2011) *The Man Who Mistook His Wife for a Hat*. London: Picador.

The information appears in this order:

1 author, last name first, and initial

2 date

3 book title

4 place of publication: publisher.

Note how the book name appears in *italics*. Always use a colon (:) between the place of publication and the publisher's name.

Citing references in text

This is how you would cite a reference in the body of your work:

> Ball (2012) argues that the challenges experienced by those undertaking midwifery practice have impacted on their ability to do their job.

or

> Current research suggests that the challenges experienced by those undertaking midwifery practice have impacted on their ability to do their job (Ball, 2012).

Multiple authors

This is how you would cite a reference by more than one author:

> Bryant and Bradley (1985, p. 24) argue that the educationalists are not...

or

> Some research argues that educationalists need to do more (Bryant & Bradley, 1985, p. 24).

If there are three authors, give all names:

> Clark, Kemp and Howarth (2016, p.189) argue that...

If there are four or more authors, give the name of the first author, followed by **et al.**, which means 'and others':

> Jones, et al. (2016, p.189) argue that...

Note that '&' is used in the brackets but 'and' is written out in full in the main text.

Referencing online information

You need to reference electronic sources carefully because websites change and you may need to find the information elsewhere. If you are referring to a web document or journal, use the systems described above. After the publisher, or instead if there isn't a publisher, give the name of the website of the organisation responsible for providing/maintaining the information (http://internetaddress/remotepath), and the date it was accessed in square brackets, e.g.

Dalrymple, J. and Burke, B. (2006) *Anti-oppressive practice: social care and the law*. 2nd ed. Dawsonera, [Online], Available: http://www.dawsonera.com [28 January 2017].

Now try this

Choose any book and reference it using a conventional system.

You could use the guide above. Make sure you include the correct information, punctuation and italics (or underlined) text.

Selecting reliable sources

When searching for sources of research into a contemporary health and social care issue, you need to select **reliable** sources.

Reliable publications

Sources of reliable secondary research include:

- professional journals, e.g. the *British Journal of Health Psychology* and the *British Journal of Social Work*
- textbooks
- periodicals such as *Nursery World*.

Reputable journals and publishers of academic books often use peer review. This is where experts scrutinise and review articles prior to publication, so there is confidence in the reliability of the sources included.

Reliable organisations

Other sources of reliable secondary research include:

- professional bodies, e.g. the Health and Safety Executive or the Nursing and Midwifery Council
- organisations involved in research, e.g. health authorities, local authorities, social service departments, charities, community organisations, the Office for National Statistics and the Care Quality Commission.

Reliable sources

When searching for reliable sources, consider these questions.

✓ Where does the information come from?

✓ Who provided the information? Are they an expert in their field?

✓ What was the motivation for the research? (For example, is there any bias in the reporting?)

✓ Is the source reliable? (For example, some institutions advise against using Wikipedia as it may not be considered a reliable source because information can be given or edited by anyone at any time, and errors may or may not be noticed.)

✓ Is the information consistent with other research? A single study is not enough to prove a point or make a case.

✓ Has the source of the funding for the research influenced the findings?

✓ Where was it published? In a reliable peer-reviewed journal rather than someone's blog, so maybe based on fact rather than opinion?

✓ Is the internet site provided by an official body, organisation or authoritative source?

Advantages and limitations of sources

When looking at the findings of research, consider any wide **generalisations** made about the whole population. Huge and representative samples are needed for valid generalisations. Even then, findings might only apply to sections of the population, not to everyone. Research articles often state the limitations of the research, including the size of the sample.

👍 One advantage of research articles is that you can judge the reliability of generalisations based on the sample used. The more representative of the population they are, the more valid and reliable they become. For example, the research into 'The state of the nation's waistline' was based on a large population (over 8,730 addresses over 560 postcodes).

👎 One limitation of research articles is that they often don't allow access to the actual data findings they are based on, so you only have the generalisations to work from.

Contemporary sources

Sources for this unit should be contemporary. This usually means that the research has taken place during the last 10 years.

Now try this

1   What is meant by 'peer review'?

2   How would you establish whether a piece of research is 'contemporary'?

3   What is one way of considering whether generalisations in some research are reliable?

Electronic searches

When searching to select appropriate secondary sources, getting the literature search right can save you hours of time. Conducting electronic searches effectively by narrowing the range of information to a manageable size will help you to produce a quality piece of work.

Refining electronic searches

Use with search term	Function	Example
Only search term	Returns information containing that word or phrase	Working together
Quote marks '...'	Search for an exact phrase so the search doesn't return every source containing those words in any order	'The nervous system'
+ or **AND**	Narrow a search by combining terms. The example will return information about people with both conditions	Endometriosis + chronic headaches
– or **NOT**	Eliminate words from your search. The example will give you facts about leukaemia but not how it is treated	Leukaemia not treatment
OR	Broaden a search to include results that contain either word	Hospital or clinic
* after a word	Will bring up all possible extensions of the word	Partner* → partner, partnerships, partners

Different search engines and library databases use different protocols, such as the symbol + or the word 'and', so use help screens to find out which you should use.

Targeting your search

You can **limit** and **refine** your searches by date, language, place of publication, author, publication or document type. A search engine such as Google has toolbars and menus for this purpose. For example:

- **Search tools** allows the user to restrict the search results to those published in a particular country or during a time span.
- **Books** restricts the search findings to publications.
- Options such as **Images** can be useful.
- **Google Scholar** refines searches to find journal articles.
- **Academic websites**: for example, some institutions have an **Athens** account, which provides access to all the sites that your institution has subscribed to, and allows access to e-resources.

Reading **abstracts** of articles can also be a quick and efficient method of establishing the reliability of sources and to what extent they are relevant to your research.

Now try this

1 Find out how to search your library database and whether you can access any online journals.

2 Browse the 'Publications' section of the Care Quality Commission website.

The range of open-access publications on the Care Quality Commission website might be one useful source in your work.

Connecting sources

As part of your research skills and assessment for this unit, you need to show connections between sources of information.

Making connections

You need to be able to connect your sources of information to each other and to your research project.

Conducting an online search, e.g. for data on prostate cancer, will generate numerous pieces of different information. Think critically about each piece and consider:

- How exactly does this piece of information fit into my project?
- Does this source of information contribute a piece of the story to my project?
- How is it significant?
- How is it relevant to the big picture?
- What information is still missing?

Making connections between your sources helps you to produce research that is reliable and valid, and strengthens the argument or rationale for your research.

Drawing conclusions

This means that you make a judgement on what the information in all your literature is saying. It might be that you see a relationship between the sources in that they all come to a similar conclusion. Think critically about each piece and make a judgement on what they are suggesting. Think critically about each piece.

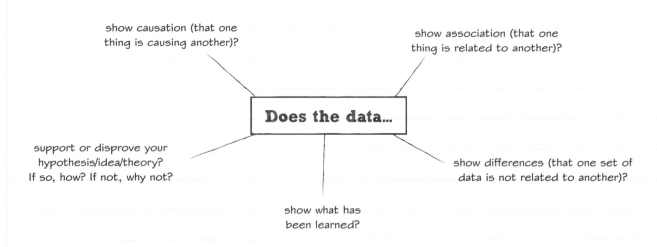

show causation (that one thing is causing another)?

show association (that one thing is related to another)?

Does the data...

support or disprove your hypothesis/idea/theory? If so, how? If not, why not?

show differences (that one set of data is not related to another)?

show what has been learned?

Now try this

1. Name **two** things you need to think about critically when reviewing sources of information.
2. Why is it important to make connections between sources?

Suitability of sources

You need to assess the suitability of secondary sources for research, to establish their reliability and validity. One way is to evaluate the **S**ource, **A**ppearance, **M**ethod, **T**imeliness, **A**pplicability, **B**alance (SAMTAB) and also to consider the ethical principles applied to the research.

S **Source:** Does it come from a reputable source (usually noted on the webpage)? Is author information included? Do you know the publisher? Note that Wikipedia may not always be a reliable source.

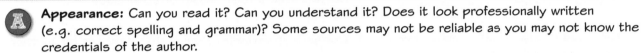
A **Appearance:** Can you read it? Can you understand it? Does it look professionally written (e.g. correct spelling and grammar)? Some sources may not be reliable as you may not know the credentials of the author.

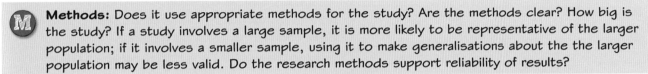
M **Methods:** Does it use appropriate methods for the study? Are the methods clear? How big is the study? If a study involves a large sample, it is more likely to be representative of the larger population; if it involves a smaller sample, using it to make generalisations about the the larger population may be less valid. Do the research methods support reliability of results?

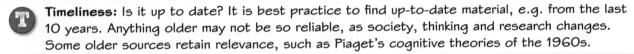
T **Timeliness:** Is it up to date? It is best practice to find up-to-date material, e.g. from the last 10 years. Anything older may not be so reliable, as society, thinking and research changes. Some older sources retain relevance, such as Piaget's cognitive theories of the 1960s.

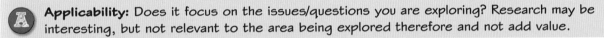
A **Applicability:** Does it focus on the issues/questions you are exploring? Research may be interesting, but not relevant to the area being explored therefore and not add value.

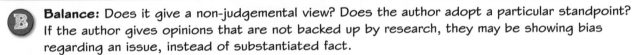
B **Balance:** Does it give a non-judgemental view? Does the author adopt a particular standpoint? If the author gives opinions that are not backed up by research, they may be showing bias regarding an issue, instead of substantiated fact.

Ethical principles checklist

Consider the suitability of sources in relationship to ethical considerations, where known:

- Have **ethical principles** been followed or referred to in the course of the research?
- Have participants given their informed consent?
- Has the author fairly represented the participants? If not, the author has not been respectful and has behaved unethically.
- Has **confidentiality** of participants been respected and safeguarded?
- Has the author acknowledged any potential **conflicts of interest** and noted how these were addressed, or suggested how these could affect the findings? If not, have you detected any concerning conflicts of interest?

Selection for literature review

In your research and assessment when you evaluate sources, you should consider:

- sources of reliable research (page 190)
- how the sources relate to each other (page 192)
- the suitability of different methods used to research an issue, e.g. qualitative (feelings), quantitative (numbers) or a mixture of both, and the reliability of results (page 192, pages 172–174)
- ethical principles (pages 177–182 and page 193).

By answering questions such as those in the SAMTAB and using an ethical principles checklist, you can assess whether each article you find is worthy of being included in your literature review.

When carrying out a literature review as part of your assessment for Unit 4, you need to match the criteria given for the research with the task brief you will be given.

Links Look at page 185 to revise keeping notes and records of sources, pages 188–189 to revise referencing techniques, and pages 204–208 for information on assessment and sources.

Now try this

Search for an article about a health and social care issue of your choice. Use the SAMTAB approach and ethical principles checklist to help assess its suitability for your research.

Interpreting quantitative data

You need to understand how data has been treated in the research papers that you read, so that you can judge the significance of results for yourself. This is an important skill in research and in your assessment for this unit, as you need to analyse the data provided, interpret the data and evaluate any quantitative conclusions drawn by the authors of the research.

Using quantitative analysis

The aim is to use numbers and **statistics** to describe a sample, in order to highlight any **significant differences** or **significant similarities** between two sample groups, or between the sample and the population.

Key terms

Correlation: a relationship or connection.

Causation: when one thing brings about another.

Dependent variable: a value that depends on another (usually the y-axis on a graph).

Independent variable: a value that doesn't depend on another (usually the x-axis on a graph).

Frequency: how often something occurs.

Raw data: data that has been gathered, before it is analysed.

Mean: average obtained by adding the values in the data set together and dividing by the number of values in the set.

Median: the middle value in a set that is arranged in numerical order.

Mode: the most common value in the set.

Standard deviation: a test to discover how much a data set varies from the mean.

Organising raw data

The first step in analysing quantitative data is organising the raw data to check its completeness and accuracy.

- Notice if any data points are outside the expected range (**outliers**).
- **Tables** can be a useful way to organise data.
- **Software packages** can help organise and interpret data.
- **Spreadsheets** can be used to record and sort data, make calculations for data analysis and draw graphs in various formats.

Analysing data

Analysing data means interpreting the information and presenting it in a meaningful way.

Statistics are often used to investigate the significance of results, giving an indication of the likelihood that a difference in two data sets could be caused by chance alone.

Interpreting quantitative data is an important aspect of the research process to help you find out how well the research answers your research questions/hypotheses.

Now try this

🔗 **Links** To revise mean, mode and median, see page 195.

1. Organise the following data set. 1, 7, 42, 6, 12, 13, 2, 7, 13, 7, 9, 2, 4, 5, 10, 10
2. Are there any outliers? If so, exclude them from your analysis.
3. Identify the mean, mode and median.

You could do this manually or you could use a spreadsheet.

Interpreting graphs and tables

You will need to understand how to interpret data from graphs and tables shown in research you have sourced. Here are some examples of the common types you may come across.

Histograms

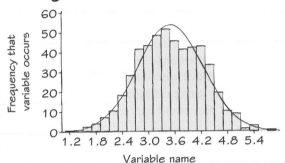

Histograms give a good idea of the overall results as well as the mean and range.

Pie charts

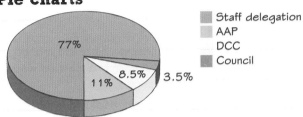

Pie charts are a good graphical form for displaying data and give an overall picture of findings. They are often used to show data sets that are parts of a whole, such as percentages.

Scatter plots

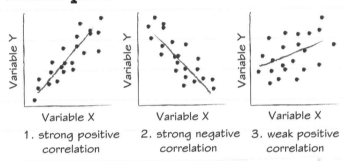

1. strong positive correlation
2. strong negative correlation
3. weak positive correlation

Scatter plots can be used to show the relationship or **correlation** between two variables.

Person graphic

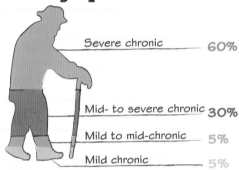

Showing **percentages** is another way of giving a good picture of overall results.

Mean, mode, median, range

1 **Mean:** add all values together and divide by the number of values:

(9 + 18 + 12 + 10 + 12 + 10 + 17 + 10 + 16) ÷ 9 = 13 (rounded)

2 **Median:** the middle value in the set when it is arranged in numerical order:

9 10 10 10 12 12 16 17 18

Note that when there is an even number of values, you find the mean of the two values in the middle.

3 **Mode:** the value that appears most often:

9 10 10 10 12 12 16 17 18

4 **Range:** the difference between the lowest and highest values:

The difference between 9 and 18 = 9

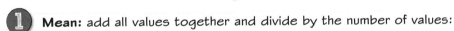

Now try this

Find the percentage for the following research findings:
(a) 45 out of 250 people like butter; (b) 7 out of 70 like eggs.

To work out a percentage, you divide the number by the total number and multiply it by 100, e.g. 35 balls bounced out of 200:
(35 ÷ 200) x 100 = 17.5%.

195

Bias in quantitative data

Bias can result from poorly planned research, and misuse of statistics can misrepresent results. You need to know about sources of bias and be aware of how statistics can be misused.

Sources of bias

 Leading questions

A leading or **loaded** question makes it more likely that a respondent will answer in a certain way, leading to bias in the results.

The proper way to conduct research is to ask **non-leading** questions.

Leading question: 'Was your experience of treatment good?'

Non-leading question: 'How was your experience of treatment?'

 Sample bias

A researcher may find they cannot collect data equally from each sample, so some samples are under-represented and some samples are over-represented. For example, it may be very difficult to access samples of some sections of the population, such as homeless people or drug users.

Misuse of data

 Sample size and generalisations

Small samples may be **non-representative** and could give **unreliable** data. Consider the statement: '98% of people in care believe care standards have dropped in the last 10 years'. 98% of what? You could generalise from 98% of 10,000 people but not from 98% of 10 people.

 Validity

It may be true to say that 80% of dentists recommend FreshBrite toothpaste. But is the statement actually **valid** if dentists were asked to recommend three brands of toothpaste?

 Selective use of data

A researcher may be selective in their use of data, picking information that supports their argument and making vague or dismissive statements about data that does not.

Recognising bias in graphs, tables and statistics

To recognise bias, be aware that:

- The scales on the axes of graphs can be manipulated to make data look more or less significant.
- A table of selected data might give a false impression.
- Bias in statistics can occur through poor questioning, or using an inappropriate sampling or research method.

Risk of bias and misuse of data

Evidence-based policy making uses research results to guide a government's policies. When research is carried out correctly, evidence-based policy making has advantages. However, the implications of changing policy and practice based on biased, incorrect or untruthful research results are huge.

The Wakefield MMR case (see page 178) shows how incorrect research results can influence the public, causing them to change their behaviour.

Links Look at pages 172 and 173 to revise open and closed **questions**, page 176 for **sampling**, page 182 for **bias** and page 190 for **generalisations**.

Now try this

1. Devise a leading question and non-leading question on a health and social care topic.
2. Predict how the leading question could influence the answers you would receive.
3. If your question was part of a wider study, how could your biased findings influence policy or practice?

Interpreting qualitative data

You need to understand how to interpret qualitative data in research and also in source material, so that you can judge the significance of results for yourself.

Qualitative v quantitative

Interpreting qualitative data is very different from interpreting quantitative data. It involves making sense of what people **say and do**, rather than finding meaning in numbers.

Making sense of qualitative data is sometimes called **interpretive** research (as the researcher has to deduce the meaning in the participants' responses), whereas using numbers and statistics can give **definitive** results.

Qualitative data

The researcher makes transcripts of interviews and recordings, uses responses from open-ended surveys and questionnaires, analyses case studies and makes observations of behaviour. This produces largely unstructured data that has to be analysed.

One person's interview may be very different from another's. To analyse interviews, the researcher has to identify common themes running through all the different transcripts.

Approaches to analysis

Different research skills are used when interpreting qualitative data. Here are some examples.

1 **Analysing transcripts**

Researchers analyse data from transcripts and make notes using:

☑ skim and scan reading skills to identify patterns and trends in people's words – highlighter pens are useful for **coding** different **themes**

☑ software such as NVivo – 'a platform for analysing unstructured data'.

Be aware that interpretation of data may depend on a researcher's perspective and so may be open to bias.

2 **Identifying themes**

Analysis of transcripts involves looking for repeating themes in data. This might be carried out manually or using technology. These themes may emerge from the data (**inductive**) or start with an idea or theory (**deductive**).

3 **Inductive approach**

☑ 'Bottom up' approach

☑ Theory emerges from the research:

Research ▶ Patterns ▶ Tentative conclusions ▶ Theory

4 **Deductive approach**

☑ 'Top down' approach

☑ Starts with an idea or theory

☑ Results confirm or challenge original theory:

Theory ▶ Hypothesis ▶ Research ▶ Confirmation of hypothesis

Now try this

1 Why is interpreting qualitative data different from interpreting quantitative data?

2 What research skills do you need to analyse qualitative data?

Interpreting words

Interpreting qualitative data involves using research skills to interpret language data, distinguish between fact and opinion, and identify bias.

Distinguishing between fact and opinion

- A **fact** is something that has actually happened or that is true and can be supported by evidence.
- An **opinion** is a belief, so can vary based on a person's perspective, emotions or individual understanding of something.

When you interpret language data you need to take an objective and non-judgemental approach, and identify bias. A professional journal is likely to contain mainly facts. A blog or Twitter post may contain mainly opinion.

Analysing data

Transcribing, coding and interpreting qualitative data is a time-consuming process which requires patience and organisation. Here are some approaches.

 Interpreting information

Qualitative data includes information about people's feelings and experiences, opinions and knowledge, expressed in their own words. The researcher needs to:

- transcribe data word by word (**verbatim**)
- interpret **non-verbal** communication
- **code and categorise** sections of text
- understand what was said and deduce what was meant.

 Coding and categorising data

This important aspect of analysing qualitative data involves subdividing large amounts of raw data and assigning these portions to **categories**.

- **Codes** are tags or labels for allocating portions of text to different themes, trends or patterns. Numbers and colours make useful coding systems.
- **Coded sections** are reorganised to bring text with similar themes together.

The researcher is looking for repeated patterns that will show connections between the sources of information in the data.

 Using different types of analysis

Content	Used with verbal or behaviour data, to classify or summarise
Narrative	Used to transcribe experiences
Discourse	Used to understand everyday usage of language (spoken and written text)
Framework	Includes transcribing, reading, identifying themes, coding by theme and interpreting
Grounded theory	Inductive method for examining a single case, generating a theory, examining the next case and revising a theory

---

Now try this

1. Ask three friends about their experiences of healthcare, either as a patient or as a relative of a patient. Have these been positive or negative experiences? As a result, how do they feel about their potential use of healthcare services in the future?

2. Are there common themes and connections that you can identify in the three interviews? Be aware of what is fact and what is opinion, and take a non-judgemental approach.

Bias in qualitative data

A key research skill is the ability to identify potential sources of bias, error or misuse of data in literature, methods, analysis and conclusions of research.

Sources of bias, error and misuse

Sources of bias that are common to qualitative and quantitative data collections include leading questions and sample bias. Additional sources of bias in relation to qualitative data are due to:

- the interpersonal nature of the data-collection process
- distinguishing between fact and opinion.

Links See page 196 to revise bias in quantitative data and page 198 to revise fact and opinion and bias.

Recognising bias, error and misuse

Researchers need to be aware of the reliability of different kinds of sources and identify bias, error and misuse of data.

Researcher bias

The researcher personally impacts on the quality of data. Body language, facial expression, tone of voice, style of language, dress, social status, race and gender can all influence the responses.

An open and relaxed questioner will receive different responses to someone who is tense, hurried, or aggressive in questioning.

Conformity error

The **Asch line judgement conformity study** is a good example of conformity error. The people in the experiment were asked to match a line length given in Exhibit 1 to one of the lines given in Exhibit 2. The answer was obvious. The aim of the study was to see which line the subject would choose if all members of the group had already given the same, obviously wrong answer. The tendency is to conform and give the incorrect answer!

2 Respondent bias

Here are some examples of respondent bias.

☑ **Acquiescence bias**: when respondents tend to agree with the researcher or respond in a way they think the researcher expects.

☑ **Dominant participant bias**: may occur in a focus group, when a dominant personality influences the responses from the group.

☑ **Social desirability bias**: when respondents give a response that is socially acceptable to make them look good, rather than truthful.

☑ **Mood bias**: the participant's mood at the time of questioning can influence results.

Changing how data is gathered can reduce respondent bias. For example, social bias can be reduced if respondents complete the survey anonymously or if confidentiality is guaranteed.

Misuse of qualitative data

Due to the more subjective nature of qualitative data, it can be easy to misinterpret research findings. Findings may also be misrepresented, just as results from quantitative data can, and the risks of doing so are the same.

Now try this

1 How can researcher bias affect data collection?
2 Give an example of respondent bias.

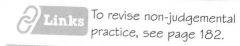 **Links** To revise non-judgemental practice, see page 182.

Recommendations for practice

Findings from research lead to recommendations for changes to working practice. Improving practice in health and social care helps to provide the best possible services for service users.

Research aims

Research in health and social care aims to:

- ✓ improve outcomes for people using services
- ✓ improve working practice by informing policy and practice
- ✓ extend knowledge and understanding
- ✓ identify gaps in provision
- ✓ improve provision
- ✓ improve life in society for all of us.

Research into working practice

Research into health and social care practice can improve working practices. From time to time, your professional body may change its code of practice or advice to professionals based on the findings of research. You should be aware of any developments in your field.

Links See pages 168–169 to revise the purposes of research, and issues in health and social care.

The research cycle

This is how the research cycle can be applied to research into health and social care practice.

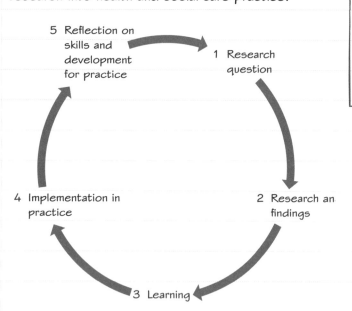

1 Research question
2 Research and findings
3 Learning
4 Implementation in practice
5 Reflection on skills and development for practice

Research log

Developments in research will guide parts of your professional development during your working life. It is good practice to keep a log where you can record learning and its impact on your professional practice. You can also record any research that has an impact on your practice.

Now try this

1 How can current research support your continued professional development to improve practice?

2 How do you intend to keep up to date with developments in your field?

 Many workplaces have a subscription to a professional journal to enable practitioners to keep up to date. Your professional body will also publish relevant articles on research findings in their magazine or on their website.

Recommendations for provision

Findings from research lead to recommendations and potential for changes to provision of services, improving outcomes for those who use the services.

Implications for provision

Research leads to changes in the treatment of health conditions. This type of research is carried out by organisations such as:

- the National Institute for Health Research (NIHR)
- the Department of Health (DH) and other government departments
- the Medical Research Council (MRC)
- pharmaceutical companies
- other healthcare companies
- technology companies.

Improving outcomes for people

An example of research leading to change in provision and improving outcomes for people was carried out by the National Collaborating Centre for Primary Care with the Royal College of General Practitioners (Nunes et al., 2009).

- The research showed that over a third of all medication prescribed to treat those with long-term conditions is not taken properly.
- This led to companies developing new technologies to allow service users and providers to monitor and improve how medication is taken; for example, using pills containing sensors, combined with drugs that pass data to a smartphone app when the pill dissolves in the stomach.
- Using such technology more widely will lead to an improvement both in the treatment of healthcare conditions and in practice when providing care and support.

Benefiting society

Some research findings lead to benefits for society as a whole. For example, much contemporary research has been conducted into childhood obesity. Oxford University published a report in the peer-reviewed *British Medical Journal* (Friedemann C., et al., 2012) of their findings that obese children are more likely to suffer heart attacks or strokes in adulthood.

The associated benefit of reducing the number of adult heart attacks and strokes is the saving in the cost of provision of care.

Benefits of research to provision

Research findings can have benefits that inform practice and provision for positive outcomes for individuals and society, and help target resources in health and social care efficiently.

Links See pages 168–169 to revise the purposes of research and issues in health and social care.

Research into childhood obesity can result in outcomes that help reduce the number of adults suffering heart attacks or strokes, also reducing other health risks and benefiting society.

Now try this

Look at a few pieces of research you have identified. Taking a non-judgemental approach, assess the possible implications of the research for the provision of health and social care services.

Reflecting on research

It is useful to reflect on both the importance of doing research and your role in the process.

Your role

Your role is important in the research process.

- As a **practitioner**, you know how research can make a difference to practice, provision and people's lives. You can use research findings to improve your own personal practice and encourage others to do the same.

- As a **researcher**, you can formulate your research questions to have positive impacts in these areas.

Your aims

You might undertake research to:

- find out new knowledge
- discover new ways of doing things
- understand things – health conditions, people's behaviours, why interventions work and don't work
- make a positive impact on policy, practice and/ or people's lives.

Now try this

What are you good at? What do you need to work at? Rate your abilities with each of the skills below. Use any system you like – a number score, traffic light system, or just make notes about what you need to do to improve and revise with the pages shown.

To be an effective researcher, you should have the skills to:

1 understand the purpose, issues and rationale for research (revise pages 168, 169 and 171)

2 use time management techniques and organisational skills (revise page 170)

3 identify and use research methods, questions and target groups (revise page 172–176)

4 identify and carry out ethical practice (revise pages 177–181)

5 identify and implement non-judgemental practice (revise page 182)

6 be able to make notes and keep records from source material (revise pages 183–185)

7 use a variety of reading techniques, such as skimming and scanning (revise page 186)

8 understand the conventions of academic writing, including the introduction, methodology, results and conclusion, and presenting bibliography and reference lists (revise pages 187–189)

9 select key sources and identify features of this literature (revise pages 190, 191 and 193)

10 show connections between reliable sources of information (revise page 192)

11 analyse data using valid methods, including compiling data, results and findings, triangulation, interpreting graphs and tables, using percentages and statistical averages, selecting relevant numerical data and drawing conclusions (revise pages 194–195)

12 be critical, picking up on bias or misuse of data, assessing the validity of generalisations and distinguishing between fact and opinion (revise pages 196, 198 and 199).

Notice that these are also the skills that you need in order to use research to become an effective practitioner!

It is important to reflect on the research process to help you understand the implications on your practice and wider provision of services. Reflection is an important tool to help identify future needs and help make a positive impact on people's lives.

Had a look ☐   Nearly there ☐   Nailed it! ☐

Your Unit 4 set task

You will be assessed for Unit 4 **under exam conditions**. You will show your understanding of research methodologies and associated issues by responding to a provided piece of current research on **either** health **or** social care, and your own related secondary research. Your assessment is divided into Part A and Part B.

Part A: set task brief and research

In Part A you undertake research that prepares you to complete your set task in Part B. You choose a provided piece of **current research** on **either** health **or** social care.

✓ You **analyse** the piece of research.

✓ You then carry out your own **related independent secondary research**, using at least **two** secondary sources.

✓ You prepare a **list of references** for your secondary sources.

✓ You make **notes** on your secondary research.

✓ You can take up to **six sides** of A4 notes into your Part B supervised assessment.

✓ You will be allowed **18 hours** across a period of six weeks to complete Part A.

> 🔗 **Links** See page 184 to revise secondary research and secondary sources.

Part B: completing your set task

In Part B you use your preparation from Part A to complete your set task.

✓ You will be given a **taskbook** at the beginning of your assessment period. You must complete it **independently** and under **supervised conditions**. It contains space for your responses and is submitted for assessment.

✓ You will need to provide a **list of the secondary sources** you have used in Part A.

✓ You are asked **four questions** based on **either** the health **or** social care research, and your **own research** in Part A.

✓ Your Part A notes will **not** be submitted for assessment.

✓ You have **three hours** over three days to complete Part B. You must not take anything into or out of the supervised assessment without permission.

Part B questions

You will need to refer to your chosen article from the set task brief in Part A and your notes on your own secondary research sources. The four questions in Part B relate to the assessment focus areas below and are worth a total of 65 marks. Suggestions are given for how you might allocate your time.

1. Understanding **research methods** and the **validity** and **reliability of results** in research. (15 marks) (40 mins)

2. Understanding the **relationship** between your **own secondary research** and the **provided article**, and how this relationship reinforces the **importance of the issue**. (15 marks) (40 mins)

3. **Planning** and **ethical** considerations for further research. (15 marks) (40 mins)

4. **Research implications** for **future provision** and/or **practice**. (20 marks) (50 mins)

You will also need to **list the secondary sources** you have used (10 mins).

> ## Now try this
>
> 1 In Part A, what is the minimum number of secondary research sources you must use?
> 2 In Part B, how many sides of notes made in Part A can you take into the assessment?
> 3 What is submitted for assessment?

Part A: Planning research

You will need to plan your 18 hours to analyse and carry out research for Part A, and bring together six A4 sides of notes that you can refer to in your supervised assessment. Your notes will then be kept securely with your taskbook until the supervised assessment sessions end.

Sample notes extract

A	Select, read and annotate the health **or** social care article provided in the task information, using the six headings noted in F below.	4 hrs
B	Familiarise myself with the article, making notes and identifying issues, using the six headings noted in F below.	
C	Note keywords for secondary research sources, to research identified issues.	4 hrs
D	Research and create records of possible sources for secondary research that best relate to the issue in the article. (Look at the bibliography and source of the article as a starting place for possible linked sources; consider the focus of the four Part B questions; consider the different research methods.)	
E	Assess reliability of secondary sources, with reference to **S**ource, **A**ppearance, **M**ethod, **T**imeliness, **A**pplicability and **B**alance (SAMTAB), ethical considerations and links in relation to the article and the four Part B questions.	8 hrs
F	Make notes on secondary research sources under six headings, also noting relationship to my chosen article: **1** What was the research piece about? (what it explored, why important, what the study looked at to find out) **2** What were the key methods used in the research and were they reliable? (e.g qualitative, quantitative, mix of both; how they supported reliability of research) **3** What were the key findings in the research? (e.g. what were the results of the study? Did they answer the research questions? What were the conclusions/importance of the issues?) **4** Were any recommendations or future research plans discussed? (e.g. do they recommend further research? Did any aspects of the research not go well? Consider proposal, methods, reliability, research skills required, ethical considerations, timescales.) **5** What could be the implications/impact on individual practice? (e.g. how can this type of research affect individuals in the workplace? How will it affect individual practice?) **6** What could the implications/impact be on service provision? (e.g. what are the implications on society? What is the cost and effectiveness of service providers?)	
G	Organise six sides of A4 notes to take into my Part B assessment for use with questions 1–4. Include my list of secondary sources, in alphabetical order, using a referencing system (e.g. Harvard). Ensure my notes are clear and easy to use. Print out six sides with my notes on all analysed articles.	2 hrs

✓ This plan breaks down the key stages for Part A in a detailed, clear and logical way. You need a plan that works for you and that you can check progress against.

✓ This plan uses a method for searching, assessing and making notes in a structured way. You need to bring together key information to draw on for the focus of the four Part B questions.

✓ The plan allocates time at the end to organise notes and list secondary sources using a referencing system, so the information is presented in a way that is easy to take in and use for Part B. Notes are being made on a computer and a clear printout will be used in Part B.

Now try this

Consider the time allocation in the plan above. Think about what is involved in each of the stages and make a note of estimated timings in more detail for each of the stages.

Part A: Assessing sources

You need to assess the relevance and validity of pieces of current secondary research that you find, in order to select the most appropriate secondary sources. One way of doing this is to consider the Source, Appearance, Method, Timeliness, Applicability, Balance (SAMTAB) and ethical principles.

Sample notes extract

Assessing reliability and validity of a source –

Source, Appearance, Method, Timeliness, Applicability, Balance (SAMTAB)

TITLE, AUTHOR, SOURCE

Use a referencing format (e.g. Harvard) for the list of sources you will use in your Part B assessment.

Roos, J.H. (2005) Nurses' perceptions of difficult patients. *Health SA Gesondheid*, 10(1), pp.52–61.

SOURCE

Does the resource come from a reputable source/journal (usually noted on the webpage)? Is author information included? Do you know the publisher? Note that Wikipedia may not always be a reliable source.

Article sourced: HSAG (Health South Africa Gesonheid), [Online], Available: http://www.hsag.co.za/index.php/HSAG/article/viewFile/188/179 [10 January 2015]

APPEARANCE

Can you read it and understand it? Does it look professionally written (e.g. correct spelling and grammar)? Some sources may not necessarily be reliable as you may not know the credentials of the author.

The appearance of the website link to PDF, plus the journal article itself, looks authentic; relevant information is given; source is reputable.

METHODS

Does it use appropriate methods for the study? Are the methods clear? How big is the study? Do the research methods support reliability of results? Is the method similar to the provided article, or different?

This article reports that a qualitative descriptive research design was adopted using 81 narratives. This was culturally specific, with nursing students in one university. When assessing reliability, the sample size will need to be considered. In relationship to the provided article...

In this extract of notes assessing secondary sources, an appropriate source has been identified. You need to make brief notes as you assess sources, then expand the notes to evaluate how useful the source will be when answering the four Part B questions. Your notes should make the relationship to the provided article clear.

Now try this

Search for a secondary research source related to 'difficult patients'. Complete a SAMTAB and brief notes using the six headings: Source, Appearance, Method, Timeliness, Applicability, Balance. Evaluate the source for ethical principles as well.

Links Look at page 193 for a complete SAMTAB and an ethical principles checklist you can use when assessing suitability of sources.

Part A: Making notes

Notes need to be relevant and detailed enough to be of use when answering the four Part B questions. The examples below cover research methods and key findings, based on Koekkoek, B., *et al*, (2011). How do patients come to be seen as 'difficult'?: A mixed methods study in community mental health care, *Social Science and Medicine*, 72(4), pp.504–12.

Sample notes extract

This extract from notes on methods records that mixed methods are used, and explains what this means.

What were the key methods used in the research and were they reliable?

Research by Koekkoek et al. (2011) used a mixed methods approach, using both qualitative and quantitative methods. The research involved reanalysing previous mixed methods research projects based on Parson's sick role concept to understand the links between previous studies and the current one, concerning 'difficult patients'.

The notes correctly include detail about:
- method used
- how it was used
- participants (number and who)
- purpose of method.

The notes are going on to show how far the methods support reliable outcomes.

- Design used mixed methods from previous literature reviews based on four empirical studies.
- Mixed methods Delphi study (a method of gaining data from people within their area of expertise to build a consensus, in this study a group of experts).
- Quantitative survey (professionals' ratings on whether they would label a patient 'difficult' using logistic regression) (yes/no; 0/1).
- Qualitative ground study (developing a theory from interviews with 21 difficult patients).
- Three case reports (experts reviewed case reports to identify possible interventions).
- The results could be considered reliable because triangulation was ...

Sample notes extract

What were the key findings in the research (conclusions/importance)?

Patients: perceived themselves as needing help and blamed professionals for being too pessimistic, and not understanding their health issues.

Professionals: saw patients as having complex interrelating issues associated with illness, e.g. unemployment, housing issues, poverty.

Experts: looked more at pyschopathological issues than social problems, defining patients using unusual help-seeking styles. They stated that professional pessimism was a contributory factor especially as, for example, personality disorders and some help-seeking styles were viewed negatively by some professionals. They looked beyond the patient/professional characteristics and noted that patients and professionals shape responses on the basis of one another. They had a view that many professionals work alone with patients and are unsure of what to do, with no support, which can affect quality and professionalism.

In this extract from notes on key findings, the notes summarise the research in quite a lot of detail to draw out key findings and main results.

The notes are structured and will be clear to draw on when answering the four questions in Part B.

Now try this

1 Explain why patients being labelled as 'difficult' might be an important research issue.

2 Search for an appropriate secondary research source related to 'difficult patients' and make notes about it.

 You could use the article used in the SAMTAB on page 206 and the six headings in the plan on page 205.

Part B: Listing sources

For Part B you will need to provide a list of the secondary research sources you used in Part A. You are required to use at least two secondary research sources. You need to follow a conventional style for referencing. The sources listed in the example here are a guide to how different sources are cited using a referencing system known as Harvard.

Worked example

SECTION 1: Health research

Article 1: How do patients come to be seen as 'difficult'?

Provide a list of secondary sources you have used in addition to **Article 1**.

Sample response extract

Carter, L. (2012) What can we do about 'difficult' patients? Nursing Times, [Online], Available: www.nursingtimes.net/student-nt/what-can-we-do-about-difficult-patients/5044825.fullarticle [20 May 2016].

Manos, P.J., Braun, J. (2006) Care of the Difficult Patient: A Nurse's Guide. Oxford: Routledge.

Roos, J.H. (2005) Nurses' perceptions of difficult patients. Health SA Gesondheid 10(1) pp.52–61.

Wanderfelt R., and Blink, B. (2012) Burnout: Dealing with difficult patients. The Only Journal on Difficult Patients. 12(2) pp.405–9.

> It is conventional to list the sources in alphabetical order.

> You need to use a conventional style to reference a source from the internet.

> You need to use a conventional style to reference a book source, with the book title in italics or underlined.

> You need to use a conventional style to reference a journal article, with the journal title in italics or underlined, and the title of the article not in italics.

> NB: this last journal article reference is fictitious and has been used to provide an example for the sample response.

Now try this

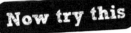

Carry out an internet search for one journal article, one book and one webpage about this issue and cite each one using a conventional style of reference.

> You can find guides on the internet for conventional ways of presenting references.

 Links See pages 188–189 to revise referencing.

Part B Q1: Research methods

In Question 1 you need to focus on how research methods have been used and the validity and reliability of results, both in the research article provided and in your own secondary sources.

Worked example

1 How have research methods been used to extract data in this article and other articles you have researched about the issue?

In your answer you should include:

- what other methods of research have been used to explore the issue
- how reliable the results of the research methods are.

15 marks

You need to use your notes from Part A to explain the research methods and use of data in the provided article and at least two secondary sources. Include the suitability of the research methods and how they support the reliability of the findings. Comment on any issues that may have affected the results. You will write around two sides of a page in your taskbook.

Sample response extract

In the study conducted by Koekkoek, qualitative and quantitative methods were used which included qualitative and quantitative data from a previous literature review, a mixed methods Delphi study, quantitative survey, qualitative ground study and three case reports.

 When referring to a provided article, you need to give a **full reference**. In this extract from a response, only a brief reference is made.

 You need to go beyond stating methods and **explain** what a Delphi study is.

 You should include the number of participants and **explain** what they did.

Improved response extract

Research conducted by Koekkoek et al. (2011) used a mixed methods approach combining both qualitative and quantitative methods. The research involved reanalysing previous mixed methods research projects based upon Parson's sick role concept, to understand the links between previous studies and the current one. Methods used included mixed methods from previous literature reviews based on four empirical studies and a mixed methods Delphi study. A Delphi study is a method of gaining data from experts to build a consensus. A quantitative survey was also used, with professionals providing a rating on whether they would label a patient 'difficult' using logistic regression (yes/no; 0/1). Other methods included a qualitative ground study, developing a theory from interviews with 21 difficult patients, and reviews of three case reports, done by experts to identify possible interventions.

 In this extract from a response, a full reference is given to the provided article.

 More information is provided to help understand the methods.

 The response **explains** mixed methods and the Delphi study using better **terminology**.

The response **identifies** the number of **participants** and **what they did**.

Now try this

Choose a piece of research. Identify: what methods were used for what purpose; the participants; and the sample type and size (for example, if a questionnaire was sent to a specified number of care homes).

 **Links** See pages 171–176 to revise research methods and target groups and samples.

Part B Q1: Suitability of methods

You should explain research methods clearly, using the correct terminology.

Sample response extract

In another study conducted by Wanderfelt and Blithe, they also used quantitative and qualitative methods. They used surveys asking people to rate how stressful it was dealing with difficult patients. They also used interviews with professionals to find out how they perceived 'difficult' patients.

 In this extract the learner is referring to their own secondary research. You need to give a **correct and full** reference, but this reference is brief and incorrect (using the wrong name for one of the researchers).

 You need to **make clear** which are the qualitative and quantitative elements of the study, and why they are suitable. Here it is not clear.

Improved response extract

The study conducted by Wanderfelt and Blink (2012) also used quantitative and qualitative methods (being a mixed methods design). For the quantitative element, the survey asked participants to rate the level of stress they experienced when dealing with 'difficult patients', using a Likert scale. This is a common method, for example a scale of between 1 and 10. The qualitative aspect of the study comprised interviewing ten healthcare professionals about who they perceived as difficult patients. Using a Likert scale is good, as it is a commonly used method, making it recognisable and easily understood. It is also easily quantifiable for analysis and does not require the participant to take a definite yes or no stand on the issue. One drawback of the method is that there might be a tendency for people not to pick the extremes of the scale even if that is their most accurate answer.

 In this extract referring to the learner's own secondary research, the learner **cites the source correctly**.

 It is clear that **quantitative** research was used. The response explains the methodology and its **suitability**, using **correct terminology**.

 The **qualitative** elements of the study are clear.

 The response shows the learner knows the **advantages** and **disadvantages** of a Likert scale.

Now try this

Using a source that you have identified, select a method of research and explain it in detail. Make sure you include how the method was used to explore the issue, and its suitability and reliability.

 Use the correct terminology for your methods and detailed explanations.

 Links See pages 172–176 to revise research methods, advantages and disadvantages, and reliability.

Part B Q1: Methods and reliability

You need to assess how reliable the results of the research methods are in your provided article and in your own related secondary research sources.

Sample response extract

Because there were so many methods used in the study, it might be that the study is considered reliable. However, the authors did rely on other research projects and chose what they wanted to put in. Also, the sample size was small.

In this extract on the Koekkoek research, only a **basic** answer is given is given to the question on how **reliable the results** of the research methods used are, with limited information.

Improved response extract

Using a triangulation of methods, as in Koekkoek et al. (2011), does help to make a study more reliable. However, in this study the authors did say they used 'secondary analysis' of recent research projects and, although they tried to stay close to the findings of these studies, they chose which parts they wanted to put into their study. This means that they were being judgemental or selective about what they chose. The samples in their study were also small, which would make it harder to make generalisations, so the study cannot be applied to everyone.

This extract provides detail on how reliable the learner finds the results of the research methods to be. Answering in this way shows how well they understand the research aims of the study, its methods and results.

Sample response extract

This study only had a small sample so the results cannot be used to say with certainty that it would apply to everyone.

In this extract on the Wanderfelt research, the response provides only basic information about the reliability of methods and how this impacts on whether the results can be relied upon. You need to clearly show how the methods used might be unreliable.

Improved response extract

Using a mix of qualitative and quantitative methods (mixed methods) is a good way to increase the reliability of any research. However, the study by Wanderfelt and Blink (2012) was based on only a small sample, so although the results can be useful in informing future research, they may not be reliable for making generalisations as there was a limited range of responses.

This extract provides detail about the reliability of methods and explains what that might mean in terms of usage and results. Providing more detailed information shows you understand the research aims of the study, its methods and results.

Links See pages 170, 172–174, 176 and 190, to revise triangulation, methods, reliability of results, samples and generalisations.

Now try this

Explain why using a triangulation of methods may help to make research results more reliable.

Part B Q2: Research issues and significance

In Question 2 you need to focus on understanding the relationship between the provided article and your own secondary research, and how this relationship reinforces the importance of the issue.

Worked example

2 Why is research that leads to a better understanding of patients who are labelled as 'difficult' important for individuals?

In your answer you should include how far your secondary research supports the conclusions drawn in the article.   **15 marks**

You should analyse the issue, leading to a **conclusion** about the **issue's importance**. Provide relevant **examples** of effects on individuals, and **support** these from the research findings. Assess **how far** your secondary research supports the conclusions of the provided article. Your response should be **objective**, based on facts and examples from the research. You will write around two sides of a page in your taskbook.

Sample response extract

This article was about how patients are labelled as difficult. This study showed that it is because the professionals don't think the patient is really ill and the patient gets cross about it. For example, my mum was told she was a difficult patient, and she is!

This extract refers to the provided article. Although the outline and conclusions are correct, there are not many examples of what professionals feel makes the patient difficult. The final sentence is not an objective judgement that summarises the article's position.

Improved response extract

This article aimed to gain a better understanding of how patients come to be labelled as 'difficult'. Conclusions from Koekkoek et al. (2011) have shown that the label of 'difficult patient' was often given by professionals when they could find no physical illness, but some aspect of the patient's behaviour, e.g. mental functioning, influenced their decisions to label patients as 'difficult'.

In this extract referring to the provided article, the response starts by providing an outline of the article and its conclusions, making clear the intention of the study.

Koekkoek et al.'s study (2011) showed the importance of professionals exploring, and being aware of, their own attitudes, behaviours and perceptions. If professionals change their perceptions, it will have a positive impact on patients as they will feel 'believed'. It may also result in cost savings as treatments will be less expensive and patients' recovery rates will improve.

The response provides an objective judgement that summaries the article's position.

The response goes on to say why the research in the provided article is important to individuals in health and social care practice. Make sure that you bring in evidence that supports your conclusions.

Now try this

Choose a research article that interests you. Write a short paragraph that outlines its purpose and main conclusions. Show why the research issue is important for individuals, supporting your points with examples from the research.

Part B Q2: Research conclusions

You need to show how far your own secondary research supports the conclusions drawn in the provided research article.

Sample response extract

Other research has also found that professionals label patients as difficult and they have said there is a need to change professionals' attitudes and perceptions so the patient thinks they are being treated positively and to make them feel more responsible and autonomous.

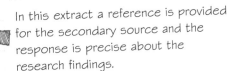

In this extract on research conclusions, a reference is made to other research findings but it is very general. You need to be **precise** about the findings and **cite the author** so that readers can find the research you are referring to.

Improved response extract

Roos (2005) asked nursing professionals about their experience and level of stress when dealing with difficult patients. Here, too, a label of 'difficult' was given to those patients and Roos stated that there is a need for clear guidelines to help professionals promote patient autonomy, motivation and empowerment. This will help the patient to still be recognised as being ill but to feel more responsible and autonomous. These views have also been found in other research (Wanderfelt and Blink, 2012).

In this extract a reference is provided for the secondary source and the response is precise about the research findings.

This response cites another secondary source which gives **further support**, **validity and reliability** to the claims that the secondary research supports the conclusions of the provided research article.

Referencing your sources

Along with stating your secondary sources at the start of Part B, make sure that you reference your sources when you refer to them in your answers so your readers know which research you are referring to and can find it themselves if they wish to.

Links See pages 188–189 to revise referencing your sources.

Now try this

Find a secondary research source that is related to the issues in the provided research article. You could use the one you found for the 'Now try this' on page 207. Write a short paragraph that outlines its purpose and main conclusions, and why the research is important for individuals. Explain how far this secondary source supports the conclusions drawn in the provided research article.

Part B Q3: Further research and methods

In Question 3 you focus on planning and ethical considerations for further research.

Worked example

3 You are planning to carry out further research into a better understanding of patients who are labelled as 'difficult'. What will you need to consider when planning this research?

You should refer to the article and to your own secondary research.

15 marks

You will need to suggest **research methods** that you could use to continue research into the issue, and **justify** why they are **suitable**. You need to cover **planning considerations**, **ethical issues** and **the research skills** required to explore the issue, including any **practical considerations**. You should **support any judgements** on the importance of these considerations. You should aim to write about two sides of a page in your taskbook.

Sample response extract

For future research I would conduct research on the ways that the patients and professionals develop relationships. I would conduct questionnaires and interviews with health professionals and some patients to ask them about how they feel that patients are diagnosed and treated. I would also conduct some observations on how patients and professionals interact.

 This extract states the methods the learner would use in their study, but the **details** and **description** of their purpose are too brief.

Improved response extract

For future research I would want to explore the ways that professionals develop relationships with patients to find out how the label of 'difficult patient' could be applied by some. To do this I would need to conduct observations of professionals and patients to see how they interact and the relationships they have. I would conduct interviews with professionals and patients in order to understand what these two groups think about diagnosis and treatment. Finally, conducting questionnaires with professionals who are not the participants, and asking for their views on diagnosis and support of patients perceived to be difficult, may help me to understand ways of improving patient and professional relationships and of empowering patients to be more proactive in their recovery and wellbeing.

 This extract explains the type of research the learner would want to carry out.

 The learner **justifies** why they use the methods of observation, interviews and questionnaires.

 The learner **expands** their response to provide a **rationale** as to why their research will be **effective**.

Links See page 170 to revise factors involved in planning research.

Planning further research

You must consider the participants, methods and ethics when planning to conduct a good piece of research. You need to consider:

- ✓ the type of research you would undertake (e.g. the research title)
- ✓ the methods that you could use (e.g. triangulation of methods; ensuring reliability)
- ✓ the participants: how many and whether they will be randomly selected or not
- ✓ how this research is effective and suitable (e.g. if it builds on previous research)
- ✓ planning considerations (e.g. ethics, research skills)
- ✓ whether and how this research will impact on health and social care practice and provision.

Now try this

Using the information from page 207 onwards, make notes of further research you would plan to carry out into the issue of patients labelled as 'difficult'. Provide justification for the research methods you would use.

Part B Q3: Further research and ethics

In your answer to Question 3 you will need to demonstrate your understanding of the ethical issues that relate to your research and the impact it will have.

Sample response extract

In planning this research one of the important things to look at is the ethical considerations. I need to make sure that I have been given permission to do the study and also that I have the consent of all the participants to do the study. For this I would need to tell them about the research I want to conduct and their involvement and get their consent. I would need to make sure that I follow the ethical codes of conduct and any legislation that is relevant.

This extract identifies the need to consider **ethical issues** related to the research but it is too brief.

The response identifies the need to follow **ethical codes** and any **legislation** relating to participants but doesn't provide detail.

Improved response extract

In planning this research it is important to consider ethical issues. I need to ensure that, firstly, I have permission from the settings to carry out my research. I also need to make sure that participants give informed consent. I need to make sure that patients have the mental capacity to give consent and understand the nature of the study. I have referred to the British Psychological Society's ethical codes of conduct and those of my organisation. I need to receive informed consent from all my participants, telling them about my study and that their participation is voluntary so they can withdraw their consent at any time. In research it is important that I adhere to legislation such as the Data Protection Act 1998 which sets out how I can store and use people's information. For example, I will keep all data in a locked filing cabinet or password-protected computer. All names will be changed.

This extract identifies the need to obtain **permission** from the settings where participants may be, as well as the **informed consent** of participants.

You need to consider whether the patients have the **mental capacity** to take part.

You need to show you are following a recognised body's code of ethical conduct.

You need to show you understand the need to gain **informed consent** by telling the participants about the study, what you want the participants to do and how you will use the information.

You need to show awareness of the **legislation** that governs **protection of personal data** and how the information will be stored.

Now try this

Use the research information from page 207 onwards and the further research plans on page 214 to make notes on the ethical considerations involved in your further research plans.

 Links See pages 177–181 to revise ethical considerations in research.

Part B Q3: Further research and planning

Your answer needs to show how you will plan and organise your further research, including the skills you need and realistic timescales.

Sample response extract

To be able to carry out future research in this area I would need to make sure that I have taken account of the skills I need to conduct the research, and also be aware of any issues that might stop me from completing the research in the time I have. I need to set realistic timescales to complete the study and set deadlines for completing each aspect. I need to be able to find research literature quickly and be able to report it accurately. I need to apply non-judgemental practice in my research.

 This extract acknowledges the main **planning considerations** but needs to give more detail and examples.

 The response identifies the importance of setting **realistic timescales** to complete the study.

 The response identifies planning needs for **research literature**, **accurate** reporting and **non-judgemental** practice.

Improved response extract

To be able to carry out future research in this area I would need to make sure that I have taken account of the skills I need to conduct the research, and also be aware of any issues I might have in completing the research. For example, I need to ensure that I set realistic timescales that take account of possible illness, holidays, participant availability and other events that could delay my research.

Research skills needed to explore this issue include being able to skim or scan literature initially to identify key information and to assess whether it provides a suitable link to the topic. A further skill is in analysing literature and reporting it accurately and objectively using set referencing conventions. Good formal writing skills will also be needed to demonstrate an awareness of the issue and objectively discuss other literature to create a balanced argument. These and other skills will help to ensure that valid and reliable judgements are made which help to provide a positive impact on informing practice and provision.

 This extract identifies the need to **adhere to timescales** and qualifies this by giving examples of the **issues that can impact** on completing on time, so the plan is **realistic**.

You need to identify correct planning considerations and also give examples of skills you need to help you give a balanced argument and produce a valid and reliable judgement that will result in positive outcomes for practice and provision.

Links See pages 170 and 202 to revise the skills you need in research.

Now try this

Review the skills needed to carry out the research you planned on pages 214–215. Make a list of any skills you would need to develop or provide, and how you would do this.

Part B Q4: Implications for practice and provision

Question 4 focuses on research conclusions and the implications of research for future provision and practice in health and social care.

Worked example

4   What implications does this research have for the practice/provision of services for patients who are labelled as 'difficult'?

You should refer to the article and your own secondary research.   20 marks

You will need to **analyse** and **explain** how the research you have reviewed could **impact** on provision and practice for patients who are labelled as 'difficult'. You should **support** and **justify** any **recommendations for change** by giving **reasons** and **examples**. Aim to write about three sides in your taskbook.

Sample response extract

The issue I have researched has shown that there needs to be clear guidelines for professionals when dealing with and diagnosing patients (Koekkoek et al., 2011). Some professionals report extreme stress when having to deal with individuals they perceive as difficult patients (Roos, 2005). These findings show that professionals need to look at how they deal with, and diagnose, patients and also how professionals should behave. If they do not, there is likely to be a negative impact on practice/provision. This might include, for example, the cost of caring for patients, the time professionals spend in appointments and constraints on providing other services. Stress experienced by professionals will increase, as will the stress of the patients, affecting overall wellbeing.

This extract starts with a reminder about the article to place the justification in context.

You need to provide an explanation of the findings and go on to provide details of how this may affect individuals.

You need to make reference to research. Including this helps to emphasise understanding of the issue.

You need to include implications for practice and provision. This describes an implication for professionals and states a negative impact if they do nothing.

The extract gives good examples of how the research could directly impact on practice/provision. In addition, some of the positive outcomes could have been mentioned.

Now try this

Using the research on these skills pages or related research that you identify, add a paragraph to the above answer. Give some good examples of implications for practice/provision, and state some of the positive outcomes.

You could include the benefits of empowering patients and encouraging confidence, promoting inclusion in the diagnosis/ treatment cycle. Patients might then open up about their issues and become part of the decision-making process for healthy outcomes. This would also have benefits in saving costs for health services when diagnosing and treating patients.

Part B Q4: Recommendations for practice and provision

You should analyse and explain the implications of research for future provision and practice, making recommendations and justifying and supporting your reasons.

Sample response extract

Future practice would benefit from drawing from findings to develop a framework for professionals to follow when diagnosing and dealing with patients labelled 'difficult' and developing strategies to help support and empower patients to take ownership of their health needs. Further follow-up studies could assess the success of these frameworks and adapt them to the changing needs of individuals and to promoting best practice.

The impact of research such as this on practice and provision is far reaching. For example, having patients become part of the decisions for treatment will help empower them and they will be more satisfied with their diagnosis, which may reduce health issues. This has a knock-on effect in that it will reduce costs to health services in the areas of patient appointments, diagnosis and treatment. Such frameworks may also reduce the stress levels of patients and of professionals who care for 'difficult patients' and may even eliminate the term 'difficult patient'.

 This extract from a response shows an understanding of how further research can be of benefit to future provision and practice.

 You need to identify future research topics and how they might impact on practice/provision.

You need to make recommendations for change and support and justify them with reasons and examples.

Implications for practice and provision

When answering Question 4, you should:

✓ **support your judgement** by referring to research, examples from the article and your own secondary sources

✓ **extend your discussion** to consider the implications of the research for:

- practice (how the research might affect individuals in the workplace and day-to-day practice)
- service provision (the wider implications, including cost and effectiveness of service providers, and implications for society)

✓ **make recommendations** for change based on implications of the research for practice and provision, ensuring these are **robust and reliable**

✓ **provide some rationale** that backs up your explanation of the implications of the research for practice and provision within your sector.

Now try this

Using the research within these skills pages and your own sources, add a paragraph to the above answer that gives your own recommendations for provision and practice. Justify them with reasons and examples.

Answers

Unit 1: Human Lifespan Development

1. Principles of growth
1   Length of body.
2   Head circumference.

2. Principles of development
Henry's development will be observed to assess his stage of development and then compared with the milestones he is expected to reach.

3. Gross motor skills, 0–8 years
1   Sit.
2   Crawl.

4. Fine motor skills, 0–8 years
Example answer:
Connor will still be using a palmar grip when he draws with crayons, but Amy can control and hold her pencil to colour using a tripod grasp. Connor only uses a spoon to feed himself but Amy is developing skills to use both a fork and spoon. Connor needs help with dressing – he tries to pull on shoes but can't manage it yet. Amy can put on her coat and do up her buttons.

5. Physical development in adolescence
Example answer:
Primary sexual characteristics refer to the reproductive organs that are already present in the body. These organs in boys and girls start to mature when sex hormones are released. Secondary sexual characteristics are not present in the body before puberty but are physical changes that happen when sex hormones are released.

6. Physical development in early adulthood
Example answer:
• They have reached maturation and are at the peak of physical fitness.
• Their motor coordination is at its peak.
• They have reached the peak of physical strength.
• Their reaction time is the best it will be.
• Their stamina is at its height.

7. Physical development in middle adulthood
Example answer:
Menopause begins because the ovaries produce less oestrogen. The lack of oestrogen reduces and eventually stops eggs being released by the ovaries. This results in menstruation becoming less frequent and, after a while, it will cease completely. Oestrogen also affects the part of the brain that regulates temperature. A reduction of oestrogen can cause women to experience hot flushes and night sweats. During women's fertile period, oestrogen helps to keep the uterus healthy. Without oestrogen the uterus will thin and shrink.

8. Physical development in later adulthood
Example answer:
1   Peter will have less stamina.
2   Peter will experience loss of muscle.

9. Intellectual development
Example answer:
• Sami will be able to count the blocks as he builds his towers.
• Sami may ask questions when exploring the sand.
• Sami can identify and choose colours to paint with.

10. Stages of cognitive development – Piaget
Example answer:
A schema is an idea or concept that a child develops. An example is when a child who has experienced one type of construction block is given a different type and has to find a way to link the new blocks.

11. Piaget – how children think
Example answer:
1   Nathan is egocentric and will not be able to see things from other children's viewpoints.
2   Nathan will develop empathy around the age of 7.

12. Language development
Example answer:
1   Saira will be able to form simple sentences using subject, verb and object in the correct order because she will have an innate understanding of language structure.
2   Saira will be following the same pattern of language development as other children because the part of the brain that supports language development was pre-programmed.

13. Theories of attachment

> 1 month old: Ruby is in the process of developing an attachment to her mother but appears content when cared for by others.

↓

> 4 months old: Ruby will have formed a closer bond with her mother. She will appear more contented when she is with her mother but still accept care from other people close to her.

↓

> 7 months old: Ruby will begin to show anxiety when parted from her mother and become anxious when cared for by others.

↓

> 9 months old: Ruby will start to form attachments with others who care for her and be more content when her mother is not there.

14. Emotional development – self concept
Example answer:
• Carly may compare herself negatively with her friends because she is not developing at the same rate as them.
• Carly may feel less attractive than others because she is getting comments about her appearance on social media.

15. Stages of play
Example answer:
Suitable resources are those that children can share but use in their own way, such as building blocks, sand play, cars and water play.

16. Friendships and relationships

Example answer:
- Saeed will develop his self-esteem because he feels accepted and liked.
- Saeed will become more confident and independent by playing cooperatively with a friend.

17. Social development and independence

Example answer:
1. Influenced by peers.
2. Like to be socially accepted.
3. Developing independence to make own decisions.

18. Maturation theory

Example answer
Practitioners observe individual children and compare each area of their development with the developmental 'norm' described by Gesell. This helps them to understand if the child is not meeting their expected milestone in any area of their development. They can then put into place additional support for that area of development. The norms of development also tell practitioners the next milestone the child should reach, so they can plan activities to help them work towards it.

19. Social learning theory

Your own observation
For example: A child watches an adult using a mobile phone. They think about what has happened. When they see the phone left on a table they pick it up and hold it next to their ear. Adults laugh, so they repeat the behaviour when they have the opportunity.

20. Nature versus nurture

Example answer:
Nature – Gesell's maturation theory is based on the belief that development is predetermined and follows the same pattern but at different rates.
Nurture – Bandura's social learning theory is based on the belief that learning happens through observing, imitating and modelling the behaviours of others.

21. Genetic factors

Example answer:
1. **Genetic predisposition to conditions** – a person has an increased likelihood of developing the condition because a faulty gene has been passed to them from a parent.
2. **Susceptibility to disease** – a person has an increased risk of developing the disease because of their genetic makeup.

22. Biological factors

Three from: small head circumference, neurological problems, abnormal growth, developmental delay, facial abnormalities.

23. Environmental factors

Example answer:
1. Will may have a genetic predisposition to heart disease passed down from his father.
2. Pollution from the traffic in the city can harm the cardiovascular system, leading to heart disease.
3. Stress and anxiety from overcrowding can harm the cardiovascular system.

24. Health and social care services

Example answer:
1. Because of his learning difficulties, Rajif may not be aware of or able to find out about services that are available to him.
2. If Rajif goes to his GP, he may have difficulty communicating his symptoms, so problems that require his referral to specialist services could be missed.

25. Social factors – family dysfunction

1. Kieran's parents have a permissive parenting style.
2. Zofia's parents have an authoritative parenting style.

26. Social factors – bullying

Example answer:
Social: In the short term, bullying may impact on Zak's ability to build new friendships because he does not know who is sending the texts.
In the long term, Zak may be wary and reluctant to build relationships because he does not trust people.
Emotional: In the short term, Zak will be frightened and anxious. In the longer term, Zak could become depressed or have other mental health problems.

27. The influence of culture and religion

Example answer:
Health benefits: higher-fibre diet improves digestive system, low-fat diet lowers cholesterol.
Health risks: lack of iron reduces production of red blood cells, lack of calcium results in weaker/brittle bones.

28. Economic factors

Your own answers, for example:
Positive
- Having an adequate income gives a feeling of security and contentment.
- Having an adequate income provides better living conditions, which is important for maintaining health.

Negative
- Poor education may lead to fewer employment opportunities, leading to low self-esteem.
- Drug use or binge drinking may lead to loss of positive friendships.

29. Life events

Example answer:
Started nursery, started school, started college/university, first job, entered into a partnership/marriage.

30. The effects of life events

Your own list of priorities. The Holmes-Rahe list:
1. Death of someone close such as a spouse.
2. Divorce.
3. Serious injury or illness.
4. Marriage.
5. Retirement.
6. Redundancy.
7. Starting a family.
8. Beginning or changing employment.
9. Promotion.
10. Moving house or leaving home.
11. Starting school.

31. Cardiovascular disease and ageing

Example answer:
Low-fat diet, regular exercise, reducing salt in diet, eating more fruit and vegetables, refraining from/stopping smoking.

32. Degeneration of the nervous tissue

Example answer:
The effects may include:
1. loss of coordination
2. memory loss
3. difficulty in speech.
Ways to reduce the decline may include:
1. taking regular exercise
2. taking part in activities such as crosswords or playing chess
3. stopping smoking .

33. Degeneration of the sense organs

Example answer:
1   The person's ability to taste is affected, which reduces their interest in, and enjoyment of, food. This can lead to missing meals or a less varied diet.
2   A poor diet can lead to nutritional deficiency, which will affect the maintenance of the body's immune system and the ability to heal and maintain skin, teeth, eyes and bones.

34. Osteoarthritis and nutrition

Three from:
• an injury to a joint
• genetic inheritance
• obesity
• being female
• joint abnormality.

35. Dementia

Example answer:
Early stage: *two from:* informal help with everyday tasks, medication, counselling, memory clinics
Later stage: *two from:* community/specialist nurse visits, respite care, medication, support in the home with personal care
Last stage: *two from:* residential/hospice care; personal/continence care; end-of-life care.

36. Effects of illness common in ageing

Example answer:
1   Social: reduces his opportunity to socialise.
    Emotional: feeling a lack of control over his health.
2   Change to a low-fat diet, take gentle exercise.

37. Psychological effects of ageing

Example answer:
Neena will be grieving because of the death of her husband, which may lead to depression.
Neena may have a feeling of helplessness because she has to rely on others for her care, which can cause low self-esteem.

38. Theories of ageing

Example answer:
Clive may lose his purpose in life, so could take up new hobbies to fill his time. This will help him to develop new knowledge and skills. He could join a club or social group so that he can get to know new people and form relationships.

39. Provision for the aged

Your own ideas, for example:
1   Acute care – stroke.
2   Healthcare – dementia care.
3   Social care – community support activities.
4   Community equipment – alarms / telecare.
5   Psychological care – medication.
6   Benefits and entitlements – cold weather payments.
7   End-of-life care – bathing / personal care.

40. Ageing and economic effects

Example answer:
1   Lack of funding to pay for pensions.
2   Shortage of housing for younger people.
3   People having to retire later.

41. Your Unit 1 exam

Example answer:
1   Testes enlarge and produce sperm.
2   Penis enlarges.
3   Prostate gland produces secretions.

42. Using case studies

Example answer:
Micah has developed social and communication skills at his life stage which will help him to take part in co-operative play with other children.

43. Short-answer questions

Example answer:
Carla should not drink alcohol as it may result in foetal alcohol spectrum disorders (FASD), causing neurological problems and developmental delay.

44. 'Which' and 'identify' questions

Example answer:
1   Loss of confidence.
2   'Can't do' attitude.
3   Will compare himself unfavourably to his colleagues.

45. 'Explain' questions

Example answer:
1   **Emotional:** Mike may feel insecure because he no longer has a family that he can go to for help and advice.
2   **Social:** Mike may find difficulty in building new relationships with others because he feels they may let him down.

46. 'Outline' questions

Example answer:
Kareem earns the minimum wage, which may affect his self-image if he compares himself with others. Because he has a low wage and relies on benefits he will have less choice, which will reduce his independence. He may feel stressed if he does not have enough money for the family's needs, which could lead to psychological problems. However, Kareem does enjoy his work. This could make him feel good about himself, which would improve his self-esteem.

47. 'Describe' questions

Example answer:
Although Padma is growing older and has retired, her social and emotional needs have not changed. She has continued to be active through her voluntary work and is continuing to develop friendships. According to activity theory, replacing what was lost from her previous lifestyle with other activities will help her to come to terms with ageing. Making new friends will mean she is less likely to feel isolated, which will help her to retain positive self-esteem. Taking part in activity will help Padma to feel valued, making it less likely that she will feel unhappy or become depressed.

48. Extended case study

Example answer:
1   Community nurse to monitor / make home visits.
2   Community equipment services to provide mobility aids.
3   Regular visits from home carer to support Tina with personal care.

49. Long-answer questions

Example answer:
At 4 years old, Lena will be able to manipulate small objects with her fingers and have good hand–eye coordination. This means that she will be able to dress and undress without help because she is able to coordinate her eye and finger movements to do up and undo her buttons and fasten Velcro fasteners on her shoes. Lena will be able to feed herself because she will be skilful when she uses a spoon and fork and is also beginning to use a knife. She should be able to care for herself with a little help.
Lena will be able to take part in the writing and art activities with other children because she can hold and control a pencil and paintbrush using a tripod grasp. She will be able to take part in craft activities because she can cut out with scissors, stick on small pieces and thread small beads. Lena can manipulate objects, so she will be able to build towers with construction pieces and play games such as jigsaws.

50. Applying theories

Example answer:

Because Jack is given opportunities to use language, he is developing quickly, because the first few years are the critical period for language acquisition. His brain has a language acquisition device, giving him an innate ability to learn language. Jack is already beginning to structure language, building simple sentences and using correct grammar by using nouns and verbs in the correct order. According to Chomsky, he is able to do this because he has an innate understanding of the structure of language.

51. 'Discuss' questions

Example answer:

Jan's experiences of family life may make it difficult for him to make friends and build positive intimate relationships. If he has a family of his own, he could show negative behaviour towards his partner and children because this has been his only experience of family relationships. Alternatively, Jan may reflect on what has happened in his own life and become determined not to follow the same patterns of behaviour towards his own children.

52. 'Evaluate' questions

Example answer: note where the answer has shown:
a) *The significance of Piaget's theory in explaining Mena's development – highlighted in yellow below.*
b) *Possible* weaknesses *of Piaget's theory in relation to Meena's development – highlighted in blue below.*

According to Piaget, Meena is in the pre-operational stage of development. At this stage she learns about her environment through hands-on play. Her teachers seem to use Piaget's theory of intellectual development to support Meena's learning by providing experiential learning activities such as water and sand. This has helped her to develop new concepts (schemas). Piaget's theory explains how, when Meena has new experiences, she will question what she already knows (a state of disequilibrium). As she comes to terms with new information she will reach a state of equilibrium and develop a new schema.

According to Piaget, Meena's intellectual development is promoted by being allowed to discover for herself through spontaneous play activities. However, critics believe that support from an adult enables children like Meena to be helped to think more logically.

Meena also takes part in pretend play, which Piaget believed was essential for cognitive development as it helps children to apply their linguistic, social and cognitive skills through symbolic behaviour. At school Meena has the opportunity to use symbolic language and objects in her play, such as using playdough as pretend food, which has promoted the development of her imagination and language.

Giving Meena opportunities for hands-on exploration and to take part in pretend play that builds on her knowledge is likely to have supported her to meet her expected intellectual development milestones. However, if she had received more support from an adult during her exploratory play she could possibly have progressed further.

53. 'Justify' questions

Example answer:

The midwife should give advice about smoking and drinking alcohol during pregnancy to deter Leah from continuing to drink alcohol and smoke. Leah may not be aware that the chemicals from tobacco and alcohol can pass from her bloodstream to the placenta and affect the baby's health and development in the short and long term. It is important that Leah knows the seriousness of the effects on the baby, including low birth weight, intellectual delay and congenital defects. It could even result in stillbirth.

54. 'To what extent' questions

Example answer:

Self-image is how individuals view themselves, influenced by how they are perceived by others. Because Tina no longer goes out, she may take less care in her appearance and hygiene so she sees herself as less attractive. This could be exacerbated by the comments of others if they criticise the way she looks. This is likely to have a significant impact on Tina's self-image and result in her self-image declining further.

55. Concise answers

Example answer:

An increased likelihood of developing a disease because of an individual's genetic makeup.

Unit 2: Working in Health and Social Care

56. Key roles in health care

Example answer:
- Nurses are trained to carry out medical duties, such as taking blood samples, whereas healthcare assistants are trained to provide personal care duties, such as help with washing and toileting.
- Healthcare assistants work under the guidance of qualified professionals, such as nurses or doctors, whereas nurses are trained to support doctors in giving treatment and prescribed drugs.

57. Healthcare settings

The scenario could include a variety of settings: perhaps GP surgery, hospital and nursing home or own home.

58. Key roles in social care

Example answers:
People who are alcohol or drug dependent.
Adults who adopt children.

59. Social care settings

Example answer:
- Alicia might go for a brief stay in a local residential care home in order to enable her daughter, Magenta, to have a break from looking after her. This might be paid for using Alicia's personal budget.
- Alicia's care assistants may be able to provide short-term respite care in her own home, allowing Magenta to leave the house for short periods during the day.

60. Responsibilities in healthcare

Example answer:

A midwife has responsibility for the pre- and postnatal care of pregnant women and their babies, including monitoring of health and wellbeing, attending the birth and advising on care of a newborn.

A nurse is more likely to be involved in the medical care of a person during their treatment for an illness or in health screening and promotion. This could take place at home, at a GP practice or health centre, or in hospital.

61. Responsibilities in social care

Key skills required by a social worker might include the ability to:
- prepare and review case files of clients in the light of current legislation, local policy and thinking on best practice
- take difficult decisions regarding the care that service users can receive, where this might happen, appropriate exposure to risk and the service user's independence versus their need to be safeguarded from harm

- work with a variety of service users of different ages, such as children and families, teenagers and young adults, adults and older adults, and being able to assess and meet the needs of all regardless of age
- ensure continuity of care when service users are experiencing care from different agencies, so that there is no need to give repeated medical histories, and duplication and omission are avoided
- communicate well
- empathise with the various parties in each situation while remaining professional and not personally involved.

62. Supporting routines

Example answer:
- Corinne's employer can ensure that she is able to use her desk and computer by providing height-adjustable furniture.
- Corrine's employer can ensure that, when she travels for work, airport staff are available to help her check in and board her flights. Note that, because she travels, Corinne's workplace is not just her office.

63. Anti-discriminatory practice

Example answer:
Direct discrimination: harassment of (making abusive comments about) a person because of their characteristics.
Indirect discrimination: pregnancy and maternity discrimination, if pregnant women or new mothers are treated unfairly or are disadvantaged.

64. Adapting provision of services

Example answer:
- The staff in the school would be trained to respond appropriately when supporting children with BESD, for example they might use positive behaviour strategies which enable them to get to know each young person as an individual.
- A GP surgery would ensure that hearing loops were available. This enables people with hearing impairments to hear when their appointment is called or to respond if there is a safety announcement.

65. Empowering individuals

Example answer:
(i) An elderly person could be empowered by being treated in a way that ensures their dignity is respected. One example is giving the person a choice about the ways they receive their medication, such as by enabling them to take it themselves rather than relying on others.
(ii) Another way would be to recognise the elderly person as an individual rather than someone with a particular diagnosis, illness, condition or frailty. This enables the elderly resident in the care home to feel more valued as a person and more willing to contribute to their own care.

66. Empowerment in practice

Example answer:
Dignity: Listen to an elderly person telling an often-repeated story with interest and without interrupting them or trying to hurry them along.
Independence: Give a disabled person the aids and adaptations they need to enable them to live at home without help.
Express needs and preferences: Patient may register an advance decision to refuse treatment.
Safety and security: Keep the details of an adopted child's new family confidential.
Equality: Make sure that all who need access to a GP have the opportunity, medication and time they need to meet their medical needs.
Freedom from discrimination: Make sure that no-one is denied the medical care they need because someone disapproves of their lifestyle choices.

67. Ensuring safety in care

Example answer:
Risk assessments are used, for example, to reduce the risk of harm from abuse, in residential care settings where services for people with learning disabilities are provided.
One reason why services provided for people with profound learning difficulties often need to be more thorough in safeguarding is because service users may be less aware of safety issues and not able to report any harm which they experience.

68. Reports and complaints procedures

Example answer:
- Marjory may not have reported the fall because she knew she should have mopped up water she had noticed earlier in the day and didn't want to get into trouble.
- Marjory may have been unaware of the reporting procedures or may not have wanted the bother of filling in an accident form when she wasn't hurt, preferring not to get behind with her work.

69. The Data Protection Act 1998

Example answer:
1 **Service users:** The Act ensures that information is kept confidential, stored securely and only kept as long as it is needed, so protecting the personal information of service users, for example reducing the risk of those in domestic abuse refuges being found by their abusive partners.
2 **Staff:** It ensures that information about staff is kept confidential, for example reducing the risk that a service user may harass them at home.

70. Ensuring confidentiality

The discussion could cover:
- the legal and workplace requirements specified by codes of practice about confidentiality
- how medical and personal information is safely and confidentially recorded, stored and retrieved only by specified people with particular privileges
- the procedures which are followed where disclosure is legally required
- how the rights of service users are respected where they request non-disclosure, or limited disclosure, of their personal information.

71. Accountability to professional bodies

Answers might include:
- Nurses have to follow the codes of professional conduct issued by the RCN.
- Nurses have to make a health and character declaration in order to be registered.

72. Safeguarding regulations

Answers might include:
- By ensuring that children are placed only with registered foster carers.
- By ensuring that people who work with children have Disclosure and Barring Service (DBS) clearance.

73. Working in partnerships

The discussion could cover:
- examples of one or two specific types of service user, e.g. an older person or a child with emotional and behavioural difficulties
- what outcomes might be expected from partnership working for each service user, e.g. independent living for the older person
- advantages: what evidence could be used to show successful partnership working, e.g. improved attendance at school for the child

- disadvantages: how partnership working did not provide the expected outcomes, e.g. where it takes a long time to place a child with emotional and behavioural difficulties in a suitable school or where someone occupies a hospital bed because no space is available in a residential care setting
- a conclusion: whether, in your opinion, partnership working provides the best outcomes for people who use health and social care services.

74. Holistic approaches

Example answer:
A holistic approach could:
- assess the individual's wider needs, e.g. physical, intellectual, emotional and social
- involve a range of health and social care professionals, such as a psychiatrist and a mental health nurse
- enable the person with bipolar disorder to express their views and concerns, e.g. that they are unable to work and support themselves
- consider the impact of the person's illness on members of their family, e.g. that they are unsure how to respond appropriately.

75. Monitoring care internally

Answers might include:
- Healthcare assistants (HCAs) are monitored on hospital wards by registered nurses, when they help patients with dressing, washing, toileting and eating.
- Nursing staff ensure that HCAs follow codes of practice and policies and procedures, e.g. the information the HCA gives to patients to prepare them for discharge will be checked by their nurse supervisor.

76. Monitoring care externally

Example answer:
External monitoring identifies the good practice already in place, highlights any weaknesses and makes recommendations and requirements for improvements. Best practice can be shared between similar organisations, ensuring delivery of quality care.

77. Public sector services

Example answer:
- It provides services through the NHS.
- It provides community services, such as GUM clinics.

78. Private and voluntary services

Example answer:
Private: e.g. residential homes and supported living facilities.
Voluntary: charities such as Mencap, which provides residential care, education services and training for people to work with those who have learning disabilities, promotes awareness of learning disability and challenges prejudice, discrimination and stigma.

79. Hospitals and daycare units

Example answer:
- **Cardiology services:** treat diseases and illnesses of the heart and blood vessels, e.g. heart bypass surgery.
- **Orthopaedic services:** treat injuries to and disorders of the skeletal system, e.g. hip replacement surgery.

80. Hospice care

Example answer:
- Jenna and her parents feel that she will benefit emotionally from living as normal a life as possible, being with her siblings and maintaining contact with her school friends.
- Jenna may have expressed her preference to stay at home.

81. Residential care

Example answer:
She does not need nursing care.

82. Domiciliary and workplace care

Example answer:
The twins may fall behind at school because they are spending time, which other young people are using to study and do homework, looking after their father.

83. Access to services

Example answer:
- Access occupations such as work, training or volunteering.
- Use local facilities and transport.

84. Barriers to services

Example answer:
- They might need an advocate to help them if they have trouble communicating their needs.
- If they are worried about keeping an appointment with their GP, they might need a person known to them to accompany them.

85. Representing service-user interests

Example answer:
Age UK represents the interests of older people. It prevents discrimination towards them by giving clear advice about their rights in, for example, employment.

86. Advocacy

Example answer:
Problems can occur if someone is unable to give their consent to having an advocate to represent their interests. Someone with a profound learning disability may be unable to express their preferences regarding their treatment and care.

87. Regulation and inspection process

Example answer:
- Following an inspection, nurses may be required to improve their supervision of healthcare assistants, which increases their workload.
- Nurses may be asked to attend a training course to improve their skills in a certain area.

88. Regulation and inspection in England

Example answer:
The CQC is the independent regulator of health and social care in England. Its role is to ensure that service users are protected, by registering, monitoring, inspecting and rating services. Services that are regulated include residential homes. The CQC may require action to be taken to improve services and may take legal action against services that are negligent, for example. It may also contribute to public debates and policy making on health and social care issues.

89. Regulation and inspection in Wales

Example answer:
The Care and Social Services Inspectorate Wales (CSSIW) is the regulator for adult and childcare and social services in Wales. One role of the CSSIW is to safeguard adults and children, making sure that their rights are protected. One way that the CSSIW does this is to inspect adoption and fostering agencies to ensure that they follow the relevant codes of practice, e.g. to provide safe care when placing children for adoption or fostering.

90. Regulation and inspection in Northern Ireland

Example answer:
The Regulation and Quality Improvement Authority (RQIA) is Northern Ireland's independent health and social care regulator. One role of the RQIA is to ensure the comfort and dignity of people who use health and social care services. It finds out information by asking the opinions of people who use services. These views are then used to improve the ways services are provided.

91. Regulation of professions

Example answer:
The Nursing and Midwifery Council (NMC) regulates nurses and midwives in the UK by:
- ensuring nurses and midwives have the right qualifications and skills, and setting standards of practice and behaviour
- requiring nurses and midwives to challenge discrimination, carrying out a review of practice.

92. Meeting standards

Example answer:
- By preparing the reception area to make sure it is safe for users
- By using appropriate professional language when talking to visitors.

93. Training for health and social care workers

Example answer:
1 Confidentiality and end-of-life care.
2 Training, both pre- and post-qualification, involves familiarisation with codes of practice (guidelines for best practice) and learning skills to enable workers to put these guidelines into practice.

94. Safeguarding employees

Example answer:
Firstly, you might try to remind your colleague about the policies the housing project has in place with regard to infection prevention.
You should then tell your line manager what you have observed. If your colleague continues to disregard the safety procedures, you should keep a record of the incidents of when your colleague fails to change her gloves or wash her hands, and give a copy of your record to your line manager, reporting exactly what you have seen and the clients who were affected. (Your line manager might ask you to do this after you report your concerns.)

95. Ill health and specific needs

Example answer:
Nurses have to prepare patients for their operation, depending on their specific needs. They might answer questions about what the patient can eat before the operation or how long will it take the patient to wake up after surgery; they might also need to reassure small children. Nurses also have to make sure that all patient records are up to date before the patient goes to the operating theatre.

96. Caring for people with mental ill health

Example answer:
- Talking about their feelings.
- Keeping active.

97. Caring for people with a learning disability

Example answer:
- Making sure the person has a say in their care.
- Providing care that is personalised to the individual.

98. Caring for people with physical and sensory disability

Example answer:
The support worker could help Molly and her family in a number of ways. Firstly, she could ask Molly's family about their feelings regarding Molly's disability. The support worker might be able to answer some of their questions and help them to get further support, such as counselling. Molly will need advice about diet and keeping healthy, and the support worker could provide this. She might be able to show Molly how to manage in an adapted kitchen. The support worker could discuss self-care, enabling Molly to take some responsibility for her own health and wellbeing. The support worker will go with Molly to healthcare appointments and might also be able to help her explain some of the symptoms. Molly and her family will need support planning her future needs, such as holidays and respite care. The support worker may be involved in discussions with Molly's employer about how she can continue working.

99. Early years care

Example answer:
- Keeping children safe in play.
- Promoting children's rights, such as keeping their personal information safe, secure and confidential.

100. Later adulthood care

Example answer:
- Preventing self-neglect.
- Preventing abuse, e.g. financial.

101. Policies, procedures and regulations

Example answer:
People who work in health and social care are required to follow regulations to prevent discrimination towards service users and other workers. This means that they have to avoid less favourable treatment of people on the grounds of, for example, sexual orientation. For example, if a patient wishes to discuss their sexual behaviour with their GP, the GP cannot refuse to do so, nor can they refuse to give any medication which the person might need.

102. Working practices in health

Example answer:
Nurses take responsibility for the care they provide and answer for their own judgments and actions – they carry out these actions in a way that is agreed with their patients, and the families and carers of their patients, and in a way that meets the requirements of their professional bodies and the law.

103. Working practices in social care

Example answer:
- They should be free to decide how far they participate in the life of the home.
- They should be able to decide whether to maintain relationships with members of their family.

104. Your Unit 2 exam

Example answer:
- Healthcare assistants would help the patient with any personal care needs, such as washing and dressing. This will stop him coming to harm trying to do these things himself and will make him feel comfortable, cared for and reassured.
- They would monitor his health and wellbeing, and check that he is taking his medication; if there is any cause for concern they would report it to the community nurses. This would prevent any further problems from developing.

105. Responding to scenarios

Example answer:
- A doctor or specialist nurse will prescribe medication, and explain how it is to be taken. They will also have to explain any possible side effects or long-term effects of the medication.
- A physiotherapist will provide physiotherapy to help manage the condition. This will be a physiotherapist who specialises in helping people with motor neurone disease, rather than a sports physio for example.

106. 'Identify' and 'Outline' questions

Example answer:
- A surgeon might operate on the injuries he has sustained in the accident.
- A nurse would monitor his recovery after his operation.

107. 'Describe' questions

Example answer:
This midwife would ask Shazia who she would like to be present at the birth. By asking this question, the midwife demonstrates knowledge of key care principles, for example involving Shazia in planning her care.

108. 'Explain' questions

Example answer:
- The school building meets the requirements of the Equality Act by making sure that corridors and doorways are wide enough, and that their teaching spaces and offices are equipped and furnished appropriately, to allow wheelchair access.
- There will be disabled toilets, ramps and parking spaces, and the canteen and staffroom should also be adapted to allow wheelchair access.
- The science laboratory where Mike teaches will have a ramp, or a special lift, up to a raised dais so he is able to see across the heads of the pupils when he is teaching.
- If the building is more than one storey, there will be at least one lift.
- The school could also have a lowered part of the reception desk, signs in Braille, a hearing loop, and provide teaching assistants to support pupils with disabilities such as with speech, sight or hearing, and a medical room to support pupils with medical conditions that require them to have access to regular medication, for example.

109. 'Discuss' questions

Example answer:
- Care workers will speak to Delusha firmly but kindly, reminding her that they don't like being sworn at and that the other residents might take offence, while coaxing her along and helping her wash, dress, use the toilet, eat and move round the home.
- They will use humour to try to make her laugh and will continue to be kind and patient, even when she is not cooperating.
- They will consult her about her care, asking her what she wants to wear, for example, and if she doesn't respond will pick something for her, saying they like it or it makes her eyes shine, so that she either goes along with their choice or says she wants something different.
- This will empower Delusha and may encourage her to be less irritable.
- The care workers will understand that she behaves as she does because she is frustrated at not being able to hear properly and feels she has lost her independence.

110. Long-answer questions

Example answer:
Fonzi's teacher could have a talk with him; explaining that exercise will help him get fitter, that he expects him to join in when the class does PE and try his best, and tell him kindly but firmly that he will not accept any excuses not to join in.
The teacher will keep an eye on Fonzi and encourage him, at the same time listening to make sure his classmates don't make any unkind comments.
He could have a quiet word with any children who make comments, explaining that Fonzi is trying his best and needs encouragement, so that his classmates urge him on and make supportive comments. This will empower Fonzi by making him realise that he is enjoying joining in with the other children and that if he lost weight he would be able to do more and enjoy it more.

111. Concise answers

Example answer:
David felt that the lack of vegetarian food discriminated against him. It meant that his needs and preferences were not being met. When he raised the issue with hospital staff, discrimination was shown in the lack of respect.

Unit 3: Anatomy and Physiology for Health and Social Care

112. Cell structure and function

Example answer:
Cells grow to maturity by manufacturing proteins which then divide or specialise. Enzymes, which are proteins, mediate many cell functions. Ribosomes, which are inside human cells, are made of RNA and protein, and they manufacture other proteins.

113. Tissue types: connective tissue

Tissue type	Function
Epithelial	**make up the coverings and linings of the body, and its organs and organ systems**
Nervous	transfer of information via electrical impulses
Muscle	**movement, and helps internal processes such as digestion and circulation**
Connective	structure, support and transport in the body

114. Tissue types: epithelial tissue

1 *Example answer:* Ciliated epithelial tissue is found in hollow organs and tubes, such as the lungs. There are goblet cells (which secrete mucous) and cilla to help move the mucous and unwanted particles towards the mouth and nose away from the lungs.

2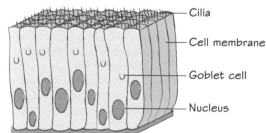

115. Tissue types: muscle and nervous tissue

Muscle tissue type	Location in body	Function
Striated	**attached to the bones of the skeleton**	**moves the bones of the skeleton**
Non-striated	**around hollow organs such as the stomach**	**used in internal body processes and functions, such as peristalsis**
Cardiac	heart	**keeps the heart beating**

116. Major body organs

Organ system	Example organ(s) *Possible answers include:*
Nervous system	brain or skin
Cardiovascular system	heart
Respiratory system	lungs
Digestive system	stomach/liver/pancreas/duodenum/ileum/colon
Reproductive system	uterus/ovaries/testes

117. Energy metabolism

Example answers:

1 Catabolism is the chemical breakdown of complex substances, such as carbohydrates, proteins and glucose, and is accompanied by the release of energy, whereas anabolism is the opposite. It is the building up of larger molecules from smaller ones, for example proteins from amino acids.

2 Aerobic respiration takes place if the body has plenty of oxygen. The products are carbon dioxide and water, which are excreted through the lungs. If there is insufficient oxygen, anaerobic respiration occurs, producing lactic acid. These types of respiration take place under different conditions and have different products.

118. Inheritance and genetic variation

Example answer:

1 Genetic variation refers to the differences in appearance between humans.

2 Females inherit one X chromosome from their mother and one from their father. Males inherit an X chromosome from their mother and a Y chromosome from their father.

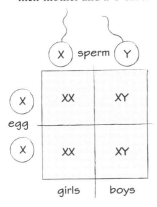

The Punnett square shows that the probability of having either a girl or a boy is in the ratio 2:2, so when a baby is conceived, there is a 50% chance that it could be a boy and a 50% chance it could be a girl.

119. Mendelian principles

Example answer:

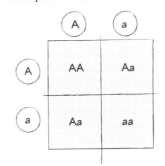

Parents with the genotype Aa could have children of genotypes AA (normal), Aa (a carrier) or aa (affected) in the ratio 1:2:1, so the probability of having a normal child is 25%, a child who is a carrier 50% and an affected child 25%.

120. Genetic and chromosome disorders, and testing

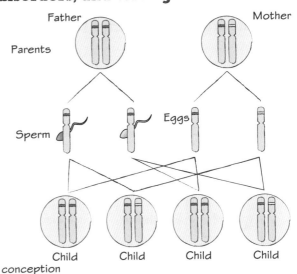

The answer shown is for a parent with normal genes and a parent carrying a dominant gene for a disorder such as Huntington's disease. Other possible answers include crosses between two carriers of the dominant gene, a carrier of a recessive gene with a normal person with normal genes, and two carriers of a recessive gene.

121. Homeostasis: temperature and blood pressure

An answer which covers the points is shown in the diagram:

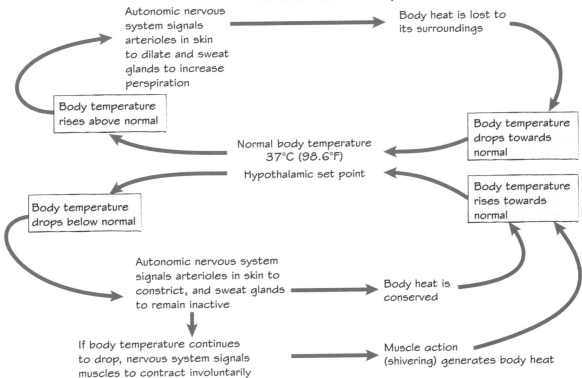

122. Homeostasis: glucose and fluids

Example answer:

1 Hyperglycaemia is an unusually high glucose level. After a meal, blood glucose rises. This increased level of glucose stimulates the production of the hormone insulin from the beta cells in the islets of Langerhans in the pancreas. Insulin regulates the concentration of glucose in the blood and increases the passage of glucose into actively respiring body cells. In the absence of insulin, very little glucose is able to pass through cell membranes and so the glucose level rises. Individuals with diabetes (caused by a lack of insulin secretion) inject themselves with insulin to make up for this shortfall and prevent glucose levels rising.

2 A hypoglycaemic episode is due to an unusually low blood glucose level. Someone with diabetes might counteract the effects of a hypoglycaemic episode by eating something sweet, such as a biscuit.

123. The heart structure and function

Cardiac muscle.

124. The cardiovascular system

Example answer:

Blood vessel	Cross section	How structure relates to function
Artery	Thicker smooth muscle layer / Fibrous layer of connective tissue / Endothelium / Lumen	Arteries have thick, muscular, elastic walls to be able to carry blood with a high pressure away from the heart.
Vein	Thicker smooth muscle layer / Fibrous layer of connective tissue / Endothelium / Lumen	Veins carry deoxygenated blood and waste products back towards the heart. The pressure in veins is much lower than that in arteries, so their walls are thinner and less muscular.
Capillary	Endothelium / Lumen	Capillary walls are only one cell thick, to maximise the rate of diffusion into and out of the blood.

125. Blood structure and function

Example answer:

Blood is adapted to carry out its four main functions as follows.

1 **Transport:** Blood consists of straw-coloured plasma (the matrix), in which several types of blood cells are carried. Plasma is mainly water which flows easily and is the carrier of various substances, such as dissolved gases like oxygen and carbon dioxide, nutrients like glucose and amino acids, and salts, enzymes and hormones. Red blood cells have no nucleus, contain haemoglobin and have a flat shape, which gives them a high surface-area-to-volume ratio for the efficient transport of oxygen.

2 **Regulation:** The plasma contains a combination of important proteins, collectively known as the plasma proteins, which have roles in osmotic regulation.

3 **Defence:** White blood cells are larger than red blood cells and there are several types. The granulocytes are capable of changing their shape and engulfing foreign material, such as bacteria and carbon particles, so defend the body against infection. This process is known as phagocytosis.

4 **Clotting:** Platelets are cell fragments which form a plug to help the blood to clot at the site of injury.

126. Cardiovascular disorders

Example answer:

Three acute disorders: heart attack, blood clot, stroke.

Three chronic disorders: *answers can include three from:* angina, anaemia, CHD (chronic heart disease), leukaemia, hypertension.

127. Respiratory system structure

Example answer:

The tissue in the nose is adapted to its function by having:

• tiny hairs (cilia) of ciliated epithelial tissue which begin the process of filtering atmospheric air
• goblet cells in the ciliated epithelial tissues which secrete mucus to trap dust and bacteria, and to moisten the air
• cilia which sweep the mucus, dust and bacteria away from the airways, preventing their entry into the body
• many blood capillaries to warm the air.

128. Respiratory system function

Example answer:

Alveoli are thin-walled and covered with tiny capillaries, which enable the exchange of oxygen into the blood and carbon dioxide out of the blood. Their structure also means they have a large surface area for gas exchange.

129. Respiratory disorders

Example answer:

If the maximum amount of air a person can expire or the amount of oxygen in the blood decreases, this can be a sign that the person's lungs are functioning less efficiently and so the person may have developed a respiratory disorder.

130. The skeletal system

A: Clavicle
B: Sternum
C: Pelvis

131. Joints and movements

Shoulder: Abduction (moves arm away from midline of body), adduction (moves arm towards midline of body), circumduction (moves arm in a circular movement around shoulder).

Knee: Extension (straightening limb), flexion (bending knee).

132. Skeletal disorders

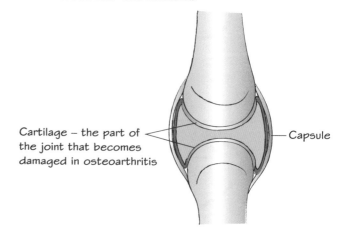

Cartilage – the part of the joint that becomes damaged in osteoarthritis

Capsule

133. The muscular system and disorders

1 Examples include overstretching, contracting too quickly, twisting, tearing or snapping due to overreaching, an awkward fall, change in direction or sudden change in speed.
2 Examples include aches, pain, tension, reduced movement, swelling, bruises, muscle spasms.

134. Major muscles

Answers should include some of each of the following two groups of muscles:
Leg muscles (quadriceps, hamstrings, gastrocnemius).
Lower torso muscles (abdominals, obliques, erector spinae, gluteus maximus).

135. The digestive system

Part of the alimentary canal	Function
Mouth	breaks food up into smaller pieces
Oesophagus	food passes from the mouth to the stomach
Stomach	**food churned up mechanically and chemically broken down**
Duodenum	mechanical breakdown of food and chemical digestion
Small intestine and ileum	absorption of the products of digestion
Large intestine	**absorption of water, and faeces formed and stored**
Rectum	**faeces stored**
Anus	defecation

136. Enzymes and products of digestion

Enzyme type	Substrate	Products of digestion
protease	**proteins**	peptides and amino acids
salivary/pancreatic amylase	starch	**simple sugars**
pancreatic lipase	**lipids**	fatty acids and glycerol

137. Absorption of digestive products

Example answer:
Food is ingested through the mouth, where it is chewed up (masticated) and formed into a ball (bolus) by the tongue to enable swallowing. It is then pushed into the oesophagus and is conveyed by peristalsis to the stomach.
In the stomach, the food is churned up mechanically and chemically broken down by gastric juices to a liquid state (known as chyme). Food is in the stomach for about five hours, during which time protein digestion begins.
Chyme then passes through the pyloric sphincter muscle into the duodenum (the first part of the small intestine). Pancreatic juice, produced by the pancreas and secreted into the duodenum, contains trypsin (a protease) which is involved in the breakdown of proteins into peptides and amino acids.
Peptides and amino acids that are produced during protein digestion pass through the capillaries into the bloodstream. They are then carried to the liver where they are regulated to make them suitable for use in body tissues. They are stored in the liver until required; any excess is deaminated and excreted as urea by the kidneys.

138. Digestive disorders

Example answer:
Villi have a good capillary blood supply and a large surface area. In the villi, the products of digestion diffuse into the blood in the capillaries and into the lymph fluid in the lacteals. The epithelial cells are covered in microscopic protrusions called microvilli. It is the villi and microvilli which enable absorption to take place.

139. The nervous system

Example answer:
The autonomic nervous system is divided into two parts.
1 The **sympathetic nervous system** prepares the body for expending energy and dealing with emergency situations. Actions include increasing the heart and breathing rates, dilating blood vessels and stimulating sweat glands. This prepares the body for the possibility of fighting or running away (fight or flight) when faced with an emergency, such as being attacked.
2 The **parasympathetic nervous system** balances the actions of the sympathetic nervous system by creating conditions for rest and sleep, slowing down many body processes, so preparing the body for calming down and reaching a healthy balance. Saliva increases and digestive enzymes are released to improve digestion, and the heart rate drops to rest and conserve energy (rest and digest).

140. Disorders of the nervous system

Could include five answers from:
- multiple sclerosis – the brain and spinal cord
- motor neurone disease – motor neurones
- sciatica – nerve coming from the spinal cord
- meningitis – membranes in the brain and spinal cord
- brain tumour – the brain
- dementia – the brain.
- Parkinson's disease – loss of nerve cells in the brain.

141. The endocrine system

Example answer:
- Regulating body activities (e.g. growth) – **growth hormone** (controls growth of long bones and muscles).
- Assisting the reproductive process – **oestrogen** (involved in development of secondary sex characteristics and regulation of the reproductive system).
- Maintaining stability (homeostasis) during times of stress – **antidiuretic hormone** (ADH) causes water reabsorption in the kidneys.

Other answers are possible.

142. Endocrine disorders

Example answer:
A deficiency of something, for example hypothyroidism (underactive thyroid), hypotension (low blood pressure), hypoglycaemia (low blood sugar level).

143. Lymphatic and immune systems

Example answer:
The lymph nodes filter and trap any cell debris or micro-organisms which may cause infection, so that the lymph entering the blood does not contain such impurities.

144. Lymphatic organs and disorders

The spleen:
- filters the blood
- stores blood
- carries out immune responses
- carries out erythropoiesis (blood cell production).

145. The renal system and disorders

Example answer:
One of the kidneys' functions is the regulation of water in the body. Kidney failure leads to a build-up of fluid, resulting in an oedema (a swelling due to fluid retention in the tissues).

146. The female reproductive system

The uterus protects and supports the developing embryo which becomes the foetus.

147. The male reproductive system

1 Androgens.
2 In the testes.

148. Reproductive system disorders

These are possible symptoms of both benign prostatic hyperplasia (hypertrophy) and prostate cancer. Prostate cancer can be successfully treated if diagnosed and treated quickly enough.

149. Gametes, fertilisation, conception and growth

Example answer:
An egg survives in a fertilisable form for as little as eight hours after ovulation. Sperm is capable of fertilising the egg for about 24 hours. So the period for conception, or fertile window, is relatively short in the monthly cycle and it may take several months to conceive.

150. Foetal growth through the trimesters

Example answer:
Babies born earlier than the third trimester, in the second trimester, will have immature lungs and soft bones and may not have fully developed and functioning organs, nerves, muscles and skeleton.

151. Prenatal development and teratogens

Example answer:
Regular antenatal care is very important during pregnancy because monitoring can help to detect potential problems early, so that action can be taken to help ensure the developing foetus remains healthy. Health professionals advise on all aspects of a healthy pregnancy and birth, not just on problems.

152. Congenital disorders

Congenital rubella syndrome = the rubella virus.

153. Clinical trials

Example answer:
- **Blinding of trials/use of placebos/use of controls:** in some clinical trials the researchers know who is receiving the treatment, but the patients do not – this is known as a single-blind trial. If patients don't know whether they are receiving a treatment or a placebo (a dummy treatment with no known medicinal properties), their beliefs cannot influence the results of the trial. In a double-blind trial neither the researchers nor the patients know who is receiving the treatment and who is getting an alternative (placebo). This is believed to be one of the most reliable styles of clinical trial. If researchers don't know which group of patients is undergoing treatment and which is the group receiving a placebo (control group), they cannot influence the results, thereby improving the reliability of the study
- **Randomisation of samples/use of controls and placebos:** participants in a clinical trial are usually randomly allocated to one of two groups: the first group is given the treatment being tested and the second group (the control group) is given either a placebo or a previously established treatment. For a fair and reliable test, conditions within the two groups must be as similar as possible, e.g. same gender mix.
- **Sample sizes:** the sample must be large enough to mean that the results cannot be a chance occurrence.

154. Epidemiological studies and data analysis

Example answer:
Death rates per 1000 for children at different developmental stages dropped in all groups from 2000 to 2005. The largest mortality rates were for under-fives, which dropped from 166 to 123, followed by infant mortality dropping from 97 to 77, child mortality from 77 to 50, neonatal mortality from 49 to 39, and the smallest mortality rates were for postneonatal mortality, from 48 to 38.

155. Data analysis skills: statistics, bar charts and histograms

1 A bar chart.
2 Smoking.
3 Yes, the greater the severity of someone's mental illness the greater the likelihood that they will smoke.
4 *Answers could include:*
   - This age group is smaller than other age groups, so there are likely to be fewer people of this age living in the area to attend the clinic.
   - Fewer in this age group are likely to attend the clinic because some will be in residential care homes or hospitals, and will be seen there by doctors rather than at the clinic.
   - Some of this age group will be unable to make the journey to the clinic due to frailty/disability/illness.
   No, it doesn't suggest that people in this age group are the healthiest, it suggests that it is a smaller age group.

156. Data analysis skills: graphs and tables

1 The trend is for more boys than girls to do the recommended amount of physical activity.
   Also, whereas at the age of 2 to 3 a similar percentage of both girls and boys do the recommended amount of physical activity, as they get older the percentage of boys rises, reaching a peak at 8 to 9 and then declines, but the percentage of girls stays much the same until the age of 10 to 11 when it rapidly declines.
2 Yes, there is a rough correlation between the number of cigarettes smoked and blood pressure. Overall, the greater the number of cigarettes smoked a day, the higher the systolic blood pressure.
3 Surgery, hormone therapy and radiation

157. Data analysis skills: pictorial presentation

1 The two food types 'bread, rice, potatoes, pasta and other starchy foods', and 'fruit and vegetables' should equally make up the greatest proportions of a healthy diet.
2 Taylor did not initiate contact with any others.
3 **a)** Breast cancer. **b)** Lung and bronchus cancer.

158. Your Unit 3 exam

An operation to deliver a baby which involves making a cut in the front wall of a woman's abdomen and womb.

159. 'State' and 'Which' questions

F.

160. 'Identify' and 'Complete' questions

Fall in blood glucose level is detected

Liver secretes **glucagon**

Glycogen converted to **glucose**

Blood glucose level **rises**

161. 'Outline' and 'In which'/'To which' questions

Example answers:

B: Platelets are vital in the clotting process. They are cell fragments that circulate in the blood and bind together to form a plug, called a blood clot, when they recognise damaged blood vessels.

C: The main function of white blood cells is to fight infection. The most common type of white blood cell is granulocytes, which can change shape and engulf foreign material, such as bacteria and carbon particles. This process is called phagocytosis. The number of granulocytes increases significantly during infections.

162. 'Describe' questions

Example answer:

When one or both of the left and right coronary arteries become narrowed due to coronary heart disease, it causes angina (a severe pain in the chest), usually on exertion.

The blockage is due to fatty plaques sticking to the artery walls (atheroma) on which clotting (thrombosis) can take place. If the artery becomes blocked, the segment of muscle it supplies starts to die. This is a heart attack (myocardial infarction) or coronary thrombosis.

163. 'Explain' questions

Example answer:

One function is to produce bile to digest fats. Bile flows down the bile duct into the duodenum, after temporary storage in the gall bladder on the under surface of the liver, to emulsify the fats (lipids). Emulsification results in the fats forming millions of tiny globules, so that enzymes can work efficiently over a massively enlarged surface area.

A second function is in the metabolism of sugar. The liver removes glucose and other sugars from the blood coming from the small intestine and converts them into glycogen for storage. The third function is in the metabolism of proteins. Surplus amino acids that are not required for manufacturing cell proteins are broken down in the liver to form glycogen and urea, which is then transported by the bloodstream to the kidneys for elimination in urine.

164. 'Compare and contrast' questions

Example answer:

The similarities between Type 1 and Type 2 diabetes mellitus are that they are both caused by lack of insulin in the body leading to raised blood sugar levels. The symptoms, which include excessive thirst, increased urination, tiredness, weight loss, thrush and blurred vision, are the same, as are the possible complications.

The differences between Types 1 and 2 diabetes are that, in Type 1, the pancreas produces little or no insulin and there is sudden onset of the illness, whereas in Type 2 either not enough insulin is produced or the body is resistant to the insulin, and onset is gradual. Type 1 is usually diagnosed in childhood, whereas Type 2 most often begins in middle age, although many younger people are now being diagnosed with Type 2. This is likely to be due to increasing obesity levels, as there are definite links between obesity and Type 2 diabetes, but no links with Type 1.

165. 'Provide a key' and 'What' questions

a) Diabetic: A (red line).
   Non-diabetic: B (blue line).
b) 220 mg/100 ml.

166. 'Deduce' questions

Example answer:

Both parents A and B must be Ff, with one normal allele and one cystic fibrosis allele, because they are carriers for the recessive condition. Parents A and B can have children of genotypes FF, Ff and ff in the ratio of 1:2:1, as shown by the genetic diagram, so they have a probability of 50 % of having a child with the same genotype as themselves, i.e. Ff.

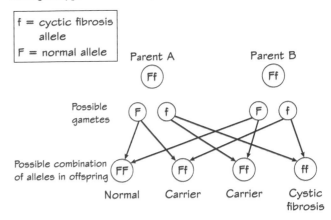

167. 'By how many' and 'To what extent' questions

Example answer:

The biggest difference between the genders was in the underweight category, with 1.9% of females having diabetes compared with 0% of males. In all other categories, males were more likely to develop diabetes than females.

Using these facts:

For those with a healthy weight, males were 3.3/1.9 = 1.7% more likely to have diabetes.

For those who were overweight, males were 6.0/4.3 = 1.4% more likely to have diabetes.

For those who were obese, males were 14.6/10.7 = 1.3% more likely to have diabetes.

Females were, therefore, most likely to have diabetes when underweight, while men were most likely to have it when at a healthy weight. Although males were more likely to have diabetes for the other weights, the likelihood decreased slightly in comparison with females as they went from normal weight to overweight to obese.

Unit 4: Enquiries into Current Research in Health and Social Care

168. Purpose of research

Example answers:

- What are the effects of dehydration among hospitalised older adults?
- Why are elderly patients more susceptible to dehydration?
- How will a programme that tackles dehydration in elderly patients in hospitals help to reduce healthcare costs?

Improving understanding of hydration will improve outcomes for older people in hospital by identifying weaknesses and improving practice.

169. Issues in health and social care

Example answers:
Health conditions: Exploring the incidence of diabetes in the elderly.
Lifestyle factors: How exercise and diet help memory retention in the elderly.
Social care and welfare needs: The impact on health services of caring for the elderly in the community.

170. Planning research

Example answers:
1 Triangulation means using different research methods to investigate the same research question from different angles. For example, by using questionnaires, interviews and observations.
2 Triangulation increases the validity of results by using several methods to reach an answer.
3 Three things to consider when setting and monitoring realistic timescales:
   - Is the design of my study realistic? Will I achieve this in the time I have been given?
   - Are there any barriers to completing the study on time, for example holidays or work commitments?
   - If something is not working, will I have time to modify (change) it?

171. Rationale for research

Example answers:
(a) **Broad topic for research:** Health conditions
   Issue: Challenges faced by autistic children in care
   Narrow issue: Autistic children in care and friendship orientations
   Rationale: Close bonds and attachments, including friendships, are essential elements in promoting children's health and wellbeing. The autistic child may experience more difficulty in developing friendships and this can impact negatively on other areas including health, education and later mental adjustment. Understanding the ways children make and maintain friends may help to develop strategies in care facilities to support healthy development of children.
   Working title: 'Friends matter': evaluating the ways that autistic children in care develop and maintain friendships
(b) **Broad topic for research:** Lifestyle factors
   Issue: Impact of lifestyle factors on services
   Narrow issue: The effects of lifestyle factors on health and wellbeing
   Rationale: Understanding how lifestyle factors can positively impact on an individual's health and wellbeing and also reduce excess costs to service providers. Findings could help to support service providers to develop strategies and programmes to support individuals early, saving long-term costs.
   Working title: The impact of lifestyle factors on longer-term health and costs to service providers
(c) **Broad topic for research:** Social care and welfare needs
   Issue: The impact on service users of change to social care and welfare
   Narrow issue: Are social care professionals confident in advising service users of their rights?
   Rationale: If social care professionals are not familiar with legislation and confident in advising service users of their rights, or what they can claim for, it can have a negative impact on service users' health and welfare, as well as impacting on the cost to NHS service providers in dealing with possible negative outcomes.
   Working title: The impact of professionals' knowledge of current welfare laws on supporting the rights of service users

172. Quantitative methods

1 Quantitative methods are used to look at the effects of one thing on another (cause and effect) using **experiments**, or to look at strength of feeling, e.g. how strongly do you feel that eating bananas helps you gain more energy?
Example answers:
2 Increasing the temperature of the environment increases metabolic rate.
   or
   Adults who were sexually abused in childhood are more likely to abuse others in adulthood.
3 Questionnaires can produce numerical data as you could ask a person to rate their feelings on an issue using a scale from 1 to 5.
   Experiments can produce numerical data, for example by comparing a group's response to taking a drug to another group's response.

173. Qualitative methods

1 Qualitative methods are usually used to look **subjectively** at human behaviour and to interpret what people say about how they feel and experience things.
Example answer:
2 Interviews can be used to find out what a person thinks about an issue or an experience. For example, their feelings about how confident they are about interacting with others after a traumatic experience.
   Observations can be used to explore whether the person acts in the way they say they would, for example by monitoring a person's interactions with others in a group over a number of sessions.

174. Advantages and disadvantages

Example answers:
1 One method could be to use a questionnaire to find out the types of therapies used and how many people use each.
2 One advantage of using questionnaires is that they can be used to gain large amounts of information quickly. A disadvantage could be that people may misinterpret the questions or not tell the truth.

175. Research questions

1 Closed question.
2 Closed question.
3 Open question.
4 Open question.
5 Closed question.
6 Closed question.

176. Target groups and samples

Example answers:
1 The children in the primary school.
2 • A stratified random sample. This means dividing the children into subsets or strata, e.g. boys and girls, and randomly selecting a proportional number of boys and girls for the sample.
   • A cluster sample could be used of just one class in the school.

177. Ethical principles

Example answer:
1 Three ethical principles are to maintain confidentiality, to obtain informed consent and to respect the human rights of participants.
2 The main purpose of an ethical code of conduct is to prevent any harm to participants who consent to take part in research.

178. Safeguarding ethics
Example answers:
1 A key procedure that researchers should follow under the Data Protection Act 1998 is to keep personal data stored in a locked cabinet or password-protected computer.
2 • Peer review – scrutiny of research findings by another expert in the field prior to publication.
 • Participant review – when people who took part in the research are given the opportunity to comment and may request that their data is excluded.

179. Confidentiality
1 Participants' names and addresses, location of study, names of any organisations, identifying features.
2 Locations, names and other identifying features of organisations and settings, as well as the names of any individual participants and gatekeepers.

180. Informed consent
1 Informed consent means that the participant has been told everything they need to know to understand the project and has agreed to take part.
2 It is important to gain informed consent so that participants are fully aware of what they are being asked to do and are able to make a judgement on whether they want to take part in the research. It is also important to ensure they are not likely to come to any harm.
3 Some people do not have the level of mental capacity to be able to understand the project, so need a responsible adult to be with them and also to give consent.

181. Legislation
Example answers:
1 Personal information must be: used fairly and lawful; accurate and up to date.
2 *One of:*
 • **Article 3:** No person should be subjected to torture or inhuman degrading treatment.
 • **Article 8:** All individuals have the right to respect of their private and family life, home and correspondence.
 • **Article 9:** All individuals have the right to freedom of thought, conscience and religion.

182. Non-judgemental practice
1 Taking a non-judgemental approach to research means that you keep an open mind about possible outcomes.
2 Bias means that you have already made up your mind about something. It can arise if you have preconceived ideas about what the answers to your research questions will be.

183. Primary and secondary research
1 Primary research gathers information that has not been collected before. Secondary research involves exploring and analysing existing data.
Example answer:
2 Two examples of primary research methods are observations and interviews.
Two examples of secondary research methods are reviewing journal articles and analysing case studies.

184. Literature review
Example answers:
1 Secondary research examines both primary and secondary research about a topic. A secondary source is an interpretation of a primary source, so it is literature that has been written about that primary source.

2 The purpose of a literature review is to gain a deeper understanding of the topic and find out what has been researched before; to gain knowledge about primary and secondary sources and to evaluate how reliable each source is by understanding where each of the researchers has gathered their information from; to inform your research study.
3 A primary source could be a document giving a person's own original ideas or research or theory, for example Piaget talking about his work. A secondary source would be someone's interpretation of this original work.

185. Notes and records of sources
Your answer should include information about your piece of literature using the headings below.
• Title
• Author
• Source and publisher
• Date of publication
• Page numbers
• Date a webpage was accessed
• URL of webpage
• Key points, e.g. research methods, key findings
• Connections with other sources of information

186. Reading techniques
Skim reading is used to get a general overview, or to make an initial assessment, of a document by running your eyes over a text and taking in basic information.
Scanning is used to find the most relevant parts of a document to assess whether it is right for your purpose, for example by reading the title and the abstract of a research article.

187. Academic reading and analysis
You should have found these sections in the article of your choice:
1 the abstract / introduction
2 the research methodologies
3 the results
4 the conclusions
5 the references / bibliography.

188. Referencing conventions
1 It is important to cite references correctly because:
 • you should always acknowledge the source of any information to avoid plagiarism
 • good referencing increases the validity of your work as it shows that other researchers have published supporting information
 • the reader should be able to access any source material that you used – good referencing will help them find your sources easily.
2 A **reference** section lists all the sources that have been cited in a text. A **bibliography** takes the same format as a reference list, but lists everything the writer has read about the topic, not only the sources that are mentioned in the text.

189. Referencing techniques
Check your answer by comparing it with the examples given on page 189.

190. Selecting reliable sources
Example answers:
1 Peer review means that experts have scrutinised and reviewed the articles before they have been published.
2 You would look at the date of the source. Research conducted in the past 10 years is classed as contemporary.
3 Generalisations should only be made on the basis of large sample sizes which are more likely to represent the whole population. If the sample is too small, the researcher cannot say that the results found would relate to the whole population.

191. Electronic searches

You should have found out how your library catalogue works and browsed the CQC publications.

192. Connecting sources

Example answers:

1 Think about how the information fits into your own project and what information is still missing.

2 It is important to make connections between sources because this helps to result in a piece of research that is reliable and valid, and strengthens the argument or rationale for the research.

193. Suitability of sources

You should have used the SAMTAB approach and ethical principles checklist to assess a research article of your choice.

194. Interpreting quantitative data

1 Organising data: 1 2 2 4 5 6 7 7 7 9 10 10 12 13 13 42

2 42 could be an outlier.

3 Mean: 7.2; Median: 7   Mode: 7.

195. Interpreting graphs and tables

a) $\frac{45}{250} \times 100 = 18\%$

b) $\frac{7}{70} \times 100 = 10\%$

196. Bias in quantitative data

Example answers:

1 **Leading question:** Don't you agree that this government's policies on welfare reform are really making improvements to practices and systems?
Non-leading question: What do you think about the government's policies on welfare reform in improving practices and systems?

2 A leading question such as this could influence the person being asked the question into giving answers that they think the researcher wants, in this case that the welfare reforms are improving practice and systems.

3 The effect of this research on wider policy or practice could result in practices and systems staying the same, when people may already be suffering as a result of current reforms, and no policies will be changed to reflect what is actually happening.

197. Interpreting qualitative data

Example answer:

1 Qualitative data looks at what people say and do so means analysing words and actions/body language. Quantitative data deals with numbers so researchers look for meanings in numbers.

2 Research skills needed to analyse qualitative data include identifying common themes running through transcripts, deducing the meaning in the participants' responses and skim and scan reading.

198. Interpreting words

Your own response.

199. Bias in qualitative data

Example answers:

1 The researcher's body language can affect data collection. An open and relaxed questioner will receive different responses from someone who is tense and hurried, or aggressive in their questioning. The respondent may feel intimidated and give the responses they think the researcher may want.

2 An example of respondent bias is social desirability bias. This is when the respondent gives a response that they think will make them look good, so it may not be a truthful response.

200. Recommendations for practice

1 Current research provides information on the latest methods and their effectiveness, so helps improve own knowledge and practice.

2 *Answers could include:* subscriptions to professional journals (either own or through workplace), reading articles published by own professional body in magazines or on its website, keeping a log to record own learning and its impact on own practice, attending training courses, learning from other more experienced professionals in the workplace.

201. Recommendations for provision

Your own response.

202. Identifying future research

Answers could include:

- ways of sharing information on assessment and care plans
- modelling, commissioning and evaluating effectiveness of care provision in prison
- effective models for providing medication, especially on entry to prison
- planning for prisoner release, to ascertain healthcare challenges.

203. Reflecting on research

Your own response.

204. Your Unit 4 set task

1 2.

2 Up to six sides of A4.

3 The taskbook.

205. Part A: Planning research

Your own response.

206. Part A: Assessing sources

Your own response.

207. Part A: Making notes

Example answer:

1 The issue of patients being labelled as 'difficult' is important because a 'difficult patient' means different things to different groups of people, resulting in patients not always having their needs met. The patients perceive themselves as needing help and can blame professionals for being too pessimistic, and not understanding about their health issues. The professionals can see patients as having complex interrelating issues associated with illness, e.g. unemployment, housing issues or poverty. The experts looked more at pyschopathological issues than social problems, having a view that many professionals work alone with difficult patients and are unsure of what to do, with no support, which can affect quality and professionalism.

2 *Answers will depend on the source selected.*

208. Part B: Listing sources

Your own response.

209. Part B Q1: Research methods

Your own response.

210. Part B Q1: Suitability of methods

Your own response.

211. Part B Q1: Methods and reliability

Example answer:

If you use several different research methods (a triangulation) to research the same issue and they all give the same results and lead to the same conclusion, this makes it more likely that the research results are reliable.

212. Part B Q2: Research issues and significance

Your own response.

213. Part B Q2: Research conclusions

Your own response.

214. Part B Q3: Further research and methods

Ideas for future research could include:

- How far was professional pessimism a contributory factor, especially as, for example, personality disorders and some help-seeking styles were viewed negatively by some professionals?
- How exactly do patients and professionals shape responses based on stereotypical expectations of each other?
- What training and support do professionals need, to enable them to work alone with patients and give high-quality and professional care?

Methods to be used, with justification, could include the following:

- Observations of current practice over a period of time – this builds a reliable picture of current practice based on primary information. Observations can be a more reliable method, especially if conducted on larger numbers of participants as results are then more reliable.
- Interviews with patients and professionals – although the responses have to be transcribed and checked for respondent bias, this is another way of collecting primary information. Interviews are a good way of gaining information as topics can be explored in depth, particularly when interviewing after conducting observations/questionnaires.
- Questionnaires and surveys with patients and professionals – if carefully constructed, these can collect a large amount of information quickly and are a cheap and non-time-consuming activity.
- All of these methods would be used in each setting for comparison purposes.
- Using triangulation of these methods helps to produce more reliable findings: the observations record actual behaviours and the questionnaires clarify meaning to the behaviours, while interviews help to explore the underlying reasons that may trigger or control these behaviours.

215. Part B Q3: Further research and ethics

Example answer:

- Gain consent and access from each setting.
- Gain informed consent from individual professionals and other participants.
- Consider the mental capacity of participants and, if they cannot make informed decisions on their own, ask a responsible adult to give consent and be present.
- Consider any potential risk or harm to participants.
- Follow ethical codes of conduct.
- Comply with legal requirements, including the Data Protection Act, for participants' data.

216. Part B Q3: Further research and planning

Your own response.

217. Part B Q4: Implications for practice and provision

Example answer:

This future research will improve policy and practice and outcomes for the patients. Through gaining an understanding of how professionals perceive and react to 'difficult' patients, further training needs of the professionals can be identified, in order to raise their own awareness of how they are reacting. Professionals may become more patient and understanding, and calmer and less formal with 'difficult' patients. This could lead to relationships improving and patients becoming empowered to take a more proactive role in their own diagnosis and treatment. They are then more likely to open up about their issues and become part of the decision-making process, so professionals are more likely to focus on their health issues rather than seeing mainly the issues that make them identify the patient as difficult. Ultimately this will lead to healthier outcomes for patients and a saving in costs to the health services in diagnosing and treating patients.

218. Part B Q4: Recommendations for practice and provision

Answers will depend on the sources used.

Acknowledgements

We are grateful to the following for permission to reproduce copyright material:

Figures
Figure on page 165 adapted from http://www.aihw.gov.au/, © Australian Institute of Health and Welfare 2016. http://creativecommons.org/licenses/by/3.0/au

Tables
Table on page 156 from https://zerocancer.org/learn/side-effects

Text
Extract on page 88 adapted from https://www.nice.org.uk/, National Institute for Health and Care Excellence (2016) 'Ways that NICE provides guidance'. Manchester: NICE. Available from www.nice.org.uk. Material was accurate at the time of going to press.; General Displayed Text on page 89 adapted from https://www.estyn.gov.wales, Copyright © Estyn All rights reserved; General Displayed Texts on page 91, page 102 from https://www.rcn.org.uk/professional-development/principles-of-nursing-practice; General Displayed Text on page 91 adapted from https://www.nmc.org.uk/, http://www.nationalarchives.gov.uk/doc/open-government-licence/version/3/; Worked Examples on page 193, page 206, page 205, page 207 from Georgina Shaw, Georgina Shaw; Extract on page 202 adapted from Health and social care services for older male adults in prison: the identification of current service provision and piloting of an assessment and care planning model, *Health Services and Delivery Research*, 1: Issue:5 (J. Senior et al.), © Queen's Printer and Controller of HMSO 2013., © NETSCC 2016; Worked Example on page 208 adapted from Nurses perceptions of difficult patients, *Health SA GESONDHEID* Vol.10 No.1 (Roos, J, H 2005)

References on page 201:
Nunes et al. (2009):
Nunes V, Neilson J, O'Flynn N, Calvert N, Kuntze S, Smithson H, Benson J, Blair J, Bowser A, Clyne W, Crome P, Haddad P, Hemingway S, Horne R, Johnson S, Kelly S, Packham B, Patel M, Steel J (2009) *Clinical Guidelines and Evidence Review for Medicines Adherence: involving patients in decisions about prescribed medicines and supporting adherence.* London: National Collaborating Centre for Primary Care and Royal College of General Practitioners.

Friedemann, C et al. (2012):
Claire Friedemann, Carl Heneghan, Kamal Mahtani, Matthew Thompson, Rafael Perera Alison M Ward, Cardiovascular disease risk in healthy children and its association with body mass index: systematic review and meta-analysis, *British Medical Journal* 2012;345:e4759 [Online] http://dx.doi.org/10.1136/bmj.e4759 (Published 25 September 2012)

The publisher would like to thank the following for their kind permission to reproduce their photographs:

(Key: b-bottom; c-centre; l-left; r-right; t-top)

123RF.com: 16b, Richard Thomas 168b; **Alamy Images**: 138, Blend Images 93, BRU News 12, BSIP SA 56, By Ian Miles-Flashpoint Pictures 79, Cultura Creative (RF) 86, Islandstock 67, Jeff Gilbert 37, John Birdsall 45, moodboard 71, Olaf Doering 75, Photo Researchers, Inc 172; **Fotolia.com**: belahoche 179, BillionPhotos.com 36l, Click Images 3bl, denys_kuvaiev 21, diego cervo 2br, highwaystarz 7t, Monkey Business 16c, 26, 173, 199, Oksana Kuzmina 15l, Photographee.eu 197, photology1971 3br, Rafael Ben-Ari 1b, rocketclips 57, vadymvdrobot 5t; **Getty Images**: Adam Gault 1t, Alija 3tr, Andersen Ross 33, Bernhard Lang 6, BJI / Blue Jean Images 64, Christopher Futcher 97, Comstock 38l, Daniel Grill 4tr, David A Land 3tc, Dean Mitchell 78, Design Pics / Kristy-Anne Glubish 58, Ed Reschke 114, Hemant Mehta 24, Herbert Gehr 18, Hero Images 70, Huntstock 140, Isaac Lane Koval / Corbis / VCG 99, JGI / Jamie Grill 201, joecicak 203, Jonathan Kirn 2tr, Jutta Klee 16t, LanaDjuric 4br, monkeybusinessimages 182, SarahlWard 168t, Tetra Images 180, UpperCut Images 84, Vincent Hazat 76; **Pearson Education Ltd**: Lord and Leverett 15br, MindStudio 81r, Tudor Photography 4tl, Jules Selmes 4bl, 10, 15tr, 59, 81l; **Science Photo Library Ltd**: Biophoto Associates 132b, Lea Paterson 177, Simon Fraser / Royal Victoria Infirmary, Newcastle 80, Steve Horrell 132t; **Shutterstock.com**: 1000 Words 169, aastock 36r, Alexander Raths 192, Anna Lurye. 38r, auremar 82, Boudikka 2bl, cesc_assawin 35, Dusit 194, Elena Elisseeva 34, Flashon Studio 8, Jaimie Duplass 22, jannoon028 175, Kuzma 184, Lisa S. 98, Pressmaster. 36c, suthin3 7b, Syaheir Azizan 2tl, Tyler Olson 92, Winnie Chao 3tl, ZouZou. 5b

All other images © Pearson Education

A note from the publisher
In order to ensure that this resource offers high-quality support for the associated Pearson qualification, it has been through a review process by the awarding body. This process confirms that this resource fully covers the teaching and learning content of the specification or part of a specification at which it is aimed. It also confirms that it demonstrates an appropriate balance between the development of subject skills, knowledge and understanding, in addition to preparation for assessment.

Endorsement does not cover any guidance on assessment activities or processes (e.g. practice questions or advice on how to answer assessment questions), included in the resource nor does it prescribe any particular approach to the teaching or delivery of a related course.

While the publishers have made every attempt to ensure that advice on the qualification and its assessment is accurate, the official specification and associated assessment guidance materials are the only authoritative source of information and should always be referred to for definitive guidance.

Pearson examiners have not contributed to any sections in this resource relevant to examination papers for which they have responsibility.

Examiners will not use endorsed resources as a source of material for any assessment set by Pearson.

Endorsement of a resource does not mean that the resource is required to achieve this Pearson qualification, nor does it mean that it is the only suitable material available to support the qualification, and any resource lists produced by the awarding body shall include this and other appropriate resources.